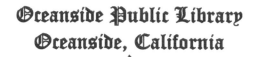

Oceanside Public Library
Oceanside, California

In Memory of

Bill Missett

Donated by

Cathie and Larry Hatter

CIVIC CENTER

The BBC

The BBC

Myth of a Public Service

TOM MILLS

VERSO
London • New York

First published by Verso 2016
© Tom Mills 2016

1 3 5 7 9 10 8 6 4 2

Verso
UK: 6 Meard Street, London W1F 0EG
US: 20 Jay Street, Suite 1010, Brooklyn, NY 11201
versobooks.com

Verso is the imprint of New Left Books

ISBN-13: 978-1-78478-482-9
ISBN-13: 978-1-78478-485-0 (US EBK)
ISBN-13: 978-1-78478-484-3 (UK EBK)

British Library Cataloguing in Publication Data
A catalogue record for this book is available from the British Library

Library of Congress Cataloging-in-Publication Data
A catalog record for this book is available from the Library of Congress

Typeset in Sabon by MJ & N Gavan, Truro, Cornwall
Printed and bound by CPI Group (UK) Ltd, Croydon, CR0 4YY

Contents

Introduction

The BBC is one of the most important political and cultural institutions in Britain, and is among the most influential and trusted media organisations in the world. Its global audience has been estimated at 308 million, while in the UK almost everyone uses its services in some form.[1] The great majority of the British public watch BBC television, most listen to BBC radio, and over half use the BBC's online services.[2] We turn to the Corporation for music, sport, drama and documentaries. But it is also a vital and trusted news service; not just a cultural institution, but an indispensible source of information about the world and our place in it.

One in sixteen adults around the world are thought to use BBC news services and in the UK around four out of five do so: a reach far greater than any other provider.[3] While most of us use a number of different news sources, half of the UK public consider it their most important source of news, and as many as one in five rely solely on the BBC. Moreover, it is not only the most popular provider of news, it is also regarded by viewers and listeners as the most accurate and trustworthy.[4]

But are we right to trust the BBC? Does it provide us with an impartial account of what is going on in the world, or does it serve particular political interests and agendas? This book argues that despite all the claims to the contrary, the BBC is neither independent nor impartial; that its structure and culture have been profoundly shaped by the interests of powerful groups in British society; and that this in turn has shaped what we see, hear and read on the BBC.

The Corporation is of course not without its critics. But debates over the politics of the BBC have been hopelessly misinformed. Although it is among the most important institutions in Britain, it is also one of the most misunderstood. It is maligned by commentators in the national press for its left-wing bias, but in fact its journalism has overwhelmingly reflected the ideas and interests of elite groups, and marginalised alternative and oppositional perspectives. It is lauded by liberal academics and journalists for its much-vaunted independence and its fostering of democratic public life, but in fact it is part of a cluster of powerful and largely unaccountable institutions which dominate British society – not just 'a mouthpiece for the Establishment' as Owen Jones suggests, but an integral part of it.[5] It is celebrated by the left as a publicly funded bulwark against the power of the corporate media, but it has long been 'infatuated with markets'[6] and of all the national broadcasters it devotes by far the most time and resources to business.[7]

This book sets the record straight on the BBC. It corrects the myths and misunderstandings and the mendacious and muddled thinking that have clouded public understanding of an institution that not only lies at the heart of British cultural and political life, but is an international exemplar of the tradition of public service broadcasting it pioneered.

As we shall see, the reactionary press and the conservative movement in Britain have done much to confound public understanding of the BBC. But so too have many liberals and leftists, who have tended to overlook the reality of the BBC's history, focusing instead on the ideal of public service broadcasting with which it is associated.

Introduction

This is a wider problem. To discuss the BBC is not just to debate the merits of a particular media institution. It inevitably invokes certain imperilled principles which the Corporation is seen to embody, most of all those fundamentals of liberal journalism: accuracy, independence and impartiality. Underpinning such principles is a deeper normative commitment to a certain kind of public life; an awareness that for a society to function democratically in any meaningful sense, citizens require accurate and impartial sources of information to inform their political judgements, or better still a public space to facilitate political deliberation, free from market forces and the state. While scandals in recent years have starkly revealed that the private media is utterly incapable of performing such a role, even the BBC's most committed defenders acknowledge that in practice the Corporation has itself too often failed to live up to such principles. Accuracy has always been taken seriously, and this has for the most part at least prevented the BBC from propagating the egregious distortions and falsehoods so typical of the reactionary press. But, as will be extensively detailed here, impartiality has been routinely construed in a manner skewed towards the interests of powerful groups.

What lies behind this partial reporting? The journalist Roger Bolton, who was twice fired from the BBC over his coverage of Northern Ireland, has remarked that 'either [the BBC] is independent, or it isn't',[8] and put in such stark terms, the simple answer has to be that it is not. It has scarcely been independent of governments, let alone the state. Part of the problem, though, is that this question has tended to be framed in such stark and narrow terms. The BBC has never been 'independent' in the sense that its most enthusiastic supporters imagine. Senior executives on the Board of Governors, more recently the BBC Trust, are all political appointees, and its major source of funding, the licence fee, and its constitution – as laid out in its Royal Charter – are both routinely set by governments: a fact which inevitably influences its reporting. Neither, however, has the BBC always functioned like a straightforward instrument of Britain's governing classes. Rather, it has always occupied a grey area – sometimes darker, sometimes lighter – between government and civil society.

The BBC started life as the British Broadcasting Company Ltd, a corporate consortium of the 'Big Six' radio manufacturers formed in October 1922 and granted an exclusive licence to broadcast by the Post Office in January 1923.[9] These companies, the largest of which was Marconi, looked to establish a broadcasting service so as to create a market for the technology they had patented. The BBC emerged as a result of their protracted negotiations with government and was funded out of a levy on the sales of radio sets. Lobbying by the private media meant the new radio service was initially prevented from broadcasting much news, which was limited to bulletins after 7 p.m. based solely on agency reports. But over time, the BBC would become one of the most important and trusted sources of news for the British public. The initial restrictions on news bulletins were lifted in 1926 with the onset of the General Strike. As we shall see, the General Strike is a particularly ignominious episode in the BBC's history, and it has rarely been quite so utterly subservient to power, or so overtly partisan. But the quasi-independence it was then afforded set a pattern that has endured to this day. In 1971, the then director general Charles Curran astutely observed that the BBC 'is a creation of the Establishment, and it depends on the assent of the Establishment for its continuance in being'. But he also noted that 'its activities are, by their very nature, which is to ask questions, constantly open to the accusation of being subversive'.[10] Indeed, simply reporting accurately and offering even highly circumscribed political debate is sometimes capable of disrupting the agendas and strategies of the powerful. More than that though, the BBC has on occasion offered more critical perspectives. While its journalism rarely presents any fundamental challenges to the social order, the liberal and radical political culture of the 1960s created pockets of critical, independent reporting, especially within current affairs. The Corporation underwent something of a cultural shift that decade under the leadership of the liberal director general Hugh Greene, adopting a less austere style of broadcasting and producing socially conscious dramas and satirical programmes. The BBC, Greene himself claimed, was no longer a 'pillar of the Establishment', it was transformed by a 'new and younger generation'.[11]

The cultural changes that the BBC underwent in the 1960s, the political significance of which have tended to be exaggerated,[12] were partly attributable to the establishment of commercial television in 1955. Having lost its monopoly, the BBC was forced to innovate in order to restore its audience share and maintain its legitimacy. But they also reflected broader social changes that were under way. Relative prosperity, technological innovation, greater equality and full employment, combined with Britain's decline as an imperial power, created a climate in which political, social and cultural norms were increasingly challenged – especially by the new generation of economically independent young adults. As Stuart Hood (controller of programmes, television) recalled, the BBC in this period for the first time attacked 'some of the sacred cows of the establishment – the monarchy, the church, leading politicians and other previously taboo targets'.[13]

While this is certainly true, it is also important to recognise that the BBC was as much a target of this hostility as it was an antagonist. In 1977, the Committee on the Future of Broadcasting noted that the sixties had seen a growth of hostility 'to authority as such; not merely authority as expressed in the traditional organs of State but towards those in any institution who were charged with governance'.[14] The BBC, the paternalist institution par excellence, came increasingly to be seen as part of a bureaucratic and unaccountable Establishment, and like other powerful institutions found its hegemony over public life increasingly contested.[15] Scholars influenced by sixties radicalism no longer took for granted social structures and the ideas which legitimated them, and sociologists powerfully undermined journalistic notions of impartiality and objectivity – professional norms that were not only strongly held by journalists, but justified the BBC's privileged position in British society. In this period, the media, and the BBC in particular, came under considerable pressure from conservative moralists and a range of social forces on the left, including the broadcasting unions. Radical sections of the labour movement also agitated for structural reforms, inspired both by class-based critiques of media institutions and increasingly popular notions of worker self-management.

In understanding this period, it is important to recognise that these political struggles played out not just at the level of formal politics, nor just between social movements and the Establishment, but between and within a range of institutions including within the BBC itself. In 1979, during a discussion by senior BBC editors of *Bad News*, a highly influential sociological study of the reporting of industrial disputes, the documentary maker Tony Isaacs complained that 'there was a whole generation now in journalism and politics who in their days at the London School of Economics in the 1960s had grown to believe that the BBC was fascist and everything else that was bad'.[16]

It is sometimes imagined that the 'death of deference' in the 1960s, and the impact this had on journalistic culture, led to the combative style of political interviewing exemplified at the BBC by figures like Jeremy Paxman and John Humphreys. While not entirely erroneous, this is something of a misreading. The social change of that era no doubt opened up space for this type of journalism; but the irreverent style stems less from the egalitarian spirit of the 1960s and '70s, and more from the bumptious posturing of the public school and Oxbridge debating societies, or the 'moots' at which would-be barristers pitch their wits against one another. Indeed, Sir Robin Day, the great pioneer of the adversarial interview, was a president of the Oxford Union and was later 'called to the Bar', the culture of which is hardly alien to the political elite.[17] The real journalistic legacies of the liberal and radical upheavals of the 1960s were not the 'tough' interview, but the ambitious, innovative and popular current affairs programmes which subsequently emerged, such as Granada's *World in Action* and to a lesser extent *Panorama* and other BBC programmes produced at Lime Grove, the BBC's labyrinthine and remote studios where Paxman trained before fronting *Newsnight*.

The journalistic legacy of the democratic and egalitarian agitation which began in the 1960s lasted well into the 1980s. But it was then subject to a vigorous counterattack which reshaped the BBC as well as the broader political culture. In the 1970s, the New Right, which cohered around Margaret Thatcher, began its long march through the institutions, the BBC among them. From the mid-1980s, the Thatcher Government and its allies launched a series of public attacks on BBC political programming, and the increasingly bitter conflict with the government was only resolved when political appointees on the Board of Governors forced the resignation of Director General Alasdair Milne, a seasoned programme maker who personified the more independent stance the BBC had assumed in recent decades. With Milne's departure, the institutional culture of the BBC was gradually transformed, first under his successor, the accountant Michael Checkland, but most of all under Checkland's deputy and successor, the committed neoliberal John Birt. In his autobiography Birt would lament that when he arrived at the BBC in 1987, the Corporation 'had not yet come to terms with Thatcherism', its journalism being 'still trapped in the old post-war Butskellite, Keynesian consensus'.[18] Assisted by a small coterie of radical reformers, he worked tirelessly to put this to rights. In the purported interests of analytical journalism, he introduced 'rigorous procedures for monitoring particularly sensitive programmes'.[19] Systems of newsgathering and editorial authority were centralised and programme scripts were routinely vetted. Later, as director general, Birt imposed a neoliberal-inspired managerial restructuring on the BBC, instituting buyer–seller relationships and competitive pressures through an internal market system which integrated the BBC more fully into the private sector. Birt also shifted the BBC's journalism in a more business-friendly direction, a trend which was accelerated significantly by his successor as director general, the amiable millionaire Greg Dyke, who was later famously forced from office by the Labour Government of Tony Blair. After Dyke's departure, editorial controls were further extended, and the BBC drifted further to the right.

This book will outline the above history in much more detail, explaining how it was that the BBC was transformed from a pillar of the social democratic Establishment into a neoliberal, pro-business, right-wing organisation; and how it is that powerful interests have been able to shape the BBC, influence its output and stifle its potential for independent journalism.

The BBC is a large organisation, the origins of which go back almost a century, and so a relatively short book such as this could not hope to do justice to the breadth of its activities or the complexities of its history. The focus here is more or less exclusively on the BBC's journalistic content, rather than its broader output, and while international issues will be covered, we will concentrate largely on the BBC's domestic operations. The task is not to provide a comprehensive history of the BBC, nor a full account of its institutional life as a whole. Rather, the central theme is that of the BBC's place in the history of British democracy and its relationship with the centres of power in British society, principally corporations and the state. Here the basic picture is clear enough, even if it is rarely acknowledged in official discussions. The BBC has never been independent of the state in any meaningful sense, while the relative autonomy it once enjoyed from corporations and the logic of the market has been steadily eroded since the 1980s.

It has already been argued that the laudable values with which the Corporation is associated should not obscure an adequate understanding of the BBC as it really is. Equally though, such values should not be casually dismissed. For such ideals have, to some extent at least, been embedded within the BBC's organisational DNA and have had some impact on reporting, albeit usually in limited ways and at the margins. This book does not take the values of liberal journalism or public service broadcasting for granted. On the contrary, while offering an historically informed, clear-sighted analysis that acknowledges the reality of the BBC's often lamentable record, this book also recognises in the Corporation, and the public service ideals that have animated it, an unfulfilled promise of independent journalism and a more democratic and accountable news media.

CHAPTER I

Under the Shadow of Power

On 12 May 1926, the BBC's founding father John Reith was reading the lunchtime radio news bulletin when an important note was passed to him by a member of staff. For over a week, the British Broadcasting Company, as it was then called, had been on what Reith referred to as 'a wartime sort of footing'.[1] The UK's first and only General Strike had been called by the Trades Union Congress (TUC) in support of the mine workers, bringing everything – including the newspaper industry – to a halt. As a result, the young broadcasting company had become both a vital source of news for the public and a vital instrument of propaganda for a government determined to break the strike.

The note handed to Reith stated, unexpectedly, that the TUC had called off the strike after nine days. He asked his staff to get confirmation of the news, but not from the TUC; continuing with his broadcast, he scribbled on the note: 'Ask No 10 for confirmation'. Shortly afterwards, the prime minister's secretary confirmed that the news was indeed true. Unbeknown to striking workers, the members of the TUC General Council had earlier that day visited 10 Downing Street to inform the government that they were calling off the strike despite not having won a single concession for the miners. This was a resounding victory not only for the mine owners, but also for the government and the City of London, which were determined to drive down wages in an effort to restore the value of the pound and maintain the British Empire's international standing.

In the 7 p.m. news bulletin, Reith read 'a verbatim account, from No 10, of what had happened'.[2] Two hours later, he relayed on-air messages from the king and the prime minister, followed by what Reith described in his diary as 'a little thing of our own'.[3] 'Our first feeling on hearing of the termination of the General Strike', he announced, 'must be one of profound thankfulness to Almighty God, Who has led us through this supreme trial with national health unimpaired.' He continued:

> You have heard the messages from the King and the Prime Minister. It remains only to add the conviction that the nation's happy escape has been in large measure due to a personal trust in the Prime Minister. As for the BBC we hope your confidence in and goodwill to us have not suffered.[4]

Reith finished his 'little thing' by reading William Blake's poem 'And Did Those Feet in Ancient Time'. Blake, ironically enough, had been a supporter of the French Revolution, but his poem had become popular during the Great War as Hubert Parry's patriotic hymn 'Jerusalem'. As Reith read out the words, an orchestra played Parry's score in the background. Once Reith was finished, the BBC choir sang the hymn's final verse, a rousing call to arms for the Christian peoples of England.

Recalling these events three decades later, Reith wrote that 'if there had been broadcasting at the time of the French Revolution, there would have been no French Revolution'. Revolutions, he reasoned, are based on falsehoods and misinformation, and during the General Strike, the role of the British Broadcasting Company had been to 'announce truth'. It was, he thought, quite proper that it had been 'on the side of the government' and had supported 'law and order'.⁵

At the time of the General Strike, the BBC was still involved in negotiations over its reconstitution as a public corporation, which had been recommended by a committee only months earlier. The postmaster general, the minister to whom the BBC was directly accountable, was William Mitchell-Thomson, who as chief civil commissioner also directed the government's semi-secret strike-breaking operations, coordinated by the innocuous-sounding Supply and Transport Committee. As postmaster general, Mitchell-Thomson could oblige the BBC to broadcast any messages the government decreed. And under the BBC's Licence – the legal basis of its operations – the government had the power to commandeer the BBC 'if and whenever in the opinion of the Postmaster-General an emergency shall have arisen'. This formal power was never exercised during the General Strike, but it did not need to be. The threat itself was a powerful inducement for compliance.

The BBC's point of contact with the Cabinet during the strike was J. C. C. Davidson, who was responsible for the government's public relations and was Mitchell-Thomson's deputy at the Supply and Transport Committee. A reactionary and a propagandist, Davidson was anxious about what he called the 'politically uneducated electorate' and the threat it posed to 'our strength in the country'.⁶ Throughout the strike, he exerted what he referred to in a private letter as 'unofficial control'.⁷ What this meant was that the BBC was afforded a large degree of operational autonomy, remaining formally independent, but on the tacit understanding that it would broadly serve the political purposes of the government.

There were those in government who favoured a more robust approach. A minority of zealous reactionaries in the

Cabinet, led by Chancellor Winston Churchill, 'regarded the strikers as an enemy to be destroyed',[8] and they pushed for the use of all means at the government's disposal to achieve that end. In discussing the status of the BBC, Churchill said 'it was monstrous not to use such an instrument'.[9] Prime Minister Stanley Baldwin, however, took a different view. He thought Churchill a liability and confided to Davidson that he had been 'terrified of what Winston is going to be like'.[10] Baldwin and Davidson favoured a more subtle and, they believed, effective approach, as did the notoriously authoritarian home secretary William Joynson-Hicks, known as 'Jix', who chaired the Supply and Transport Committee. Davidson described the rationale behind their preferred strategy in a letter written shortly after the strike:

> Winston was very strong in his insistence that the Government ought to assume complete possession [of the BBC]. I was equally strong and Jix shared my view, that it would be fatal to do so for the very simple reason that the people that you want to influence are those who would have at once ceased to listen had we announced that all news was dope, while on the other hand the diehard element who criticised us for our impartiality are on our side in any case.[11]

The 'moderates' in the Cabinet used the threat posed by these 'diehard element[s]' to coerce the BBC. Baldwin, Davidson wrote, 'played a very skilful game in postponing a decision by the Cabinet on the question repeatedly raised by Winston and F. E. [Smith] of taking over the BBC'. Indeed, it was not until 11 May 1926, a week into the strike, that the Cabinet finally decided that the BBC would not be brought under direct government control.[12]

The fact that the BBC escaped being commandeered has sometimes been seen as a victory for independent broadcasting. But the historical record suggests, fairly unambiguously, that the BBC was allowed as much independence as was thought strategically expedient from the perspective of the government. As Andrew Marr has put it, the BBC escaped 'a straightforward takeover by panicky or gungo-ho politicians'.[13] But the alternative position which it found itself in was not one of independence. As Reith himself later noted, during the strike it was 'neither commandeered nor free'.[14]

In the meantime, the BBC leadership were in any case not mindful to report impartially on the dispute. Reith maintained close contact with the Cabinet at all times and was flattered that the BBC had been trusted to responsibly represent the 'national interest'. He famously remarked that the government 'know that they can trust us not to be really impartial'. Indeed, so 'partial' was Reith that at one stage he assisted the prime minister by inserting lines into a key speech he was about to broadcast from a desk in Reith's home study. The BBC's first director general later wrote that he and his wife, 'thought we would get a little brass plate put on the desk as the speech was such an important one, and was really instrumental in breaking the strike'.[15]

In the aftermath of the strike, Reith wrote a 'highly confidential' letter to senior BBC staff in which he referred with pride to the prime minister's 'gratifying trust in the Company's loyalty and judgment'.[16] BBC staff replied with a memorandum commending Reith's 'magnificent leadership', which they said had 'carried the BBC through the crisis with its prestige not only maintained but greatly increased'.[17]

In his efforts to avoid the BBC being commandeered, Reith had made arguments which were strikingly similar to those advanced by the Cabinet 'moderates'. He wrote to Baldwin urging him that if the BBC were 'commandeered or unduly hampered or manipulated now, the immediate purpose of such action is not only unserved but prejudiced'. 'This is not a time for dope,' he argued, 'even if the people could be doped. The hostile would be made more hostile from resentment.'[18] Whether Reith persuaded Baldwin and Davidson of this position, or vice versa, or they arrived at it more or less independently, is less important than the fact that their interests were closely aligned. Both the government and the BBC wished the latter to be *perceived* as independent. But while the BBC naturally favoured total freedom, from the perspective of the government the question was how much pressure was expedient for its purposes.

Moreover, the convergence of interests at the senior levels of the BBC and the government was not just a meeting of minds. During the strike, the BBC was further integrated into the infrastructure of the British imperial state. Reith moved into an office in the Admiralty, where Davidson and his team were based.[19] With him came several other BBC members of staff, including Walter Fuller, who had recently been appointed editor of the *Radio Times*, and the BBC's deputy managing director and head of public relations, Gladstone Murray.[20] Both men shared an office with Davidson's liaison officer[21] where they worked together in 'close collaboration', drafting news bulletins from information received from the regional civil commissioners and other government sources.[22] News from Reuters, which itself had come under covert government control during the First World War, was passed on from the BBC to the Admiralty before being approved or amended as deemed appropriate and sent back for broadcasting. All bulletins were submitted to Davidson for approval, and Reith recalls that he too personally vetted 'almost every item'.[23]

The BBC's chief engineer at the time recalls 'the stagger-
ing experience' of witnessing 'bias by elimination', despite
having been 'proselytizing the BBC as the impartial public
servant'.²⁴ This crucial evidence has rarely appeared in
accounts of the strike,²⁵ which have tended to focus on
controversial editorial judgements rather than the fact that
BBC news was routinely shaped around a partisan political
agenda.

The failure of the BBC to assume anything resembling
an impartial position during the General Strike has been
readily acknowledged in the many histories of the BBC and
British broadcasting, although the extent of these failures
and the level of collusion between the BBC and the government has been hugely underplayed. The classic account
is offered by the Corporation's first official historian, Asa
Briggs, who writes that the BBC 'maintained a precarious
measure of independence throughout the strike'.²⁶ This is
broadly correct. Reith worked hard to ensure that the BBC
was not 'commandeered', and this meant at times making
significant compromises. But the conventional readings,
which see the episode as something of a bumpy start on
the road to more substantive independence, are miscon-
strued. They overlook the extent to which the compromises
reached during that early period of crisis set in place terms
of the BBC's relationship with governments, its incorporation into the Establishment, and arguably the state itself.
A precarious independence has in fact defined the BBC's
institutional existence ever since, and the highly circumscribed notion of impartiality it developed in parallel with
state institutions has also proved enduring.

Briggs's successor as the BBC's official historian, Jean
Seaton, concludes her discussion of the General Strike
by noting that the compromises and accommodations
reached between the broadcaster and the government

during that early period of crisis gave rise to an enduring 'ethic of political neutrality' at the BBC, drawing on a tradition of propaganda based not on the dissemination of falsehoods, but a strategic 'selection and presentation' of information.[27] Indeed, both J. C. C. Davidson and Reith shared this same 'ethic'. They associated propaganda with explicit falsehoods, or emotive material, and saw themselves as responsible distributors of accurate information, distributed in the national interest. In a confidential report following the strike, Davidson wrote:

> When the Deputy Chief Civil Commissioner was appointed it was understood that he would be the member of the Government responsible for publicity and it was agreed that he should not make himself responsible for any propaganda but should confine himself to acting in the capacity of collector and distributor of Government news, censored when necessary but undoctored.[28]

This was a notion of propaganda that would be operationalised again by the BBC and the British state during the Second World War, and one that would become deeply engrained in the BBC's institutional culture.

The 'ethic of political neutrality' led to some curious contradictions. This is well illustrated by a memo from the BBC chairman during the General Strike, which decreed that the Corporation should 'maintain an objective news service' and

> try to convey to the minds of the people generally that the prolongation of the general stoppage is the one sure process calculated to reduce wages and the standards of living which it is the avowed endeavour of the Trade Unions to maintain and improve; and to try to make it clear that the

sooner the General Strike is satisfactorily terminated the
better for wage earners in all parts of the country.[29]

Seaton characterises the BBC's stance during and after the
General Strike as a 'denial of politics'. But her account is
less suggestive of a naive idealism than an unquestioning
acceptance of the authority of the state. Not so much a
denial of politics, as a profound identification with, and
subordination to, a particular set of institutions and governing arrangements which profoundly influenced the
Corporation's culture and editorial practices. An internal
BBC report drafted in the years after the General Strike
noted that there was no censorship in its early news
service, but since the BBC maintained 'close touch with the
appropriate departments ... the bulletins fell in line with
Government policy'.[30]

Given the close embrace between the BBC, the government and the Establishment, should the BBC be understood
as a 'state broadcaster'? Champions of public service broadcasting in politics, journalism and academia have sought to
distinguish the approach pioneered by the BBC from more
overtly politicised models elsewhere, more readily referred
to as state broadcasters. Seaton, for example, claims that
the BBC 'never has been a "state" broadcaster', since it has
'income separate from a state grant', and elsewhere she
has noted that its senior personnel work independently
of government direction and do not change with changes
of government.[31] But the BBC's income has been readily
wielded as an instrument of political influence throughout its history, while the other features Seaton points to
are shared by a good number of non-partisan state bodies.
Indeed, the British Civil Service shares with the BBC its
core values of political impartiality and objectivity, as set
out in the Civil Service Code. Reith, for his part, considered

that the BBC had been established as a body constitutionally committed to public service, and 'certainly not as a department of state',[32] and while this much is true, it hardly provides a definitive answer to this question.

As Ralph Miliband notes, the state 'is not a thing' but a diverse set of interacting institutions, which in his account comprises 'the government, the administration, the military and the police, the judicial branch, sub-central government and parliamentary assemblies'. The administrative institutions of the state, Miliband notes, 'extend far beyond the traditional bureaucracy' and include 'a large variety of bodies, often related to particular ministerial departments, or enjoying a greater or lesser degree of autonomy – public corporations, central banks, regulatory commissions, etc.' Though Miliband did not consider the BBC to be part of the state system, the fact remains that it could quite comfortably fit within his definition.[33] Thus, the sociologist Tom Burns concluded from his detailed study that the BBC should be understood as a 'Quango', that is, a quasi-independent body created to act independently but expected to act 'in conformity with Government purposes' and kept under 'essential instrument[s] of control'.[34]

Indeed, the BBC is arguably comparable with the classically repressive organs of the modern state such as the police, the domestic monopolists of Max Weber's 'legitimate use of physical force'. The Metropolitan Police was formed out of more organic and disparate 'policing' practices and rationalised and brought under the authority of the Home Office, a history which bears obvious comparisons to the early formation of the BBC. Despite the incorporation of policing functions under the authority of a secretary of state, a constitutional arrangement emerged according to which the home secretary would not interfere with the 'impartiality' and 'operational independence' of the police.

While the Metropolitan Police was created by statute, the BBC was formed by Royal Charter. In this sense, it is not even formally accountable to Parliament, but to the Crown. The subsequent renewals of the Royal Charter, as well as the appointment of BBC governors and trustees, have formally been made by an Order of the Privy Council – an arcane and rather mysterious body which exists to advise the monarch on the exercise of the Royal Prerogative, that is, on the exercise of the residential powers of the absolutist state which have never been subject to democratic controls. These powers include, for example, the declaration of war, the granting of honours and the appointment of civil servants. Orders in Council, such as those which appoint BBC trustees as well as senior civil servants, are, in essence, absolutist decrees of the central government, signed-off by the monarch of the day. They are the constitutional basis not only for the BBC, but for hundreds of 'chartered bodies', including Oxford and Cambridge and other historic universities, colleges and public schools, hospitals, professional associations, the numerous trade associations and guilds of the City of London, banks and colonial enterprises. Some of these chartered bodies, while thoroughly Establishment organisations, are best understood as part of 'civil society'. But a good number occupy central places in the cluster of state, quasi-state and non-state institutions which together constitute the central power structures of British society, notably the City of London itself (chartered in 1327) and the Bank of England (chartered in 1694). Where the BBC should be positioned on this spectrum will always remain somewhat indeterminate, precisely because the BBC's 'independence' is so inherently ambiguous.

For the anthropologist Georgina Born, a 'critical factor in the political character of the BBC is its constitutional status'.[35] Somewhat curiously, this status has been seen by both the BBC and the broader British Establishment not as a threat to the Corporation's impartiality, but as the very basis of its celebrated independence. In 1964, the then director general Hugh Greene wrote that the BBC's independence, which he considered to be a major reason for its national and international prestige, derived precisely from its 'constitutional position'.[36]

The BBC's claim, which was common in that period, to be both 'within the constitution' and yet somehow 'independent', or apolitical, may seem contradictory.[37] But from the perspective of the British elite, it is an accurate reflection of what is meant by the constitution: those set of institutions and practices that exist above, or perhaps beneath, the realm of official public contestation. To say that the BBC achieved 'constitutional status', then, is to say that it attained a position above politics in much the same way as the monarchy or the City of London or the Bank of England. What is remarkable is how quickly the BBC attained this position. Speaking at a time when the Establishment had come under criticism, John Reith recalled this achievement with some pride:

> Perhaps if I had thought more or known more I would have tried to avoid the BBC becoming part of the establishment, but perhaps not. Establishment has a good deal to say for itself. And indeed such a charge was surely a considerable tribute to the BBC – that anything of such recent appearance should have attained to such entitliture.[38]

Of course, this does not answer the question of whether the BBC is part of the state. But this is a question that inevitably descends into semantics. Certainly, the BBC needs to be understood in the broader context of the historical development of the British state, particularly the emergence of a professional and ostensibly impartial civil service and the development of extensive capillary functions, some undertaken by institutions with a considerable independence from ministers of the Crown.

The 1936 Ullswater Committee, one of the many official committees of inquiry on broadcasting, reported that: 'The position of the Corporation is one of independence in the day-to-day management of its business, and of ultimate control by His Majesty's Government.'[39] This situation has not changed nearly as much since the interwar period as liberal commentators would have us believe. Certainly, the degree of freedom the BBC has enjoyed has been politically significant, and at times it has even served as a site of opposition to powerful interests. But it has always remained, as the future director general John Birt once noted, 'under the shadow of the state and the other main repositories of power'.[40]

The former *Panorama* producer Meirion Jones has written that 'the fundamental corporate bias is pro-government, regardless of party':

> The only periods when I saw the BBC's loyalty to the government wavering was under John Major after Black Wednesday, and during the Gordon Brown administration. In each case a cynic might say the corporation could see the PMs were dead on their feet, and the other side was about to be elected and control the BBC purse strings.[41]

This kind of candour is rare. The journalist and academic John Naughton has described the 'notion that the BBC is independent of the government of the day' as 'one of those quaint constitutional myths by which Britain is governed'.[42]

For eighty years, the BBC's legal personality resided in its Board of Governors, only superseded in 2007 by the

BBC Trust. The personnel who have made up both these bodies have been independent, but appointed by the Crown on the advice of the prime minister, another quaint constitutional myth. In reality, the Corporation's governors and trustees have been appointed by the leader and close advisors of the current ruling party. By convention, they have been non-partisan appointments, unable to interfere with programme making. But these appointees, most of all the BBC chair, have often been highly politicised and interventionist. Especially notable in this regard was the Thatcher period. The potential for the powers of the Board of Governors to serve the interests of an authoritarian government was acknowledged with great prescience in 1977 in a speech by the then director general Ian Trethowen:

> Governments of both parties have so far been scrupulous in making sure, through the appointments, that the Board [of Governors] reflects a wide spectrum of opinion. In practice, in my experience, the Governors of the BBC have consciously seen themselves as an important part of the defence of our independence, and they have so acted. The fact remains that a Government with more sinister intentions could find in the power of appointment to the Board of Governors an uncomfortably convenient weapon.[43]

Another convenient weapon in the government's arsenal has been the control over the BBC's finances. It is often argued that the licence fee is an important guarantor of the BBC's independence from government since it affords revenue directly from the viewers and listeners, to whom the BBC is therefore said to be directly accountable. A 2015 parliamentary briefing paper on the renewal of the BBC's Charter, for example, claims that the BBC has a 'unique structure' in that 'it is largely independent of the state and funded by those who watch television'.[44] This is true to a point; if the BBC were dependent on general taxation, this would likely result in even greater government influence. But the relative independence provided by the licence fee mechanism should not be exaggerated. What really matters is not who provides the money, but who controls it, and here the BBC's audiences have in practice had no choice in the matter. The level of the licence fee is set by government and, like the powers of appointment, it has proved to be a useful means for exerting influence.

During periods of relative affluence, the BBC has tended to enjoy greater autonomy from government. However, during periods of austerity, a government's financial leverage tends to become much greater. Stuart Hood, a former controller of television programmes, has suggested that the more liberal and independent culture at the BBC that emerged during the 1960s under the director generalship of Hugh Greene is partly attributable to the substantial income the BBC was still receiving from the take-up of television licences:

> Because of the rising graph of TV licences [the BBC] enjoyed a parallel rise in its income. This meant that it did not have to go to the government to ask for an increase in the licence fee … The BBC was a beneficiary of the 'you have never had it so good' period under Macmillan. At a moment of prosperity and against a background of social changes, the cracks in the monolith could be and were exploited by broadcasters.[45]

This more favourable financial context changed markedly from the mid-1960s. Before this period, the BBC enjoyed steady increases in its income, but subsequent inflationary pressures meant it had to regularly request licence fee increases from the Labour Government. Naturally, such a situation where the BBC leadership is at the mercy of a government's financial largesse has political consequence. As Michael Bett, the BBC's director of personnel in the late 1970s, recalls,

> the licence fee became a bigger and bigger political issue. Therefore it mattered very much what the government thought about you and you couldn't rely on the general reputation. You had to please the government.[46]

More recently, the current Conservative Government was criticised for drawing the BBC into its politics of austerity when it imposed a sudden and dramatic cut in the BBC's income following an already harsh licence fee settlement in 2010. Shortly after the Tories' unexpected electoral victory in 2015, the government announced that it would withdraw funding for free licence fees for the over-75s. Making the announcement, the Chancellor George Osborne reasoned that the BBC is 'a publicly-funded body, so it is right that it, like other parts of the public sector, should make savings'.[47] That policy, agreed at secret meetings with Director General Tony Hall, was later described by the former director general Mark Thompson as 'totally inappropriate'.[48] Sir Christopher Bland, who chaired the BBC Board of Governors from 1996 to 2001, warned that the policy drew the Corporation 'closer to becoming an arm of government',[49] while the Blairite Labour MP Ben Bradshaw, a former BBC journalist and culture secretary, called it 'a significant assault on BBC independence'.[50]

Perhaps the greatest threat that the government holds over the Corporation though is its ultimate discretion over the BBC's very existence. Originally constituted as a public corporation under a royal charter in 1927, shortly after the

General Strike, the BBC was originally granted the right to operate for a ten-year period. Since then, the BBC Charter has been periodically renewed and amended, but has never placed the Corporation on a sure and permanent footing. The official Licence and Agreement, the other major constitutional document, negotiated with the relevant secretary of state, is by convention debated in Parliament, but need not even be subject to that limited degree of democratic oversight.

Whether or not these various mechanisms and processes are considered to undermine the BBC's independence depends on how the term is understood. The Corporation has enjoyed independence in the more limited sense of operating without direction from government, and the various mechanisms of influence are all at least one step removed from programme making. On the other hand, these mechanisms plainly allow for political influence over the BBC's output and the management of its affairs, even if only indirectly, by affording influence over the internal distribution of resources and editorial and managerial authority. More obviously, these mechanisms place the BBC in an ultimately subordinate position, which in turn makes the BBC hopelessly vulnerable to more overt political pressure.

Georgina Born considers the BBC a 'contradictory' institution, which, although kept 'on a short lead', has still exhibited signs of genuine autonomy.[51] This is accurate, and also points to a problem with the whole notion of independence as a starting point for examining the BBC; namely, that it implicitly assumes it to be a broadly homogeneous body. In fact, it has been a site of considerable political contestation, including over its own institutional character, the nature of its independence, and its relationship with governments and the state. The picture is made more complex by the fact that these 'contradictions' are not merely internal wrangles, but are related to broader struggles over the distribution of power in society. The very idea of the independence of the BBC plays an important part in these political conflicts. It emerged as an idealised expression of the terms on which broadcasting was incorporated into the Establishment, and arguably the state, and over time became a political principle invoked in struggles, as both broadcasters and politicians have sought to renegotiate the terms of this historic but ever-evolving settlement. Independence remains, therefore, a profoundly important ideal that should be upheld whenever powerful interests seek to influence the BBC. But it is nevertheless a poor starting point for an analysis of the Corporation and its place in British society. Not only does it tend to obscure internal contestation, it also unduly focuses attention on instances where the BBC and the government, or other sections of the Establishment, sharply disagree. This obscures collusion and cohesion and overlooks the extent to which the BBC is the product of the same ideological and material forces which have shaped other elite political institutions. A more fruitful approach than asking whether the BBC is authentically independent of government or the state, therefore, is to ask what social forces have shaped its institutional structure and culture and to what extent these arrangements have encouraged or discouraged particular journalistic practices – and whose interests.

In examining a hierarchical organisation like the BBC, it makes sense to take things from the top – and at the apex of the Corporation have been the governors and, from 2007, the trustees. These grandees, led by the powerful chair of the BBC, are charged with setting the Corporation's 'overall strategic direction', approving strategies and budget allocations, and overseeing the decisions of BBC management. They have been appointed by central government and have naturally enough tended to be over-whelmingly 'Establishment' figures drawn from privileged backgrounds.[52]

The governors, and later the trustees, have been respon-sible for appointing the 'chief executive officer' and 'editor-in-chief': the director general – the most powerful figure in the BBC. He (there has yet to be a female DG) has overall responsibility for the BBC's output, though naturally much of this is delegated, and heads the BBC's senior manage-ment. This consists of a complex matrix of policy-making bodies overseen by the Executive Board, which in recent years has included 'non-executive directors' drawn mainly from the corporate sector. Together, the members of the Executive Board are directly responsible for the BBC's management and output. They have the power to allocate resources to particular programme areas, and they wield the powers of appointment and promotion that shape the lower levels of the BBC hierarchy.

A 2014 report of the quasi-official Social Mobility and Child Poverty Commission had no qualms about identify-ing these top BBC executives, and over a hundred other senior BBC managers, as members of 'Britain's elite' – along with politicians, civil servants, the super-rich, FTSE 350 CEOs, newspaper columnists and other groups. The Commission's survey of 125 BBC executives found that 26 per cent had attended private school (compared with 7 per cent of the population), 33 per cent had attended Oxbridge (compared with just 0.8 per cent of the popu-lation) and 62 per cent had attended one of the Russell Group of leading universities (compared with 11.4 per cent of the population) – figures which were comparable with those for other factions of Britain's power elite, as the report shows.[53] Senior BBC managers are also extremely well paid: in 2014/15, the seven executive members of the BBC's Executive Board earned an average of over £424,000.[54] Meanwhile, around eighty BBC executives are thought to earn over £150,000,[55] even after policy measures were put in place to reduce executive pay following fierce criticism from the press. Among this executive cadre are around a hundred or so senior managers in editorial policy who on average earn just over £100,000, and the most senior of whom can earn two or three times that.[56]

Below these senior editorial managers, we see similar patterns of privilege. In 2006, the Sutton Trust examined the educational backgrounds of 100 leading news journalists in the UK, of whom 31 worked at the BBC. It found that 54 per cent were privately educated and a remarkable 45 per cent had attended Oxbridge.[57] Educational background is of course an indicator of shared class background. But it is also in itself a profoundly important basis for elite cohesion, forging along with other formative experiences, if not a shared set of ideas, then at least a shared demeanour and set of dispositions. Elitist recruiting practices – which are naturally justified in meritocratic terms, even if they are recognised to create serious problems in terms of legitimacy – thus create subtle forms of institutional and cross-institutional cohesion.

In the case of the BBC, recruitment has also been much more explicitly political. In combination with the strong Oxbridge orientation, there has, since the 1990s especially, been a greater movement of personnel between the BBC and Westminster. Before this – from the 1930s to the 1980s – the Security Service exercised a secret veto power over appointments to thousands of positions in the BBC which were referred to as 'counter-subversion' posts. As we will see later, this practice was not concerned with excluding agents of the Soviet Union from the BBC for the purposes of national security. Rather, it was mechanism intended

to prevent the employment of persons whose politics
MI5 regarded as too radical for admission to public life.
Moreover, the practice was not imposed on the BBC by the
secret state. It was encouraged by the BBC leadership, who
regarded it as a useful mechanism for the maintenance of
'impartiality', complementing and protecting other systems
of editorial control. Here, once again, we see the classic
conflation between 'objectivity' and the national interest as
defined by the British state.

What are the more mundane mechanisms of editorial
control which operate at the BBC? The sociologist Philip
Schlesinger describes how BBC journalists see 'themselves
as working in a system which offers them a high measure of
autonomy' and are generally not cognisant of the fact that
'orientations first defined at the top of the [BBC] hierarchy'
work their way downwards through a 'chain of editorial
command', becoming 'part of the taken for granted assumptions of those working in the newsrooms'. He found BBC
journalists to be 'a mass of conformists' who adopted 'the
model of corporate professionalism provided for them by
the BBC by degrees varying from unreflecting acquiescence
to the most full-blown commitment'.[58] The former BBC
executive, Stuart Hood, at around the same time, similarly
wrote of the taken-for-granted assumptions of the editor or
producer as a 'programme ethos – a general view of what is
fitting and seemly, of what is admissible and not admissible,
which is gradually absorbed by those persons involved in
programme making'.[59] The learning process that establishes
these rules and conventions is evident in historical accounts.
Hendy notes in his history of Radio 4, for example, that:
'Over time, producers had learned to adjust their ideas
to what they knew to be acceptable.' For instance, the
celebrated radio producer Geoffrey Bridson tried

offering the Home Service [the forerunner to Radio 4] a series of trenchant documentaries on subjects such as nuclear armament, Soviet Russia, McCarthyism, poverty or racial conflict, but soon found that even these were rejected, mostly for being 'too controversial or too political'. The BBC, he concluded, had come to regard the Home as the place 'to reflect the most respectably orthodox opinion as it already existed'.[60]

As is fitting for an Oxbridge institution, the BBC's 'programme ethos' has been fostered in a subtle, almost collegiate manner, but in a decidedly hierarchical context. Tom Burns notes that it 'is drummed into producers ... that if there is any doubt in their mind about a topic, or viewpoint, or film sequence, or contributor they must refer up to their chief editor, or head of department'. He also observed, though, that the significance of 'referring up' was more 'symbolic rather than operational', and quotes Anthony Smith's observation that: 'There is seldom any doubt about what the man above you thinks on any important issue. You can therefore avoid referring upwards by deciding them in a way which you know he would approve of.'[61] In a 1973 policy document called *Tastes and Standards in BBC Programmes*, Huw Wheldon, the managing director of BBC television, was quoted as saying, 'The wrath of the Corporation in its varied human manifestations is particularly reserved for those who fail to refer'.[62]

The process of 'referring up' controversial political matters to your superior, Schlesinger notes, was developed as part of a broader system of bureaucratic authority which ensured that staff conform to what he calls the BBC's 'corporate ideology'. Broader organisational control, he explains, is exercised through the development and distribution of internal policy publications and the selection and promotion of staff, which acts as an informal 'sanctioning process'.[63]

These various mechanisms are not just 'ideological'. A journalist need not accept the dominant news values of editors, and may even find ways of subverting them. But a bureaucracy like the BBC functions in such a way that makes the opportunities for this somewhat limited. Furthermore, the pressures for conformity are not merely internal to the BBC. Class and educational background influence who is recruited in the first place, and those lucky enough to win out in the competition for a highly prestigious post will not only have to develop a strategic understanding of 'office politics' and what is expected of them by colleagues and superiors: they will also enter a broader set of relations with individuals and institutions outside of the BBC. A political correspondent, for example, is not only required to develop a certain understanding of what BBC editors expect in terms of what they report and how. They are also required to familiarise themselves with the broader world of formal politics and authoritative political commentary. This is all part of the BBC's Establishment culture. Indeed, its 'corporate ideology' is essentially an institutionalisation of political compromises negotiated and renegotiated between senior BBC management and the broader Establishment of which they are a part. As Tom Burns perceptively remarked in his study, 'the relationship between the producer and his superiors reflects the relationship between the BBC and the powers that be outside'.[64]

A good illustration of this is from January 1970, around the time of Burns's study, when Charles Curran, the new director general, summoned a group of BBC journalists and producers for a meeting at his office. Curran had succeeded the liberal Hugh Greene the previous year, and his instincts

were more conservative. He opened the meeting by referring to the perception that BBC journalists had adopted
an anti-Establishment line, and that they reserved their
most severe questions for people associated with authority.
The journalists and producers countered that it was their
job to remain sceptical of authority, but always free from
personal bias. Curran, however, concluded the meeting by
explaining that while he acknowledged it was part of a
BBC journalist's role to put critical questions to authority,
it was nevertheless part of his job as director general to see
that authority was treated fairly.[65]

Another revealing incident from that same period is a
1975 dinner meeting between the then BBC chair Michael
Swann and the Labour prime minister Harold Wilson.
Over dinner, the two men discussed the influence of sixties
radicalism at the BBC. A memo of the conversation states:

> Talking about the 'hippie' influences at the BBC, Sir
> Michael Swann said that, while he would not pretend that
> the BBC was completely clear of problems of this kind, it
> was a picnic compared with Edinburgh University [where
> he had been vice chancellor]. Nonetheless he thought too
> many young producers approached every programme they
> did from the starting point of an attitude about the subject
> which could be summed up as: 'You are a shit'. It was an
> attitude which he and others in the management of the BBC
> (Sir Michael Swann particularly mentioned Huw Wheldon)
> deplored, and they would be using their influences as
> opportunity offered to try to counter it.[66]

That the prime minister sympathised with these efforts
is evident from another file recording a meeting between
Swann and Wilson two years earlier, the minutes of
which noted that 'discussion about the authority of the

Governors, the [director general] and senior staff seemed to cheer [Wilson] up no end'.[67]

Both these incidents illustrate the close relations between the BBC hierarchy and the political elite. This has shaped editorial policies and practices, making the BBC much more amenable to elites than democratic and egalitarian movements. BBC journalists may have, to differing degrees, advanced more substantive notions of independence, and even absorbed elements of oppositional politics into their professional ideology. But they remain answerable to their superiors who, like many of them, are often drawn from the same social strata as politicians and state officials and are, moreover, responsible for maintaining good relations with senior politicians and other elites who ultimately determine the BBC's future.

CHAPTER 2

'A satisfactory liaison':
The BBC and the Secret State

Late one Thursday evening in May 1935, the BBC broadcast a discussion on modern poetry between the American poet and playwright Paul Engle and the Anglo-Irish poet Cecil Day-Lewis, later poet laureate.[1] Day-Lewis had previously featured several times on local radio in 1934 and most recently, in March that year, had appeared on a BBC series called *Youth Looks Ahead*. From a privileged background, he had attended English public school and then Oxford, where he became close to W. H. Auden. But like a good number of other elite intellectuals of his generation, he was attracted to left-wing ideas and in 1933 came to the attention of the secret state when he signed an anti-war manifesto. The head of MI5, Colonel Sir Vernon Kell – the co-founder with Mansfield Smith-Cumming of the Secret Service Bureau, which subsequently split into MI5 and MI6 – then wrote to the chief constable in Day-Lewis's Cheltenham, asking for details of the man, who 'appeared to be a supporter of the communist movement'.[2]

When Day-Lewis appeared on the BBC in 1935, the producers were concerned about his politics and his apparently scurrilous claim made in his broadcast 'that developments in literature cannot be divorced from social life'.[3] They had attempted to temper his script, but he insisted that he should, as he put it, at least make 'some adequate reference to the relation between politics ... and literature'. This, according to Day-Lewis's biographer, 'caused some disquiet among the BBC producers' and 'contributed to a growing perception of him amongst broadcasters and literary journalists as "Red Cecil"'.[4] The day after his later BBC broadcast with Paul Engle, Day-Lewis wrote a letter sent care of the Communist Party's publishing company, Martin Lawrence, which was intercepted by MI5. He apologised for not having attended a demonstration, explaining that he had been 'closeted at the BBC all afternoon', and referred to a 'terrific shindy' in the BBC studio when 'Co. Dawnay suddenly woke up at the 11th hour and realised there was a viper in his bosom'. He also referred in his letter to an inquiry at the Talks Department at the BBC, claiming that 'vested interests were doing their best to get them [leftists] all turned out'.[5]

The reference to 'Co. Dawnay' in Day-Lewis's letter was to Colonel Alan Dawnay, the BBC's Controller of Programmes, who had for two years been secretly in contact with MI5. An Old Etonian and career soldier, Dawnay was recruited by Reith from the War Office, where he had served as a Colonel in MI2,[6] the section of British military intelligence responsible for Russia and Scandinavia. His contact at MI5 was Brigadier Oswald 'Jasper' Harker, who headed its counter-espionage and counter-subversion branch. A 'fearsome character', Jasper Harker later succeeded Kell as MI5's director general. He had previously worked in the Indian police, and had initially been loaned to the Security Service by the India Office. Acting on Kell's instructions, Harker met with the BBC's Colonel Dawnay for lunch on 21 December 1933 – a meeting which appears to have been the first official contact between the BBC and the Security Service. He reported the following back to Kell:

Colonel Dawnay at the outset gave me a very clear indication of the line which the BBC were anxious to pursue with a view to maintaining a reputation for reasonable impartiality on political subjects.

I gather that the general line is the one which we ourselves try to follow; that is to say that any political views which look upon the ballot box as the proper solution of their problems are reasonable politics; anything that goes outside the ballot box – such as communism or Fascism – is considered to be subversive if not seditious.[7]

Harker had agreed at the lunch meeting that if MI5 suspected what he called 'subversive propaganda' was being 'attempted through the medium of the BBC', or if that 'undesirable persons were obtaining employment', then he would give Colonel Dawnay 'a friendly hint'. Dawnay in turn agreed that he would also communicate any doubts he had about BBC employees to Harker. The two men agreed that the arrangement would be kept secret and that communications would be sent to Dawnay's home in Chelsea rather than to the BBC itself. 'It was decided that, as far as the BBC were concerned at any rate,' Harker noted in a subsequent report, 'it was most undesirable that Colonel Dawnay's contact with me should be generally known.'[8] Harker concluded his report with the words: 'I think I have effected a satisfactory liaison.'[9]

After an exchange of letters in January 1934, Harker and Colonel Dawnay met twice in March that year. At the first of these meetings, held on the evening of 14 March 1934, the main topic of discussion was an incident a week earlier which had upset the BBC management and apparently alarmed the Security Service: a left-wing trade unionist, who was to speak as part of a series on 'The National Character', had broken from his script and accused the

BBC of censorship live on air. William Ferrie, a representative of the National Union of Vehicle Builders, had been asked to respond to a talk given by the motor mogul Sir Herbert Austin. In his speech, entitled 'Modern Industry and the National Character', Sir Herbert had argued that recent developments in industry had seen huge improvements for working people.[10] Ferrie's draft response gave an account of the conditions of working-class life in Britain and advocated a radical solution. 'The conveyor-belt is our master,' Ferrie argued. 'If the management in the factory decide to increase speed by 10%, a thousand hands work 10% faster. I'm not exaggerating when I say that those of us who work on the conveyor-belt are bound to it as galley slaves were bound to the galley.'[11] The BBC pushed for Ferrie to tone down his talk, and he had originally complied. However, when it came to the time of broadcast he delivered not the watered-down speech, but the following statement:

> Last week a big employer of labour, Sir Herbert Austin, gave a talk about the British working man, and I have been invited to say what I think about the British worker. I am a working man myself, but what I wanted to tell you has been so censored and altered and cut up by the BBC that I consider it impossible for me to give a talk without it being a travesty of the British working class. I therefore protest against the censorship of the BBC and will give the talk instead to the Press.[12]

The issue for MI5 and the senior BBC management was not why Ferrie had departed from the amended draft, and certainly not why he had been obstructed from broadcasting his original speech, but how it was that he had been invited to broadcast in the first place. Dawnay explained to

Harker that he had been recommended as a result of contact with a number of figures he described as 'very left-winger'. Most notable among this group were two academics who had become disillusioned with the Labour Party and were turning towards more radical politics: Harold Laski of the London School of Economics and Hyman Levy of Imperial College, both of whom were being monitored by the Security Service. After Ferrie's on-air protest, Colonel Dawnay interviewed Hyman Levy, who had assured him that he had no prior knowledge of Ferrie's broadcast and said he did not know that he was associated with the Communist Party. Neither Colonel Dawnay nor Jasper Harker were convinced by Levy's account, but Harker warned Dawnay that 'he would need to have some fairly definitive corroboration to satisfy him that Levy was a double-crosser and a liar'. Colonel Dawnay asked Harker if MI5 could look into 'Levy's reliability', and Harker reassured Dawnay that he would do his 'best to clear up the situation'.[13]

The conversation between the two men then moved on to the critical press coverage the BBC was receiving from the right-wing tabloids and what Colonel Dawnay called 'the extremist press on the left'. Dawnay asked Harker if he thought this might be part of a conscious left-wing conspiracy. Harker wrote in his note to MI5 director general Vernon Kell,

> Colonel Dawnay asked me whether I thought – so far as the attack from the left was concerned – it was part of a definitive plan to discredit the BBC in the eyes of the public, so that the way could be made clear for a Left-Wing Government – should it come to power – to take over the BBC, the most powerful instrument for propaganda in this country, without arousing any very hostile public criticism.

This may or may not be a far fetched idea, but it certainly is one which is worth considering.[14]

When the two men met again a week later, Harker told Dawnay that he was satisfied that there was no 'intrigue' behind the 'concerted attack on the BBC from the Left Wing Press', and Dawnay told Harker that he was satisfied there was no 'treachery on the part of the staff inside the BBC'. They agreed to stay in contact regarding anything interesting or suspicious.[15]

In October 1934, MI5 passed on a dossier to Colonel Dawnay, which it said had come from a 'very anti-Communist source' not identified in the files. The dossier complained about a number of figures who had been allowed to broadcast lectures by the BBC whose views the 'source' found to be unacceptable. These included the former Labour minister Hugh Dalton and the liberal political economist J. A. Hobson. Also singled out were one J. L. Stocks, for being 'an active member of the Relief Committee for Victims of German Fascism' and 'one of the signatories to the Anti-Fascist Manifesto', and John MacMurray of London University, for having been 'a speaker at an Anti-War Conference at Hampstead'.[16]

What individual or organisation produced this document and what Colonel Dawnay thought of it is not recorded in the National Archive files, but when Harker and Dawnay met again later that month, Dawnay asked Harker if the Security Service would start vetting the present staff of the BBC. Harker reported back that he was 'impressed by Colonel Dawnay's argument, and though in detail I think this may be a long and troublesome business, I am inclined to think it is one which we should be wise to undertake'.[17]

Another notable aspect of the report forwarded to Dawnay was its claim that 'Socialist intellectuals' had been overheard claiming that they 'had the Talks Department of the BBC in their pockets'. The Talks Department was at that time headed by Charles Siepmann, whom MI5 regarded as 'an individual to be regarded with suspicion'. At one of their first meetings, Harker had asked Dawnay about Siepmann without revealing that they knew anything about him. Dawnay had replied that, though Siepmann was 'distinctly Labour Left', he was 'a most loyal and hardworking subordinate' and 'would have no dealings with the Communists'.[18]

Siepmann again came under suspicion in 1934 after a retired naval officer approached the Admiralty with a view to resigning his commission from the Reserve List. The officer, who had since been recruited by the BBC, explained to his superiors that he was now a committed pacifist, having been 'converted' while working at the BBC. According to the Admiralty's account of the interview, the officer 'made a remark to the effect that perhaps we were not aware of the pacifist nature of the Birmingham section of that Corporation, mentioning in particular the Director of Talks'. Alarmed by what they had heard, the Admiralty alerted MI5, forwarding an account of the interview. They also got in touch with Reith's deputy, Admiral Carpendale, who reassured the Admiralty that the Birmingham section was under the complete control of London and that they 'have really no chance of broadcasting any pacifist theories or exercising any influence on the general public'. Carpendale said he would 'keep an eye on the personnel there as some cranks might form a cell which would not be healthy'.[19]

Whether due to the attacks from the right-wing press, the anti-communist report, the Admiralty's intervention, or a combination of all three is not clear, but Siepmann did not last much longer as director of talks. In May 1935, when a number of appointments were announced at the BBC, the *Observer* noted that: 'The talks department is one on which the limelight beats with exceptional fierceness, and it may well be that Sir John Reith will take this opportunity to remove Mr. Siepmann to a less exposed post and provide a new target for the critics of talks.'[20] Sure enough, Siepmann was effectively demoted to head of publications that July. Hilda Matheson wrote in the *Observer*, 'Mr Siepmann's service to talks, and particularly to adult education, has been of a high order. It seems regrettable that his great abilities should be relegated to a post with so little apparent scope as that of director of regional relations.'[21]

In April 1935, Harker lunched again with Colonel Dawnay, this time to discuss 'the best way of dealing with the vetting of the staff employed by the BBC' and was joined at the meeting by Admiral Carpendale. Harker reported,

> We came to the conclusion that nothing short of a general vetting would be satisfactory (leaving out the personnel such as charwomen etc, and all who would never, by any possible means, be in a position to do anything against the interests of the BBC).
>
> Admiral Carpendale will therefore send me, in small batches, the names, (and, if possible, addresses) of the permanent staff, for us to say whether we know anything against them.
>
> The names of all new hands whom they propose to employ, will be sent to us, if possible before they are taken on.
>
> Admiral Carpendale would like us to communicate with him personally at his private address, which he will send to me (together with his telephone number) in due course.
>
> Admiral Carpendale was very alive to the fact that, owing to the majority of the staff of the BBC being employed as engineers on the technical side, any undesirable member of

the staff could at any time sabotage the whole show – this point being especially applicable to a period of crisis within the country.

From what I saw of Admiral Carpendale I think that he will co-operate with us discreetly, and I impressed upon him the necessity of not taking any action with regard to investigation or dismissal without first consulting us.[22]

Colonel Dawnay subsequently spoke to John Reith, and they agreed that any suspicions about BBC staff would be passed directly to MI5, rather than through the Metropolitan Police.[23]

Dawnay's resignation from the BBC was announced in March 1935, effective that September. His replacement was Cecil Graves, the director of the Empire Service who would later become the BBC's joint director general. Graves, like Dawnay, was a military man and a former intelligence officer. Educated at Sandhurst, he joined the BBC in 1926 after spending several years at the City, prior to which he had worked in the Intelligence Branch of the War Office.[24] Graves met with Harker and Dawnay a month before the latter's departure, and it was agreed that MI5 would thereafter maintain contact with Graves directly. There followed a discussion of what Harker called 'the communist problem vis-à-vis the BBC'.[25]

The problems, the men agreed, fell into three categories. First was the question of 'communist sympathisers' and 'communist agents' working at the BBC. Second was the possibility that 'communist inspired speakers' might be able to put their views across via programmes. The third problem the men discussed was, they agreed, the most difficult. This was the possibility that the BBC itself might become the location of industrial conflict and that the management of the Corporation might in a moment of 'national crisis' find itself vulnerable to 'sabotage' by BBC engineers. The BBC management had at that time recently been involved in a pay dispute with engineering staff, which had been supported by the *Daily Worker*, and Graves and Dawnay wanted MI5 to provide them with any intelligence they might have on communist sympathis-ers among engineers and 'the present feeling regarding the recent improvements in the conditions of the engineering staff'.[26] In the event, no systematic 'anti-sabotage' vetting was developed, and neither would those appearing on BBC programmes be systematically monitored.[27] BBC staff, however, would be vetted, secretly and systematically. The 1935 meetings set in motion a system of political vetting which was formalised with a written agreement in 1937. The practice was maintained for fifty years, abandoned only in 1985 after being exposed by a team of investigative journalists. Much of what is known about political vetting, stems from the revelations at that time and the declassified BBC files that have become available since.

The vetting procedure MI5 and the BBC established was referred to by those in the know as 'formalities', while MI5 was referred to in BBC files as 'The College' or 'Box 500', after the official PO Box address used by the Security Service. The whole process was managed at the BBC end by the so-called Special Duties office, which was headed by a security liaison officer and later by the BBC's special assistant to the director of personnel. At the time this vetting was exposed in 1985, it was headed by Ronnie Stonham, a career soldier who had joined the BBC in 1982 from the Ministry of Defence, where he had written the classified history of the British military's Northern Ireland campaign. Brigadier Stonham worked out of Room 105 in Broadcasting House and reported to Director of Personnel Christopher Martin, himself a former Royal Marine. To maintain 'the security of the formalities system', his Special Duties office held the only written records, with policies 'promulgated by personal verbal briefing of those directly concerned'.[28]

What was referred to as 'positive vetting', a practice which applied only to very senior staff, and with their knowledge, was used for a small number of posts at the BBC which involved 'constant and regular access to highly classified Government information'. In 1985, this included the director general and just seven other senior positions. Covert political vetting – referred to in the BBC files as 'negative vetting' – applied to two separate categories: 'access posts' and 'counter-subversion posts'. Access posts were those entailing knowledge of BBC plans for wartime broadcasting; those involving the receipt of the Foreign Office telegrams routinely received by the World Service; those involving access to other classified information; or those involving knowledge of the vetting system itself. In 1985, this included 539 posts, most of which were within the Wartime Broadcasting Service.[29]

Counter-subversion was a much larger category. These posts were vetted by MI5 to 'avoid slanting of BBC output i.e. political bias or distortion in programmes or the dissemination of any propaganda'.[30] In 1969, a joint BBC/MI5 working party agreed the appropriate criterion for counter-subversion vetting was those posts involving 'an unhindered opportunity to slant broadcasting material for a politically subversive purpose'.[31] This was slightly revised in 1983 to read 'posts affording direct opportunity to influence broadcast material for a subversive purpose',[32] though what consequences this rephrasing had for the practice is not clear.

The names of subjects for vetting, mostly potential recruits to the BBC, were, according to the co-authors of *Blacklist*, Mark Hollingsworth and Richard Norton-Taylor, submitted to MI5's C Branch and then to F Branch. The former was the division of MI5 responsible for vetting, while the latter was responsible for 'counter-subversion'. Counter-subversion was, in 1972, defined by F Branch director John Jones as 'activities threatening the safety or well-being of the State and intended to undermine or over-throw Parliamentary democracy by political, industrial or violent means'.[33] Counter-subversion became an ever greater priority for MI5 and a broader network of private propagandists and former intelligence officers as the crisis of the 1970s took hold and the left gained in strength, and F Branch's resources and remit grew steadily at the expense, it should be noted, of MI5's counter-espionage activities.

F Branch's judgements on potential recruits to the BBC and on existing staff considered for promotion was provided to BBC line management via the Special Duties office in the form of 'advice', leaving in theory the final decision on hiring with the BBC. In practice though, discretion was only exercised within parameters set by MI5. Those suspected of contact or sympathy with 'subversive organisations', and therefore potentially barred from employment or promotion, fell into three categories. Category A meant that the individual should not be given 'a post affording opportunity for subversive activity'. Category B meant that while the candidate was not definitely unreliable, 'substantial suspicion' remained, while Category C meant that 'the record of the candidate or of his close relatives or associates leaves room for slight doubt as to the candidate's reliability'.[34] An 'unfavourable BBC management judgement', Stonham noted in a 1985 memo, would usually be based on 'membership of, or contact with members or sympathy with the aims' of 'subversive organisations'. In 1985, these included the fascist groups the National Front

47

and the British National Party, as well as prominent radical left organisations the Communist Party of Great Britain, the Socialist Workers Party, the Workers Revolutionary Party and Militant Tendency.

The political vetting process was intended both to avoid 'recruiting the "undesirable"' and to prevent certain existing staff 'holding "influential" posts'.[35] Short- and long-term contract staff were also vetting as per full members of staff, and from 1975 the names of the regular producers and directors on the BBC's freelance list (the 'F List') were also submitted to MI5.[36] Separate personnel files labelled 'secret' and stamped with a green triangle symbol resembling a Christmas tree were maintained by the Special Duties office.

According to the official history of the Secret Service, MI5 vetted around 5,000 out of 12,000 posts in 1952 and sent 'adverse reports' on one in ten applicants. Over the years, the numbers of staff vetted remained broadly similar, although the relative proportions decreased as the BBC's staff numbers grew. A declassified BBC document from January 1984 provides a breakdown of the number of vetted posts within the BBC that decade, excluding those within Engineering and those areas covered by the 'Access List'. In 1981, a total of 5,728 out of 23,888 BBC posts, roughly a quarter, were classified as 'formalities posts'. The highest proportion of vetted posts in 1981 were those in Local Radio, where over 63 per cent of positions were subjected to political vetting. This was followed by External Services and News, where around half of all posts were vetted.[37]

Since not all posts within the BBC were vetted, it was still possible even for those considered by MI5 to be Category A subversives to be employed at the BBC, and only later come to the attention of MI5. Vetting procedures were therefore fairly open-ended, with procedures in place for the Security Service to notify the BBC if and when staff came to their 'adverse notice', or to revise previous assessments.[38] In the case of 'subversives' employed within the BBC, the policy (in 1983) was to operate 'a "tight" control policy ... for any "A"s and "B"s who have slipped into the staff'. These controls would then be 'progressively relaxed if/when "supervisors" are content', after which they could, like any Category C subversive on the payroll, be subject only to 'normal professional editorial control'.[39] The situation was explained by Stonham in a memo to Martin:

It is Corporation policy not to appoint those given an A assessment. There are, however, currently 10 'A's on the staff, 5 of these being with External Services; all of the remaining 5 either started their career in 'non-vettable' posts or the adverse information came to light after initial clearance. The difference between A and B assessments is one of 'shading' only; employment of those given a B assessment is, therefore, actively discouraged. There are, however, currently 22 'B's on the staff, 12 of these being with External Services. The Security Service does try and give us any new information on A and B category assessments, as it becomes available to them. However, in view of their work load, we do not rely on such information being provided automatically. Our current procedures, therefore, include requesting reviews for those members of staff with A or B assessments, either when required (e.g. consideration for promotion, transfer, etc.), or every three years, as appropriate. The Security Service agree that these reviews are necessary and accept that small additional load; hopefully such reviews downgrade assessments or remove the security objection entirely.[40]

Stonham also favoured MI5 periodic reviews for those members of staff categorised as 'C'. However, as MI5 refused to do so, he recommended 'a 3-yearly BBC internal review system for staff with C assessments' to be conducted by the Special Duties office, which would examine 'the subject's performance, views and attitudes over the previous 3 years'. While conceding the possibility that the subject may be 'covertly active', he considered that 'on balance', providing that if 'any doubt exists, the original assessment is allowed to stand', the risk was 'acceptable'.

This assessment was made during the 1983 review of the BBC's 'formalities' procedures, the last of a number of reviews over the fifty years during which counter-subversion vetting operated at the BBC. The first two such reviews were carried out during and shortly after the Second World War, in 1943 and 1947 respectively, while two further reviews were carried out in 1954 and 1958.[41]

Although many of the early accounts of vetting assumed that the procedure was imposed by the Security Service, during these periodic reviews the BBC generally pressed MI5 to maintain, or even extend, the political vetting of its staff, while MI5, as the BBC noted, 'repeatedly requests us to reduce the numbers submitted to vetting'.[42] The 1958 review meeting led to the setting up of a working party that suggested a narrower selection of posts to vet. The working party's report was accepted by the MI5 director general, but the BBC argued that the recommendations were 'likely in the long run to increase the risk to the security of the service, and sooner or later, to confront us with some difficult staff problems'.[43] While MI5 favoured vetting only promotions, the BBC argued that without vetting at the recruitment level, 'communists or near communists' would 'gradually accumulate into the Corporation' and would 'become disgruntled when not promoted beyond a certain point'.[44] It was the BBC, not MI5, that sought to conflate personal politics with national security concerns:

> In view of the overriding requirement of impartiality and integrity in its news service, the importance of the reputation which it has built up in this sphere and the great practical difficulty of guarding against unreliable sub-editing in the conditions of a broadcasting newsroom: the BBC feels it is essential that the political reliability of all newsroom staff should be beyond question ... It is the BBC's view that security is jeopardised, even in peacetime conditions, by occasional lapses of political judgement in BBC news broadcasts which might be thought to indicate a pro-Communist bias, precisely because such lapses undermine public confidence in an institution and a service to which everyone turns for stability and encouragement in an emergency such as war.[45]

In 1959, MI5 wanted to restrict vetting to what was then the 'Senior Sub-Editor class', but the BBC pushed for the vetting of 'all News Staff, right down to Sub-Editors'.[46] According to Seaton, MI5 was 'surprised and impressed' when in return for maintaining the vetting of its staff, the BBC offered to continue 'providing general information and photographs about artists and contributors, about staff, programmes, use of rooms on BBC premises, special liaisons with the Monitoring Service, and general assistance to Special Branch'.[47]

The BBC director general at that time was Ian Jacob, who in 1960 was succeeded by his protégé Hugh Greene, a liberal anti-communist who hoped to expand counter-subversion vetting at the BBC. According to an MI5 minute quoted in the 'authorised history', Greene 'wanted us to vet far more widely than we were prepared to do because they did not wish to employ anyone who might damage their reputation for impartiality'. MI5's director general, a former journalist who had been recruited to F Branch, however, noted after one meeting that there was 'an irreconcilable difference' on vetting: 'We were concerned with defence interests but they were really concerned with the avoidance of embarrassment.'[48] According to Christopher Andrew's authorised history of MI5, Greene's successor, Charles Curran, 'attached less importance to vetting', and MI5 complained that it was the BBC's 'deliberate policy to offer jobs to some people with ultra left records whom they considered to be imaginatively creative and desirable'. Andrew writes that 'the mood changed' after Michael Swann was appointed chairman in 1973, but does not point to any evidence indicating any change in policy.[49]

In 1978, five years after Swann's appointment, the proportion of 'formalities posts' at the BBC was reduced when the vetting of 'assistant' level posts outside of News, Production and Research was abolished. However, a recruitment drive for Breakfast Television and Local Radio in the early 1980s meant that the actual number of vetted posts nevertheless increased significantly.[50] By 1983, the Special Duties office was overloaded with work, while MI5 was not only concerned at the increase in the numbers of staff for vetting, but 'also very sensitive and concerned over the possible implications of these increases in terms of prejudicing the security of their whole operation for the BBC'.[51] These concerns led to a review that resulted in a significant reduction in the number of vetted posts.[52]

In preparation for the BBC's meeting with MI5, Ronnie Stonham suggested some laxity with regards to those members of staff who had been designated as Category C subversives. In particular, he suggested making some allowances for youthful indulgences, and wrote that 'in view of the changing values in today's society, it is considered that there is some scope for improvements and changes in the system for handling these assessments'. He suggested that the 'date of the adverse information', and particularly if the subject was an undergraduate at the relevant time, should be treated as 'major factors in making balanced judgements' when it came to the 'Special Duties office' making recommendations and the relevant department making a final decision.[53]

Despite this apparently more liberal approach, Stonham opposed any major overhaul of the vetting system. He considered that the 'current formalities system is sound, practical and is working well', and that what was required was 'some "loosening of the reins" and some modification of procedures, rather than any radical changes or reorganisation'. Indeed, while recommending greater laxity in some respects, and a further decrease in the number of vetted posts, Stonham also recommended that the staff with A and B assessments should be reviewed more regularly, every two rather than three years. And in response to a proposal that a system of 'selective vetting' be followed, he remarked that, were that institutionalised, 'we ... could have in the Corporation several candidates (of which I have quoted only three) who would have been potential sources of concern/trouble, if not actually subversive, and of which we would have been unaware'. This, in turn, he suggested, 'would deprive Line Managers of the reassurance, which they now have, of the "negative" information that their staff in the areas concerned have "nothing recorded against" and can be accepted as "reliable".'[54]

On 18 May 1983, Stonham, his superior Christopher Martin and Assistant Director General Alan Protheroe met with five representatives from MI5 at Broadcasting House. Martin told the officers that 'the BBC valued highly the information received from the Security Service', claiming that it 'was of the greatest assistance in helping to ensure that objectivity and impartiality and balance were maintained throughout the Corporation'. Once again, MI5 stated its wish to minimise the number of posts subject to vetting, in part due to 'the additional risks of embarrassment'.[55] In a secret discussion paper drafted in preparation for this meeting, the BBC had described news and current affairs as 'our most "sensitive" area and one in which we should not compromise'.[56] MI5 agreed, and the high level of vetting in this area was maintained. It was also agreed that the high level of vetting in Local Radio would continue, 'in view of the freedom of action and involvement in local affairs of all programme staff' in this area.[57]

Conversely, one category for which it was agreed vetting could be discontinued was television announcers and news readers, the rationale being that they were in any case subject to 'direct controls', meaning presumably that since they merely read from a script there was no threat to 'objectivity and impartiality and balance'. The vetting of equivalent posts in radio, however, was to continue since they enjoyed more leeway, and Stonham and MI5 later agreed that the policy on television continuity announcers was to be reversed on the basis that they 'frequently have unsupervised microphone access'.[58]

The review of the vetting system, which began that April, was completed in December and resulted in the BBC abolishing vetting for around 2,000 posts, reducing the total number of 'formalities' posts from 5,703 to 3,705.[59] This brought the percentage of positions subject to 'formalities' down from 24 per cent to 14.5 per cent. The greatest proportional decrease was in television, where the number of vetted posts decreased from 21.5 per cent to just 8 per cent, even accounting for its incorporation of staff from News

Division, who were extensively vetted, following an administrative overhaul. The number of 'formalities posts' in radio, meanwhile, also decreased, although only slightly.[60]

For fifty years, political vetting at the BBC was conducted unbeknown to most BBC staff and to the public. Some broadcasting unionists, however, did strongly suspect that left-wing candidates were being barred from employment and repeatedly raised the issue with the BBC, while newspaper journalists on several occasions attempted to expose the practice. In February 1968, for example, the *Sunday Times* cartoonist Mark Boxer seems to have got wind of the practice and arranged to meet with BBC Director General Hugh Greene and Director of Administration John Arkell, who 'stuck very firmly to the line given by the Security Service'.[61] According to Arkell's account, Boxer claimed to know about political vetting, said he had been told that the BBC was 'very rigid about the employment of Communists' and asked 'very pointed and penetrating questions'. Arkell, however, 'denied that security clearance was a pre-requisite for employment' and claimed that 'we went out of our way to be fair' to known communists.[62]

Vetting was finally exposed in the *Observer* by investigative journalists David Leigh, Paul Lashmar and Mark Hollingsworth. In their article, they identified Room 105, the home of the Special Duties office, named Ronnie Stonham, and detailed a number of people thought to have been denied jobs as a result of vetting.[63] A key source for the story was Aubrey Singer, the former deputy director general, who had taken forced retirement a year earlier.[64] Presented with their evidence, Christopher Martin had refused to comment,[65] but after the *Observer* ran the story BBC TV News quoted a former executive confirming that an MI5 clearance system did indeed exist. It also quoted John Arkell as saying: 'It would be surprising if a broadcasting organisation did not take some protective steps to prevent extremists having undue influence over the air, in the interests of security and of fairness to the public.'[66]

Following the exposé, the BBC, the Home Office, the Cabinet Office and MI5 held 'exploratory discussions into the possibility of introducing new procedures', during which Stonham proposed that a system of 'overt' vetting be introduced, under which staff requiring access to classified information would be required to fill out a security questionnaire.[67] His proposal, however, was not taken up and the whole system was 'revised and radically changed'.[68] Counter-subversion vetting was abolished and vetting thereafter was only carried out post-appointment for those proposed for involvement in the Wartime Broadcasting Service, or positions in the World Service involving access to Foreign Office material – those who would have originally been on the 'Access List'.[69]

How should we assess this history of covert political vetting at the BBC? First, it is important to note that while the practice was extensive at the broadcaster, it was not widespread across British society during the Cold War. MI5 stated at the May 1983 meeting that 'counter-subversion vetting was carried out only for the BBC and the British Council'.[70] Second, the standard justification that 'counter-subversion' activities by MI5 can be justified with reference to 'national security' concerns is not convincing. In the particular case of vetting at the BBC, there was a clear distinction between posts thought to represent some sort of security risk, 'access posts', and those which afforded the post-holder the opportunity to disseminate political views deemed unacceptable by the officers of MI5. One key question in terms of how we understand the

BBC more generally is to what extent it resisted pressure from the secret state. Here, the evidence is very revealing. David Leigh, one of the journalists who originally exposed the practice, writes that MI5 'forced the broadcasters to lie about the vetting, even to the BBC's own governors'.[71] Certainly, the latter felt bound to follow the dictates of the former, and obliged to maintain a high level of secrecy around vetting. 'The BBC is under a firm instruction', Stonham noted in one memo, 'not to make known to any extent whatsoever its relationship and contacts with the Security Service.'[72] In another, he states that the 'secrecy of the complete vetting operation imposed upon us by the Security Service … is not of our making'.[73]

The declassified documents also show that the BBC unsuccessfully tried to persuade MI5 to allow it to at least admit to the vetting of staff involved in the Wartime Broadcasting Service, as well as foreign nationals working in the World Service, on the grounds that this would be reasonably expected. MI5, it was noted in another document, 'ruled that [the BBC] should not make known to any extent whatsoever [its] relationship and contacts with the Service'.[74] All this evidence supports Leigh's argument that the BBC, far from acting independently on 'advice' provided by the Security Service, was in fact subordinate to 'the College'.

On the other hand, Leigh's suggestion that political vetting was imposed on the BBC is contradicted by compelling evidence cited by Christopher Andrew and Jean Seaton in their official histories of both institutions. Both show that, far from being forced to comply with the edicts of the secret state, the BBC's senior management repeatedly argued for an extension of political vetting, while MI5 looked to scale back its operation. Out of the two official historians, Andrew offers the more critical assessment. He

concedes that political vetting 'now seems seriously dispro-
portionate', while Seaton considers that, though it 'could
be damaging, and shocking if applied in error', it nevertheless 'helped the BBC defend itself against infiltration and
attacks from the government'.[75] She defers to the claim
by Stonham's successor Mike Hodder – which contradicts
much of the documentary evidence – that membership of
'extremist' parties was no bar to a career at the BBC and
that such persons 'enriched' the BBC by ensuring a 'wide
range of views'.

Overall, Seaton concludes that: 'Vetting was defensible and proper, but the BBC failed to make a case for it.'
This is a remarkable conclusion given that, while apparently approved by successive governments, political vetting
seems to have developed without any democratic approval.
At a review meeting with the BBC in October 1958, MI5
noted that their mandate from the government was 'limited
to vetting those who have access to Secret information',
but that this 'had been extended by the director general
of the Security Service in the case of the BBC to include
vetting against subversive activity'.[76]

Seaton's assessment is characteristic of a broader analytical problem with her work, which tends to assume
the legitimacy of compromises reached between the BBC
management and politicians and state officials, and then
to take for granted that the outcomes of such delibera-
tions are in keeping with the BBC's democratic purpose.
Her almost sentimental deference to British pragmatism
means she fails to adequately recognise the BBC as a site
of political contestation, or to see that its internal politics are related to broader struggles. To some extent, we
see a similar problem in the opposite position on vetting
advanced by David Leigh, who implicitly sees the BBC as
an independent sphere compromised by the encroachments

of the secret state. Normatively speaking, this is all well and good. But in analytical terms it is limiting. Like most liberal accounts, it assumes the BBC to be an independent and broadly cohesive institution, albeit one often subject to political pressure. But the BBC is not a bounded institution and neither does it embody particular values – such as independent journalism – in any straightforward fashion. Rather, it is a complex institution where individuals and groups with very different levels of authority advance competing visions of its character and purpose. Most importantly, they do so not in isolation, but as part of broader networks of people and institutions, and, at the most senior level, in the context of formal and informal connections to some of the most powerful people and institutions in British society.

More extensive documentation will perhaps give a more detailed picture of how the politics of vetting played out over time. But the existing evidence, as we have seen, clearly shows that the practice was initiated as a cooperative arrangement between MI5 and a small number of senior figures within the Corporation. After the exposé, counter-subversion vetting was quickly abolished under both external and internal pressure, including from broadcasting unions active in the BBC which were also involved in broader campaigns for greater journalistic freedom, including struggles against the corporate consolidation of the private news media. From the perspective of such groups, vetting by the secret state was a serious threat to journalistic freedom. But for senior management, the secret state was seen not as a threat to the BBC's independence, but as a valuable ally and asset. In this respect, a passage in a secret BBC discussion paper prepared in preparation for its meeting with MI5 in 1983 is particularly revealing:

In these 'programme areas' [subject to MI5 vetting] the numerous checks and balances which exist by virtue of normal 'editorial control' ensure that objectivity and impartiality are preserved; thus, the risk to the reputation and credibility of the BBC is minimal; some would say non-existent. However, the problem is to select the lowest workable and practicable 'influential' level for each editorial category, i.e. Production, Editorial, Direction and Reporting, at which to start applying formalities in order to ensure that the required balanced 'editorial control' is maintained.[77]

The importance of this cannot be overstated. Political vetting was not just an isolated practice which barred certain individuals from working at the BBC. It was one element within a broader system of editorial control which subtly tied the culture of the BBC to the interests of elites. It is significant in this regard that the BBC's counterparts at MI5 also appreciated the importance of 'normal editorial control'. In the mid- to late 1970s, MI5 believed that 'a Trotskyist element' was responsible for Granada's investigative current affairs programme, *World in Action*, but that there were 'virtually no instances of subversive bias in the presentation of news bulletins by the BBC'. This was attributed by MI5 not to the covert political vetting of BBC staff, but to the 'careful selection of key personnel by [BBC] management' and 'their careful monitoring of the product in the interests of objectivity'.[78]

The relationship between the BBC and the secret state has not been limited to the vetting of staff. The documents on vetting reveal, for example, that from 'at least January 1973', a small group of BBC staff, including the editor of News and Current Affairs (later the assistant director general) received a quarterly, and later biannual, 'Survey of Subversive Activities' from MI5. This practice was discontinued in August 1985, but a record of a meeting that November shows that the BBC agreed to continue to meet enquiries from MI5 for 'establishing identification'.[79] This service (what specifically it entailed is not clear from the document), it was noted, was potentially 'time consuming and embarrassing' for the BBC, but 'very useful' to MI5.[80] Another notable document in the disclosed vetting files is a letter to MI5 from Joan Reader, who worked in the Special Duties office. Reader enclosed with her letter a memo she suggested 'may be of interest to you and your colleagues'.[81] The memo, which does not itself appear in the released files, concerned a 'Bulgarian Embassy Warning' and had been forwarded to the Special Duties office by David Witherow, then the BBC's controller of resources and administration at the World Service and a former head of BBC Monitoring Service.[82] The World Service and BBC Monitoring are both semi-autonomous sections of the BBC which have been directly funded by government, rather than the licence fee, and deeply embedded in the foreign policy, security and intelligence apparatus of the British state. These snippets of correspondence point to a broader flow of information and personnel between the Corporation and the security apparatus, and arguably a deep affinity between the BBC and the secret state. In her introduction to *Pinkoes and Traitors*, Seaton refers to the BBC, approvingly, as having acted as 'the communicating part of the security state'. 'BBC engineers were in the front line of the Cold War battle for hearts and minds in Eastern Europe', she writes, 'a conflict the BBC helped decisively to win.'

Whether the BBC really contributed to the US and its allies winning (by default) the Cold War is another question, but it certainly fought hard. One of the BBC's foremost cold warriors was its most liberal director general, Hugh Greene, who, as we have seen, pushed for greater vetting of his staff by MI5. A 'journalist and psychological warrior' by his own account, Greene had worked at the *Daily Telegraph* before the Second World War, during which he headed the BBC's German service, and after which he became Controller of Broadcasting in the British Occupied Zone in Germany.[83] A privately educated Oxford graduate, Greene was a liberal, but he was very much an Establishment man and no stranger to the world of security and intelligence. His brother, the novelist Graham Greene, worked for MI6 during the war, as did his sister Elisabeth, who married the MI6 officer Rodney Dennys.[84] Greene himself became head of the BBC's Eastern Europe service in 1949, where his role was 'to pillory the Communist regime and display it as being ridiculous as well as cynical and evil'.[85] A year later, he was seconded by the BBC to the Colonial Office, where he was appointed head of propaganda for Harold Briggs, the British Army general overseeing a brutal counterinsurgency campaign in Malaya. Greene's mission there was to 'attack the morale' of the resistance, 'drive a wedge between the leaders and the rank and file' and to create 'an awareness of the values of the democratic way of life which is threatened by International Communism'.[86]

Greene's mentor at the BBC was Sir Ian Jacob, a former military officer who had served as part of Churchill's inner circle during the Second World War and would precede Greene as BBC director general. Jacob had been offered the position of head of MI6 after the war, but declined, accepting instead the post of Controller of the BBC's European Services in 1946. In September that year, he approached the Foreign Office for guidance as to how the European Services should report on the Soviet Union and communism. They responded by inviting him to join its Russia Committee, which had been set up that April to develop and coordinate the British state's anti-communist propaganda. The committee even moved the day of its weekly meeting to accommodate Jacob.[87] A key member of the committee was Ivone Kirkpatrick, a Foreign Office official who had worked as a director in the Ministry of Information and as controller of the BBC's European Services during the war. Kirkpatrick and Jacob would form a close partnership in those formative years for what would later become the BBC World Service.

One particularly significant initiative of the Russia Committee was the establishment of the Information Research Department (IRD), a Foreign Office propaganda outfit which sought especially to foster anti-communist sentiments on the left, and which would serve as 'a complementary weapon alongside the BBC in the war against Communism'.[88] The IRD was initially headed by Ralph Murray, a former BBC journalist who had worked on covert propaganda operations during the war and would later serve as a BBC governor. He was later succeeded by John Rennie, a former advertising executive and wartime propagandist, who would later be appointed head of MI6. Ian Jacob ensured that the BBC cooperated closely with the IRD, and appointed his controller of Overseas Services and editor of European Services to act as liaisons with Murray.[89] The BBC thereafter worked extremely closely with the IRD. The Labour politician Christopher Mayhew, who was instrumental in setting up the IRD, described it as having been its 'best customer'.[90] IRD material, Paul Lashmar and James Oliver write in their seminal account:

> poured into the BBC and was directed to news desks, talks writers and different specialist correspondents. IRD

provided background briefings, analysis, articles and suggested speakers. In addition, IRD specialists were available for consultation. Significantly, IRD soon boasted of its influence: 'the British Broadcasting Corporation Overseas Service is obviously a most important vehicle for anti-Communist publicity. We have the most cordial relations and daily contacts with those running this service at all levels and supply them with guidance and material [of] which they make excellent use in their news bulletins, talks and commentaries.'[91]

The flow of propaganda from IRD to the BBC's External Services was just one aspect of a much broader and deeper relationship that developed between External Services and the various foreign policy and propaganda organs of the British state. Alban Webb has described a 'hierarchy of evolving linkages from the most senior level of the BBC down', a 'network of institutional and personal links' through which 'the material nature of the relationship was revealed and worked through'. At the top of the BBC hierarchy, the director general and the chairman consulted with government ministers, while at less senior levels there were regular meetings and discussions, and daily guidance from officials.[92] This symbiotic relationship was built upon a basic class congruity, as much as more formal bureaucratic ties, with BBC personnel and their state counterparts being drawn from similar backgrounds and sharing an implicit understanding of how the 'national interest' should be construed. There was also something of a revolving door operating between the BBC and IRD. In 1954, for example, External Services recruited the head of the IRD's Soviet Desk to work on 'Communist affairs'. There, he worked closely with the BBC journalist and author Walter Kolarz, one of IRD's most prolific writers.[93]

The relationship between BBC External Services and the British government in the postwar period was deliberately kept complex and undefined, but was broadly speaking a cooperative one, albeit with the Corporation in the subordinate position. The BBC, Collier notes,

> were seemingly quite content to be directed by the FO [Foreign Office] as to how to deal with Middle Eastern personalities, and enquired whether it was desirable for them 'to deal in a more or less bare-fisted manner with any of the leading statesmen (or their principle spokesmen).'[94]

A good illustration of the nature of the relationship between BBC External Services and the British state comes from 1947, when it was still taking shape. Looking to define 'a proper understanding ... of the relations between the Foreign Office and the BBC', its Near East news editor, Gordon Mackenzie, wrote that 'the duty of the BBC is to follow in its broadcasts the general policy of HMG, but it is allowed the widest freedom in the selection, editing and presentation of day-to-day broadcast material'. His colleague Stephenson in turn emphasised that BBC support for 'some point of policy' should 'always be a matter of mutual agreement', but conceded that in the interests of maintaining 'a proper atmosphere of cooperation and assistance', when 'the FO particularly press us ... I think we are usually well advised to accede to such a request'.[95]

A further element of the BBC's close relationship with the secret state has been BBC Monitoring, which has played an important role in this matrix of broadcasting, intelligence and propaganda. Originally established to monitor and translate enemy broadcasting, BBC Monitoring served as a valuable asset for the British state during the Second World War, providing 'open source' intelligence.

Its materials, transcribed and translated by hundreds of linguists, were then gradually distributed more widely and freely and would prove absolutely fundamental to IRD's foreign propaganda efforts, especially its efforts to defeat the Nasser-inspired independence movements in the Middle East.[96]

In summary, during the Cold War period the BBC was not only distributing propaganda material in close cooperation with the British state, it was also supplying the intelligence on which that propaganda was dependent.

There is a temptation to view all this as merely a feature of the Cold War, of little relevance to the contemporary BBC, much as historical evidence of British atrocities from that period are readily dismissed as features of a bygone era of ideological fervour and geopolitical rivalry. Certainly, the intelligence and security services will have changed significantly, just as the BBC has, since the period for which the still extremely sparse documentary records are available. Moreover, by the very nature of this topic, it is extremely difficult to research. Nevertheless, with the onset of the so-called War on Terror we have seen a clear expansion in the powers of the British state's security, intelligence and propaganda apparatus, and there is no good reason to think that there is not still significant collusion of the type we find in the historical records, even if the nature of the relationships have undoubtedly changed significantly.

In response to the September 11 attacks, the British government immediately launched a number of propaganda initiatives to accompany its military response, and as part of this 'public diplomacy', the BBC World Service expanded its output to the Middle East and what strategic planners call 'AfPak', in some cases doubling its hours of broadcasting.[97] Within months, the BBC had appointed its Middle Eastern correspondent, the former Territorial Army captain and investment banker Frank Gardner, to the new post of security correspondent, the name being chosen because war on terror correspondent 'would have sounded ridiculous'. Gardner, who admits he was once interviewed for a job by MI6, is candid about having been in close contact with officers from both MI6 and MI5 since shortly after he took up the post, leading to the suspicion among his colleagues that he himself was an MI6 agent or asset.[98] Indeed, Gardner appears to have acted as a go-between for MI6 at the BBC following the death of the British weapons inspector Dr David Kelly. Further evidence of Gardner's close relationship with the government's propaganda apparatus emerged in 2008, when a document of the Home Office's Research, Information and Communication Unit (RICU) was leaked. The document, entitled 'Challenging Violent Extremist Ideology Through Communications', revealed a RICU propaganda initiative intended to 'taint the al-Qaida brand' and stated: 'We are pushing this material to UK media channels, eg a BBC radio programme exposing tensions between AQ leadership and supporters.'[99] It was soon noted that Gardner had fronted a BBC Radio 4 *Analysis* programme called 'al-Qaida's Enemy Within', which precisely mirrored the propaganda strategy outlined in the document. The BBC admitted that Gardner and another BBC colleague had been in contact, and had met with, RICU officials while making the programme, but denied that any material they provided had been used, or that the programme had been made at the prompting of officials.[100]

Whatever the truth of the matter, this plainly illustrates the ongoing close relationship between the BBC and the secret British state. It is also noteworthy in that, according to counter-terrorism propaganda expert Emma Briant, the

BBC director general's office receives a direct briefing from the Joint Intelligence Committee, the body which coordinates the activities of MI5, MI6 and GCHQ, 'on the right line to take on whether something is in the national and operational interest to broadcast'.[101]

BBC Monitoring, meanwhile, still maintains a close relationship with the security and intelligence agencies. Its 'key customers' are the Foreign and Commonwealth Office, the Ministry of Defence, the Cabinet Office and the security and intelligence agencies. Its overall performance is overseen, in an advisory capacity of course, by a Monitoring Consultative Group, which meets twice a year. This is chaired by the BBC and includes representatives from the Ministry of Defence, GCHQ, MI5, MI6, the Foreign and Commonwealth Office and the Cabinet Office.[102]

Until recently, these 'key customers' funded BBC Monitoring via a ring-fenced grant from the Cabinet Office, while the World Service has been funded out of a parliamentary grant-in-aid via the Foreign and Commonwealth Office. In 2010, the Conservative-led Coalition Government announced that this government funding would be cut back and that from 2013/14 the total cost of the World Service and BBC Monitoring would have to come out of the licence fee. The cuts to the World Service, and the planned withdrawal of funding, were strongly opposed by the Commons Foreign Affairs Select Committee, which argued that 'it would not be in the interests of the UK for the BBC to lose sight of the priorities of the FCO, which relies upon the World Service as an instrument of "soft power".'[103] Indeed, one Foreign Office official is quoted by a media academic and former BBC World Service journalist as referring to the World Service as a 'huge part of [our] soft power arsenal'.[104] The select committee's efforts led to some of the cuts being reduced and in November 2015, the

Conservative Government partly reversed the withdrawal of World Service funding. The announcement was, significantly enough, made in the government's 'National Security Strategy and Strategic Defence and Security Review', which stated that the Conservative Government would thereafter invest £85 million a year in the World Service as part of its strategy to 'further enhance our position as the world's leading soft power promoting our values and interests globally'.[105] Welcoming the announcement, BBC Director General Tony Hall described the World Service as 'one of our best sources of global influence'.[106]

CHAPTER 3

War and Peace

In April 2003, the editor and the lead presenter of BBC Radio 4's flagship news and current affairs programme *Today*, Kevin Marsh and John Humphrys, enjoyed lunch in a 'functional but expensively panelled ante-room with green tinted windows' overlooking the Thames. The dining room was in the headquarters of Britain's Secret Intelligence Service and the journalists' three dining companions were the then 'C' – as the chiefs of MI6 are known – Richard Dearlove, his deputy Nigel Inkster, and a third senior MI6 officer, Nigel Backhouse. It was a timely meeting. In opposition to majority public opinion in the UK and around the world, and in contempt of international law, the British government had recently participated in the US-led invasion of Iraq. This prima facie act of aggression – among the most grave crimes in international law – had been launched on the flimsiest of grounds, justified by complete fabrications, and MI6 were apparently uneasy as to how events might unfold. That very day, according to Marsh, Baghdad had fallen to the invading armies, and over prawns, chicken and mineral water, 'C' told him and Humphrys, to their apparent amazement, that: 'Iraq was not the main threat.' Dearlove's deputy, Inkster, then asked the BBC men: 'What do you think the reaction would be in the media if we never found any WMD?'

MI6, according to Marsh, had for several months been

giving 'strong hints that they wanted a more open relationship with some parts of the media', and Richard Dearlove
had reportedly held another meeting with a 'senior BBC
executive' at this time, to whom he made 'clear that Iraq
was not viewed by the intelligence services as the primary
threat'.[1] Marsh and Humphrys had agreed to their lunch
meeting on the condition that it, and nothing that was said
at it, would be reported, and though details were later published by the *Observer*, Marsh insists that he kept his word.
Such conversations, he writes, are 'the kind every editor
has daily ... where you pick up bits of gossip, background,
confidences. Someone's perspective'. That particular lunch,
however, proved to be especially significant. It persuaded
Marsh that 'even at the top of MI6, they didn't believe
Saddam was the urgent, imminent threat Blair and the
dossier said he was'. Combined with briefings Marsh had
been receiving from Clare Short, then still a Cabinet minister, it persuaded him of the legitimacy of concerns raised
by the anti-war movement and broader public about the
official justification for the invasion.

An estimated one million people had marched against
the planned war, the biggest protest in British history. But
more significant for Marsh were the sceptical voices among
the Establishment that were 'difficult to ignore'. Indeed, he
later recalled that 'the noise from the intelligence community over their dissatisfaction about the way in which the
case for war had been framed was deafening.' This context
is vital to understanding what followed.

On the morning of 29 May 2003, *Today* broadcast a
story by its defence and diplomatic correspondent, Andrew
Gilligan. The anonymous source for the story, it was later
revealed, was the Ministry of Defence weapons inspector Dr David Kelly. Kelly had met with Gilligan a week
earlier and informed him that the government's September

2002 dossier, *Iraq's Weapons of Mass Destruction – The Assessment of the British Government*, had been amended by Downing Street 'to make it sexier'. The intelligence services, he said, were unhappy with the document, particularly the now infamous claim that weapons of mass destruction could be deployed by Iraq within 45 minutes, a claim based on only one source. Following the report, there was a furious response from Downing Street. Blair's bullying chief spin doctor, Alastair Campbell, who already 'regularly bombarded the BBC with grievances, complaints, criticisms and implicit threats',[2] embarked on a crusade against the Corporation, which he and the prime minister claimed was pursuing an 'anti-war' agenda. Pressure mounted when David Kelly was found dead, having apparently taken his own life.

The inquiry into Kelly's death was headed by Lord Brian Hutton. Such inquiries headed by the 'great and good' have a tendency to exonerate the powerful, but Lord Hutton's findings shocked even seasoned and cynical political journalists. A triumphant Campbell declared, 'The Prime Minister told the truth, the government told the truth, I told the truth. The BBC, from the chairman on down, did not.' The scandal eventually led not to the resignation of Blair, Campbell and their co-conspirators, but to the forced resignation of the BBC chair and director general and a subsequent overhaul of the BBC's governing structures.

The BBC chair Gavyn Davies resigned immediately after the report's publication. With Davies gone, the Board of Governors, which had until then protected the Corporation's journalists, was headed by the Conservative peer Richard Ryder. With support from Pauline Neville-Jones, another Conservative peer on the Board, and a former chair of the Joint Intelligence Committee, Ryder successfully pushed for the resignation of Director General

Greg Dyke. He then apologised 'unreservedly' to the government, in a statement first approved by Downing Street,[3] and announced that the BBC had already 'begun to implement major reforms, including outside journalism, compliance systems, editorial processes and training of new recruits'.[4] These new compliance systems and editorial processes included, for example, the development of the Managed Risk Programme List (MRPL), a 'red flagging' mechanism 'monitored at senior editorial meetings in the BBC'.[5]

The MRPL is a system described by the BBC as 'an early warning system to highlight programmes with specific editorial, legal, commercial, intrinsic or reputational risks'. Under this system, a BBC programme-making team or private production company is responsible for notifying the manager of their departmental Managed Programme List of any controversial programmes due in the next three months. The Managed Programme Lists then feed into divisional lists which are discussed by executives on divisional boards and forwarded to the BBC's Editorial Standards Board, which produces the final BBC-wide MRPL.[6] Risk categories on the MRPL include: 'High Profile'; 'Political Sensitivity'; 'Political Controversy'; 'Adverse publicity for the BBC'; and 'Cultural Sensitivities'.[7]

Commentators differ as to how such post-Hutton initiatives have impacted on the BBC's journalism. The former BBC journalist John Kampfner was particularly forthright after the inquiry, claiming that the BBC had been 'muzzling journalism and deliberately avoiding giving offence to the Government and the Establishment', and Marsh writes that 'the conventional wisdom [is] that the BBC became more cautious, more risk-averse, less ready to challenge government and authority after Hutton', and admits that the BBC's journalism became more risk averse under

Dyke's immediate successor, Mark Byford.[8] The influential media commentator Steven Barnett, however, dismisses the argument that the BBC was cowed as a result of Hutton, seeing its institutional response – he mentions specifically the creation of the BBC College of Journalism – as an affirmation of the BBC's 'core values' in opposition to 'Dyke's populist approach'. For Barnett, Gilligan's report and the BBC leadership's response revealed failings at the top of the organisation, which were rightly redressed by the departure of Davies and Dyke. He argues that a lack of journalistic rigour had set in as Dyke sought to free up journalists from the managerial controls imposed by his predecessor. Yet Barnett also praises the BBC for running Gilligan's story, claiming it illustrates how indispensible independent, publicly funded journalism is to democracy.[9]

None of this is in the least bit convincing. While it is hard to see how the question of Hutton's impact on BBC journalism can be definitively resolved, and though there may have been managerial failures exposed by the episode, the fact that new 'mechanisms of accountability' were introduced following a campaign by central government leading to the resignation of the BBC chair and director general speaks volumes. And although the BBC did perform an important public service duty in running the story, on closer examination it is clear that it did so in response to Establishment voices, rather than either popular pressure or attention to the available evidence, which in any case was clear enough. Indeed, if the episode reveals anything, it is the highly circumscribed capacity for the BBC to fulfil its vital democratic function.

Despite the ferocious attacks and vociferous denials from the government, not to mention the heavy price the BBC would pay, Gilligan's story turned out to be remarkably accurate. The document the Blair government published on 24 September 2002, which came to be known as the 'dodgy dossier', was officially produced by the Joint Intelligence Committee (JIC), the government body that brings together the heads of MI5, MI6 and GCHQ, the chief of Defence Intelligence and senior officials from the Foreign Office, the Ministry of Defence, the Home Office and other departments. The dossier was compiled by combining intelligence assessments produced over the previous eight months and was supplemented with last-minute 'intelligence' requested by the government and duly supplied by MI6 – the basis for the notorious 45-minute claim.

At the time that the dossier was originally compiled, the existing JIC assessments suggested that Iraq *might* have retained some chemical and biological agents and munitions from the stocks it manufactured prior to the first Gulf War, but it was not known what had been retained or whether they would still be effective. In terms of delivering these hypothetical chemical and biological agents, it was believed that the weapons systems most likely to be used were artillery and rockets – battlefield weapons, rather than strategic missiles. Moreover, it was the assessment of the JIC that the Iraqi command *might* use these hypothetical chemical and biological weapons against neighbouring states or concentrations of Western forces, meaning that the threat of any WMDs being deployed would be *increased* by the planned invasion.

After Blair requested a dossier be published, however, these various ambiguities were toned down and combined with new and wholly inaccurate intelligence which created the completely false impression that Iraq posed an imminent threat. The Butler Inquiry, which followed Hutton's whitewash, noted that caveats and uncertainties appearing in earlier JIC assessments did not appear in the final published dossier, 'implying that there was fuller and firmer intelligence behind the judgements than was the case'.[10] This in itself does not support Gilligan's contention about the role of Downing Street, but it is also very clear from the evidence supplied to the various inquiries that the then head of the JIC, John Scarlett, and the other officials involved in producing the dossier worked closely with Campbell, making a number of 'presentational' amendments on his recommendation. As for the 45-minute claim, despite Dearlove referring to it as 'a piece of well sourced intelligence' to Hutton,[11] in evidence to the Chilcot Inquiry, an MI6 officer described the claim as having been 'based in part on wishful thinking', adding that 'we marketed that intelligence ... before it was fully validated'.[12]

If there was a problem with Gilligan's report, it was that it pointed the finger at Downing Street while underestimating the broader role played by other state officials. Gilligan had suggested that pressure from Number 10 was responsible for 'sexing up' the dossier against the wishes of the intelligence services. But the evidence from the inquiries suggests that, while many in MI6 were uncomfortable with the intelligence being shaped around the policy agenda, on the other hand senior figures in the intelligence and security apparatus worked closely with Downing Street and other government departments to ensure that the 'dodgy dossier' went, as Butler put it, to 'the outer limits of the intelligence available'. Moreover, it is now clear that MI6 was largely responsible for producing the supposed 'intelligence' which led to the inclusion of the 45-minute claim. That Gilligan focused on Downing Street rather than the spooks is perhaps not surprising given the information that was available to him. But it meant that when it came to the official inquiries, Downing Street could be shielded from any political fallout when the rest of the British state closed ranks. Particularly important in this respect was

John Scarlett, who insisted that he kept 'ownership' of the dossier, a loyalty which was apparently repaid when he was appointed as successor to Dearlove over Inkster. Gilligan's key error was his assertion that the government knew the 45-minute claim was inaccurate – a claim which was in any circumstances likely to be impossible to prove. This carelessness, although not especially significant in terms of the substance of the story, went unnoticed by the government for some time but left the BBC more vulnerable when it came to the detailed scrutiny of Lord Hutton.

When the BBC became a public corporation in 1927, it adopted the official motto 'Nation shall speak peace unto Nation', a phrase which adorned its official coat of arms and the front page of its official magazine, the *Radio Times*. The BBC, though, has seldom reflected this pacifistic spirit. Though the motto was never officially rescinded, it fell out of favour during the 1930s as the prospect of war grew.[13] During that decade the BBC quietly prepared itself for war. In 1934 Reith met with the director of operations and intelligence at the War Office to discuss plans for wartime broadcasting, and in 1936 he was involved in planning for the establishment of a wartime Ministry of Information, which he would head for a time.[14] The director general designate of the planned ministry in the interwar period was Stephen Tallents, a professional propagandist who had served as deputy director general under Reith and would go on to become founder and president of the Institute of Public Relations. In September 1938, the BBC's arrangements for the outbreak of war were finalised, along with arrangements for staff, including wartime pays scales.[15]

The BBC's output at that time reflected the dominant opinion among the British elite, which favoured the appeasement of Nazi Germany. Though apparently resigned to the inevitability of war, the BBC maintained what one former editor derided as a 'conspiracy of silence' about the prospect.[16] Speakers hostile to fascism were barred from broadcasting and Winston Churchill, who was unusual among his class for his antipathy to Nazism if not fascism per se, complained in 1938 that he had been 'muzzled by the BBC' following his last broadcast on German rearmament four years earlier. Churchill also claimed that 'the BBC seemed to have passed under the control of the Government'; and he was correct.[17]

Reviewing the BBC's coverage of foreign affairs during the 1930s, the leading scholar of interwar broadcasting, Paddy Scannel, concludes that though the BBC had formerly maintained a perilous independence, it was now 'in pawn to the state'.[18] Its reporting on fascism was not only in general accordance with the prevailing mood among Britain's political elite, but was also formed directly in response to government policy. In March 1937, Cecil Graves, the BBC's controller of programmes, reported back on a meeting with Robert Vansittart, the permanent under-secretary of state for foreign affairs. Vansittart, who like Churchill is remembered for his opposition to appeasement, indicated to Graves – a former military intelligence officer who would become joint director general during the war – that the Foreign Office would like the BBC to report more favourably on the fascist forces in Spain, who under General Franco were set to overthrow the centre-left democratic government. Graves's memo of their meeting states,

> With regard to Spanish news, he says there is now little doubt that Franco will be in Madrid and in due course in control of Spain. He says that Franco feels that the BBC and *The Times* are against him and therefore the [British]

Government must be against him too. He says this is
deplorable, since it will send Franco more into the arms of
Italy and Germany than ever ... He would be very grateful
if we could at least put out no more [Spanish] Government
news, irrespective of the amount that comes in, than insurgent [i.e. fascist] news. It is quite obvious, in fact, that he
would be glad if we could become sufficiently obviously
pro-Insurgent to convince Franco that we, and therefore the
Government are not anti-Franco. He would, in addition,
be very pleased if we could see our way to dropping the
term 'insurgent', which apparently is resented on that side,
adopting perhaps 'Nationalists' ... I think we can without
inconvenience do what he wants with regard to Spanish
news, but I don't think we can adopt the new term. We
might, however, drop the old one.[19]

With the outbreak of war two years later, BBC reporting
was subordinated to the interests of total war and became
the 'most potent source of white propaganda in Britain
during the entire war'.[20] Having formerly been accountable to the Post Office and the Foreign Office, the BBC
was now brought under the authority of the Ministry of
Information.

The wartime management of information and propaganda was initially somewhat haphazard, but John Reith,
who served as minister of information for a short period
in 1940, put it 'on a more efficient footing', drawing on his
'interest and knowledge of propaganda'.[21] Reith 'believed
that it was essential to have news and propaganda controlled by the same authority',[22] arguing that news was 'the
shocktroops of propaganda',[23] and under his initiative the
control of news, the responsibility of MI7, was integrated
into the ministry's propaganda operation. After some initial
fiascos, an efficient system of censorship was established.

The Post Office, which controlled Britain's communicative infrastructure, rerouted the wires services which supplied the BBC and the press with domestic and international news, so that reports could be censored before reaching the media.

The BBC's relationship with the government followed a similar rationale. In February 1940, BBC Director General Frederick Ogilvie met with John Reith, who had recently been appointed head of the Ministry of Information. Reith considered it would be easier if the BBC were simply taken over by the government, referring back to his difficulties during the General Strike. Ogilvie, however, emphasised that the 'constitutional independence of the BBC was of supreme importance', arguing that since democracy was one of the issues at stake in the war it would be better if the BBC remained independent. He stressed though that any change 'did nothing in itself to improve what chiefly mattered, namely the day to day work of broadcasting', since in any case the BBC 'was already in the closest touch with various Government Departments', not just the Ministry of Information, but also Department EH, the enemy propaganda department later subsumed into the Special Operations Executive.[24] The BBC would once again be trusted to reflect the national interest, and do so working closely with government departments. While notionally still independent, and generally acting on guidance rather than direction, the BBC readily agreed to 'bow' to all the Ministry of Information's decisions,[25] while the ministry for its part 'soon learned that it was better to leave news communications to the experienced professionals and that the credibility and integrity of their coverage could only be enhanced by an outward appearance of independence'.[26]

In May 1940, Churchill succeeded Chamberlain as prime minister and Reith, whom Churchill strongly disliked, was removed as minister of information and replaced by the Conservative politician Duff Cooper, an Old Etonian and Churchill ally. With the change of guard, the BBC was brought even more firmly under government control. Cooper met with the BBC leadership, and it was agreed that a 'greater degree of control' would henceforth be exercised. The then BBC chair and director general said they would 'gladly accept any directions whether general or particular in all matters which the Minister considered to be in the national interest', and it was agreed that all 'broadcasts of political importance' would first be approved by Cooper. It was also agreed that the ministry's director of Broadcasting Division would attend policy meetings at the BBC and that the BBC's controller of Home Division would attend the meetings at the ministry every day, and the director general twice a week.[27]

The BBC's wartime policy was that those who 'had taken part in public agitation against the war effort' were barred from broadcasting, a policy that excluded not only fascists and, for a time, communists, but also pacifists.[28] In August 1940, the BBC Board of Governors, which by then comprised just two men, considered that broadcasting was 'a vital war weapon – the most important war weapon after the armed forces' and ruled that 'there could be no place in the Corporation's service for registered conscientious objectors'.[29] While somewhat displeased with having this policy imposed on the Corporation, Ogilvie complied, the policy fitting with his own aim of making the BBC into a 'fully effective instrument of war'.[30]

At a meeting in December that year, the War Cabinet discussed whether it was necessary to introduce new measures to ensure the 'effective control' of the BBC by the government. It was decided that, rather than the government assuming 'complete control of the BBC', two 'advisors' would be appointed to the Corporation, each to 'have supreme direction in his own particular sphere', while any conflict with the BBC director general would be ultimately decided by the minister of information.[31]

Thoroughly integrated into the machinery of total war, the BBC developed a close relationship with the Political Warfare Executive, broadcasting its propaganda into Europe while the RAF dropped its leaflets during bombing raids.[32] Although the BBC generally avoided broadcasting completely false reports for strategic reasons, figures were routinely massaged to boost morale and news was 'cut, edited and censored'.[33]

In 1942, the BBC still struggled with military restrictions on its war reporting, which was criticised by the minister of information, 10 Downing Street and the Board of Governors.[34] Cecil Graves urged the Ministry of Information to 'put [the BBC's] national propaganda on a modern war-time basis' and argued that it was a matter of 'vital importance' that a common plan of action be developed involving the BBC, the Ministry of Information, the Political Warfare Executive, the US Office of War Information, and the British and US General Staffs.[35] The BBC's newsgathering capacities, which up until then were extremely limited, where thereafter greatly increased. This was just one area where the BBC's status and reputation was greatly enhanced by the war – its staff numbers had increased almost threefold from 4,000 in 1939 to 11,000 in late 1940.[36] Furthermore, though initially seen by the public as untrustworthy and elitist, the BBC sought – closely supervised by the Ministry of Information – to broaden its appeal, promoting a more egalitarian nationalism that appealed as much to 'ordinary' culture as to the symbols of nation and Empire, a trend exemplified by the participation of left-wing intellectuals such as J. B. Priestley and George Orwell. While 'clinging on to many of its established traditions', the BBC's 'pre-war cultural elitism [was] modified into an uneasy kind of elevated classlessness',[37] and the wartime BBC arguably helped craft the more inclusive, collectivist political culture on which the more egalitarian post-war political economy was built.[38]

In the interwar period the BBC had served as a 'willing, even evangelical, propagandist of empire'.[39] But in the post-war period, British elites were forced to adapt to the realities of imperial decline and US global hegemony. A significant and symbolic episode for the new US-dominated international order was the so-called 'Suez crisis' of 1956, during which Britain secretly colluded with Israel and France to depose President Nasser of Egypt and regain control of the Suez Canal. The Suez crisis represents one of a number of landmarks in liberal histories of the BBC, which describe its gradual move out of the shadow of the state to become an authentically independent broadcaster.[40] During the crisis, the BBC angered the government by giving airtime to the Labour leader Hugh Gaitskell, and it was able to overcome the restrictive 'fourteen day rule', which had prevented broadcasting of issues due to be debated in Parliament.

While the Suez crisis features in many a journalistic and scholarly account of broadcasting, by far the most extensive study has been conducted by the historian Tony Shaw. In a close review of the evidence, he casts considerable doubt on conventional interpretations of the crisis. Revisiting the BBC's part in the crisis in light of the 2003 invasion of Iraq reveals some striking parallels. In both cases, the prime minister secretly planned for the illegal invasion of a former colonial state and, behind a pretence of international diplomacy, sought to win over domestic and international opinion through a campaign of propaganda and disinformation. In both cases, the BBC was a crucial battleground in the propaganda war and came under enormous pressure via its high-level contacts with politicians and state officials. As we shall see, during the Suez crisis the BBC *to some extent* resisted governmental pressure and endeavoured to reflect Establishment opposition to the war. But it also faced accusations of anti-government bias, despite failing to adequately interrogate the case for war and reporting in terms largely favourable to the government.[41]

Shortly after the crisis, the BBC Board of Governors conducted a review of the BBC's coverage, which concluded that it had 'fulfilled [its] obligation for impartiality, objectivity and for telling the truth'.[42] Shaw finds that, on the contrary, while the BBC's news bulletins 'were on the whole admirably straight and impartial', its current affairs programmes 'consistently strayed from the "factual" and consistently in the government's favour', evincing 'a discreet, yet distinct, pro-government bias'.[43] Though, as liberal commentators have emphasised, the BBC was able to dispense with the restrictions of the fourteen-day rule and reflect some of the public controversy over Eden's handling of the crisis, it did so 'in a decidedly unbalanced way', and when its 'commentaries did brave the waters of controversy, they invariably came down on the government's side'.[44]

In the weeks after the nationalisation of the canal on 26 July 1956, the BBC, Shaw writes, adopted 'an actively hostile position in relation to Nasser himself'. 'From the very start of the dispute, BBC commentaries were in no doubt about the illegality of Nasser's action and the government's subsequent right to take military "precautions"'.[45] As the government stepped up its information operations in early to mid-August, BBC bulletins 'put a sudden and increased emphasis on official statements which stressed the need for a tough line with the Egyptians'.[46]

BBC officials at this stage became concerned that their one-sided coverage might impact negatively on the Corporation's reputation and, seeking to adopt a less partisan line, they rejected a request from the Australian prime minister to broadcast in support of Eden, reasoning that the foreign secretary was already scheduled to appear. This decision led to an intervention by Eden via the BBC chair, Alexander Cadogan. A former civil servant, Cadogan had been appointed by Churchill in 1952 and was close to Eden, having served as his deputy under-secretary. In addition to his role at the BBC, he was also the government director of the Suez Canal Company. Cadogan's appointment reinforced the already close relationship between the BBC and the British state. He had arrived in the same year as Director General Ian Jacob, who had taken a year's sabbatical as chief staff officer to the minister of defence. Both men were deeply integrated into the British Establishment. Ian Jacob was at dinner at 10 Downing Street when the news of the nationalisation came in, and Cadogan later that night agreed to attend 10 Downing Street, despite already being in his pyjamas.[47]

Ian Jacob, according to Shaw, actively defended the BBC's independence against Eden. But Cadogan 'showed himself to be a firm and energetic supervisory chairman, cancelling talks, insisting on advance scrutiny of selected scripts and prescribing modifications'.[48] After the BBC declined the Australian prime minister's request to broadcast, Cadogan instructed Jacob to reverse the decision, 'no matter what our traditions and inhibitions might be'.[49]

Shortly afterwards, a plan to interview Nasser was abandoned when the famed BBC producer Grace Wyndham-Goldie insisted that Downing Street should first be consulted and Eden replied that the plan was 'unwise'.[50] When, on 15 August, the BBC organised a roundtable discussion featuring an Egyptian official, Ian Jacob was called back from his holiday by Eden and it was indicated to him that the government might install an advisor at the BBC as it had during the Second World War.[51] According to Shaw, though Jacob defended the need for independence in such encounters,

> overall, the Corporation's current affairs programmes continued to show a distinct pro-government bias. Nasser was consistently portrayed either as desperate, with his fellow Arabs having turned against him, or as the archetypal megalomaniac whose irrational hatred of Britain was being exploited by the Russians.[52]

Along with the anti-Nasser propaganda being supplied to the BBC by the Information Research Department, governmental pressure 'had the combined effect of slanting its coverage of the Suez crisis significantly in favour of the government'.[53] On 16 August, an international conference was convened in London to resolve the dispute, to which the Egyptian government was not invited. At the behest of Cadogan, BBC staff were instructed to be 'especially careful while the Conference is sitting' and to broadcast just 'straight news' and no programme which might offend the government.[54] This followed a letter from Eden to Cadogan emphasising the BBC's 'very heavy responsibility' at a 'crucial time' when 'people will judge the strength and determination of Britain by what they hear on the BBC'. In September, it was agreed by the Board of Governors 'that the BBC should do nothing to underline the existence of party division and disunity'. Even when polls suggested a majority of British people were turning against any military action, the BBC continued to toe the government line.[55] A combination of quiet persuasion, veiled and explicit threats, and direct censorship via the issue of D Notices, proved to be quite effective, and pressure increased as the planned invasion drew nearer.

Less than a week before, the government advised the BBC of its plans to introduce dramatic funding cuts to its External Services and to install a Foreign Office official 'to advise the BBC on the content and direction of their overseas programmes'.[56] Most famously, the 10 Downing Street press secretary, William Clark, disingenuously suggested to Harman Grisewood – who was effectively acting as director general in Jacob's absence – that plans were afoot for the government to take direct control of the BBC. This threat to take over the Corporation features prominently in accounts of the crisis, and was certainly significant, but it has served as something of a distraction from a broader pattern of intimidation and collusion. This campaign culminated in Grisewood and Director of Administration Norman Bottomley, the BBC's two most senior figures under the director general, visiting the Ministry of Defence, where they were shown the War Room. They were advised that military operations would soon begin and that, when they did, full wartime censorship would be introduced.[57]

Nonetheless, the Suez crisis is still celebrated as an episode demonstrating the BBC's capacity for independence and impartiality.[58] Although not completely without merit, this risks seriously mischaracterising the extent and nature of the BBC's independence then and now. Central to such accounts is the fact that the BBC granted Gaitskell a 'right of reply' to Eden's broadcast of 3 November, in which he portrayed the invasion as a 'police action' and described himself as 'a man of peace, a League of Nations man'. Gaitskell's address followed a key Board of Governors meeting two days earlier, at which Cadogan, again acting for Eden, argued against the BBC broadcasting any critical material once the invasion was under way. Cadogan was opposed by Grisewood, who argued that, since the External Services had broadcast criticism in its press reviews, it would be untenable for the BBC to suppress critical perspectives in its domestic broadcasts. Grisewood won out in the split and so Cadogan as a result had little choice but to reluctantly allow Gaitskell to broadcast, especially given that as leader of the opposition he was entitled to respond to any controversial broadcast, and Eden himself had referred to his own address in such terms. The broadcast was certainly politically important. But it's significance in terms of the BBC's independence is much exaggerated. Coming from the leader of Her Majesty's Most Loyal Opposition, it was the very definition of Establishment dissent and, moreover, it was supported by large sections of the national press, including the *Daily Mirror*, the *Daily Herald*, the *News Chronicle*, the *Manchester Guardian* and the *Observer*. Even before Eden delivered his 3 November address, Clark had expected that the Board of Governors would likely grant Gaitskell a response, and Eden accepted as much.[59] Afterwards, Cadogan described Gaitskell's broadcast as 'disgraceful' and noted with satisfaction that the BBC had 'given him enough rope!'[60] Grisewood's defence, meanwhile, rested upon his belief that 'the system of control' that had been established over BBC programme makers was 'in good order', and that its relations with Parliament were 'better and closer than they had been'.[61]

To put the Suez episode in its proper context, it is important to consider how non-elite dissent on issues of war and peace was treated by the BBC during the same period. Anthony Adamthwaite, who has examined the BBC's files from the

forties and fifties, describes in detail how peace movements were marginalised by the BBC during that period,
even after the emergence of CND in 1958, while official
perspectives predominated, reflecting the close connections between senior BBC personnel and Whitehall.[62] The
BBC willingly brought its output in line with government
policy, including through the censorship of programmes,
only displaying an authentic independence when its public
reputation was at stake.

A particularly revealing incident in terms of how the
BBC–Whitehall relationship worked in practice took place
two years before the Suez crisis, when the BBC came under
pressure from the Conservative government over a proposed programme on the hydrogen bomb. In the summer
of 1954, a features producer began work on an hour-long
programme exploring the impact of nuclear weapons.
The government was at that stage planning a white
paper announcing its intention to develop new nuclear
weapons and was therefore keen to limit any public controversy. When it got wind of the planned programme, the
postmaster general, acting for Prime Minister Winston
Churchill, wrote to Cadogan stating that the question
of thermo-nuclear weapons 'raise[d] important issues of
public policy' which might 'require the issue of guidance
or directions to the Corporation in pursuance of section
15(4) of the Corporation's Licence.'[63] This was a threat
to use the legal powers the government had to veto any
BBC programme. Cadogan replied with a strong defence
of the BBC's independence, writing that 'the Corporation
cannot agree to accept and follow Government guidance
over particular fields of output except where security is
concerned. To do so would be to abdicate from respon-
sibilities given to the Governors by the Charter.' So far
so good.

But what then happened is revealing. First, the BBC leadership ruled that no programme on nuclear weapons would be broadcast until the government had clarified its position in response to Cadogan's reply. This meant that the government achieved what seems to have been its immediate aim: to prevent any critical broadcast on nuclear weapons prior to the publication of its white paper. Second, and even more significantly, the governmental pressure eventually resulted in a new policy, tightening editorial controls over the production of such programmes. Cadogan's request for clarification led to a meeting the following month attended by both Cadogan and Jacob and a governmental delegation which included Minister of Defence Harold Macmillan and Cabinet Secretary Sir Norman Brook. At the meeting, Macmillan, according to Jacob's note, indicated that the government was concerned that the planned programmes might

> stimulate the feeling so easily accepted by the British people because it agreed with their natural laziness in these matters, that because of the terrible nature of the hydrogen bomb there was no need for them to take part in any home defence measures or similar activities.[64]

Cadogan remarked he 'entirely agreed with the Ministers proposal and confirmed that the Corporation had no desire to embarrass the Government on this very delicate matter'. It was then agreed that the issue would be handled on an 'informal basis' without 'hampering documents'.[65] The postmaster general reported back to Churchill that it had been agreed with the BBC that

> the Corporation should keep in close touch with the Ministry of Defence on all matters relating to the presentation of

the hydrogen bomb to the public. We all thought that this was a more satisfactory and practical solution than that the Government should try and lay down precise rules in writing.[66]

Later, Jacob drafted a policy paper entitled *Thermo-nuclear Weapons and Broadcasting*, which stated that the BBC had a duty to act 'responsibly' and 'in the national interest' on this issue. Presenting the paper to senior executives, Jacob said that it would 'be advisable for Directors and Controllers to keep a careful watch on what is proposed, and to bring up for central consideration at a very early stage projects that have doubtful features'.[67]

This episode has relevance for the Suez crisis a year or two later. The then postmaster general, Charles Hill, who was later appointed BBC chair, wrote that while the powers allowing for formal intervention in BBC output were limited, 'informal consultation' had proved successful in that earlier case and 'is generally satisfactory'.[68] Another episode covered by Goodwin, which has been far more extensively covered in the literature on the BBC, is the banning of a dramatised documentary in 1965 which depicted the aftermath of nuclear war. *The War Game* was cancelled by the BBC on the basis that it was 'too horrifying for the medium of broadcasting', causing enormous public controversy. Prior to the planned broadcast, the former cabinet secretary Sir Norman Brook, who was now chairman of the BBC, initiated an 'informal consultation' with Whitehall over the programme. He wrote to the cabinet secretary, stating that the

showing of the film on television might well have a significant effect on public attitudes towards the policy of the nuclear deterrent. In these circumstances I doubt whether

the BBC ought alone to take the responsibility of deciding
whether this film should be shown on television ... It seems
to me that the Government should have an opportunity of
expressing a view about this ...[69]

What followed was a special showing of the film attended
by civil servants from the Home Office, the Post Office, the
Ministry of Defence and the Defence Staff, who noted in
discussion after the showing that the film might increase
support for CND.[70] After the subsequent banning of the
programme, critics alleged that the BBC caved in to government pressure, while the BBC for its part publicly claimed
that the decision had been the Corporation's alone. It has
never been clear from the available files who made the
final decision to ban the programme and why, but there
is strong evidence that Lord Normanbrook and director
general Hugh Greene banned the programme at the behest
of the government, while publicly taking responsibility for
the decision. One document obtained by the media scholar
John Cook under the Freedom of Information Act states the
following about a lunch meeting between Normanbrook,
Greene and the then lord president Herbert Bowden.

If as Lord Normanbrook and Sir Hugh Greene undoubtedly assume, the conclusion were to be reached that the
film should not be shown Sir Hugh Greene said that he
would be prepared to issue a press statement to the effect
that the BBC itself had decided that it would be against
the public interest for the film to be shown. If this were
to be the outcome, it would undoubtedly go some way
towards preventing embarrassment which would be caused
if the Government were known to be implicated in the
decision.[71]

The offer by Greene is also evidenced in a memo written by Cabinet Secretary Sir Burke Trend, who had briefed Bowden before that lunch meeting. Trend wrote that Normanbrook and Greene had

> indicated that, if it were decided on grounds of public policy that the film should not be shown, the BBC might be prepared to issue a statement to the effect that they themselves had decided on these grounds not to show it ... The difficulty, for the BBC no less than for the Government, is to think of some reason for suppressing the film which would not stir up controversy or provoke suspicion that it was motivated by political prejudice, whether of the pro- or anti-CND type.[72]

Evidence of a very similar arrangement, reached much later, in 1981, has also emerged. That year, BBC *Panorama* planned to make a programme exploring the accountability of the security and intelligence services. Substantial cuts were then made to the programme at the behest of Director General Ian Trethowan, who publicly denied that anyone in government had seen the film or had put the BBC under pressure. In fact, Trethowan was under considerable pressure from the Conservative Government, with which he had been in close contact, and he had met with the heads of MI5 and MI6 and agreed to make the cuts after privately viewing the film with MI5's legal adviser.[73] That incident took place a year before the conflict between Britain and Argentina over the Falklands/Malvinas, when the BBC once again came under enormous political pressure, and during which comparable patterns of reporting to those during Suez are evident. During the Falklands/Malvinas conflict, the BBC faced particularly strong criticism over its neutral description of British troops, which infuriated right-wing critics like Norman Tebbit, who wanted the BBC to describe the military as 'we' or 'ours'. This view seems to have had some support within the BBC leadership. During the conflict, one senior executive reminded editors 'that the BBC was the *British* Broadcasting Corporation' and that its 'detached style' was causing 'unnecessary irritation' to the public.[74]

A week later, the director general told the News and Current Affairs meeting that 'one benefit to come out of the [public] savaging of the BBC had been the clear proof it provided to outside countries of the BBC's independence from government'. Yet senior editorial figures were also candid in private about the balance of their coverage. Defending a *Panorama* programme that came in for particularly strong criticism, the programme's producer, George Carey, noted that 'the introduction to the programme had emphasised that the British cause was utterly right'. At the same meeting, it was also admitted that 'the weight of BBC coverage had been concerned with government statements and policy' and noted that in its 'vilification of the BBC, the government seemed to have entirely overlooked this'. The Glasgow University Media Group, which conducted a study of television coverage of the conflict, writes that:

> Some programme makers, mainly in BBC current affairs, had taken the 'balance and impartiality' argument seriously and had dipped the Corporation's toes into the waters of dissent. When these waters proved too hot, the BBC withdrew, while attempting to preserve its apparent independence from the government.[75]

The Glasgow University Media Group's study also examined coverage of anti-nuclear activism in 1983. The report suggests no complicity and emphasises that the BBC and other news outlets resisted the Conservative Government's characterisation of protesters as agents of the Soviets. But it did find that coverage of demonstrations tended not to address the substantive issues at stake behind the protests; that in so far as they were afforded airtime anti-nuclear campaigners were routinely 'balanced' with pro-nuclear views in a way that officials were not; and that polling suggesting public support went unreported by the BBC.[76]

Does the high-profile conflict between the BBC and the government in 2003 over the Iraq invasion suggest that the BBC later adopted a more independent and critical stance? If so, then it was a brief interlude to an otherwise consistent pattern.

In an email sent in the weeks after Gilligan's 'dodgy dossier' report, his boss, Kevin Marsh, criticised his 'loose use of language and lack of judgment in some of his phraseology' and complained of 'the loose and in some ways distant relationship he's been allowed to have with *Today*'.[77] Gilligan's original appointment was part of a loosening of editorial restraints at the Corporation which took place when Greg Dyke took over from John Birt.[78] Part of the rationale for Gilligan's appointment specifically, according to Richard Sambrook, who was director of BBC News during the Iraq invasion, was that 'for many years the BBC defence correspondent had simply reflected the Ministry of Defence's point of view'. This, Sambrook remarked to the Hutton Inquiry, 'may be legitimate in one sense, but actually in terms of journalism we needed a correspondent who would ask questions and hold to account as well'.[79] Sambrook's very public remarks led to a complaint from a former BBC defence correspondent, Mark Laity, who had left the Corporation in February 2000 to become a media advisor and spokesperson at NATO. Laity –

who would later be awarded a medal for his work as a media advisor for the occupying forces in Afghanistan – said he was 'shocked' by Sambrook's 'damaging and totally inaccurate remark'. While conceding that he had followed 'a rather more traditional BBC approach', he noted that in his eleven years in the role, 'no such imputation was ever made by anyone in BBC News or its management – indeed quite the contrary'.[80]

As Laity's remarks suggest, the 'traditional BBC approach' has not been to 'hold to account', as Sambrook puts it, but rather to report largely from the perspective of, and within the terms set by, the British state. This is usually ignored in journalists' accounts of broadcasting and armed conflict, which tend to focus on moments of tension and conflict between journalists and officials, while ignoring empirical evidence on the actual patterns of reporting. On this latter question, the evidence is fairly clear: media reporting during and leading up to periods of armed conflict has tended to be overwhelmingly pro-war, with critical perspectives appearing largely in accordance with the level of elite dissensus.[81]

The evidence on BBC reporting of foreign policy issues and controversies is in keeping with this. David McQueen's examination of BBC *Panorama*'s coverage of the Iraq war, for example, finds that the BBC initially 'excluded expert and activist opinion opposed to the war', but that as 'oppositional views grew louder' it began to reflect opposition from 'a variety of establishment and (to a much lesser extent) non-establishment actors'.[82] Once the invasion was under way, according to another study, only 2 per cent of BBC reports dealt with the original purpose of the invasion or its outcome.[83] Another academic study, commissioned by the BBC itself, found that its television coverage tended to reflect pro-war assumptions and was 'informed mainly by American and British government and military sources'.[84] Significantly, that study found that the BBC was much more reliant on government sources than all its domestic competitors and was much less likely to use independent sources or to report Iraqi civilian casualties.[85]

Such findings are reflective of a general journalistic culture at the BBC that routinely defers to powerful interests in the way issues are selected, presented and contested. But it also reflects the extreme political pressure which the BBC comes under during periods of crisis. This is clearly evident in the documents that have come to light in the case of Iraq. 'It is our firm view that Number Ten has tried to intimidate the BBC in its reporting of events leading up to the war and during the course of the war itself', Sambrook wrote on 27 June 2003.[86] This pressure came particularly from 'the odiously aggressive Alastair Campbell', as former BBC Governor Kenneth Bloomfield describes him,[87] whose public criticism of Gilligan's report was taken by the BBC as an accusation that the Corporation was pursuing an anti-war agenda.

Campbell has claimed that 'the BBC became very, very hostile in its coverage of Iraq' and didn't provide enough airtime to the 'considerable amount of support for the government's position'.[88] The feeling within the anti-war movement, by contrast, was that the BBC was much more pro-war in terms of its output than commercial television and, as we have seen, unlike Campbell's claim this is supported by the evidence. Lindsey German, a founder and long-time convenor of the Stop the War Coalition, is typical in her assessment that: 'the BBC were awful, absolutely awful. We got much better coverage from Sky, we got much better coverage from the ITN news channel.' German suggests that this is partly down to government pressure and partly down to an 'ethos that demonstrations are beneath them, whereas the more commercial channels go with what they think is interesting'.[89]

This analysis accords very closely with the explanation provided by Kevin Marsh. On the question of the coverage of the anti-war movement, Marsh told the author, Ian Sinclair:

> It is partly because we are more sceptical about the motives of demonstrations. You've got to remember the BBC has been in the firing line for a long time ... We don't just cover a demonstration because it is noisy, or because there is a lot of people there. We are not guided by the numbers of a demonstration ... Sky and ITN have a much more traditional journalistic view. They take the view that part of their job is to grab people's attention. Numbers grab people's attention. Demonstrations grab people's attention, even if they don't turn violent. So that is part of the answer. The other answer is, and this is certainly true of *Today* and Radio 4 and to some extent true of the main bulletins on BBC 1, there was a hell of a lot going on. Real things happening. UN talks on the second resolution, trying to get France on side, meetings between Bush and Blair and so on. We felt that that was our priority: to look at the real movements that were happening that meant that war may or may not happen ... [W]e, rightly or wrongly, see ourselves as public policy journalists then necessarily we look at what is happening in public policy i.e. politicians and officials.[90]

There is a passing allusion here to government pressure, on which Marsh makes the following more substantive remarks:

> Campbell would deluge us in letters. Anything and everything: a single word, a phrase, the way in which a headline

was presented – all the way through to 'You're lying'. The whole gambit. And this was a regular thing. I genuinely don't know how he and his office found the time to send as many letters and faxes as they did. Because they must have been faxing other people as well, it can't have been just us. So when you talk about the tremendous amount of pressure the BBC was under from the Government, when parliament returned in 2002 it was pretty much daily pressure from Alastair Campbell: 'You've got this wrong', 'You've got that wrong', 'This isn't true'.[91]

Blair himself complained privately to Dyke that the BBC had 'not got the balance right between support and dissent; between news and comment; between the voices of the Iraqi regime and the voices of Iraqi dissidents; or between the diplomatic support we have, and diplomatic opposition.'[92] Such complaints, it should be remembered, could not be ignored by the BBC leadership, which ultimately depends on governmental support. Even before his resignation, Davies had already written of 'threats, veiled and not so veiled, from "government sources" to take revenge on the BBC by reducing its funding, removing its director-general and changing its charter'.[93]

In response to one letter from Campbell, Sambrook cited 'the many reports we have filed from Iraq about mass graves, torture and political repression – evidence which has been used to justify the war'.[94] He might also have noted the efforts the BBC leadership had gone to in order to ensure that the government's line was well represented in BBC reporting. Dyke, who personally was in favour of the invasion, recalls in his autobiography that he 'made strenuous efforts to ensure that the Government position was fairly reported', setting up and chairing 'an ad hoc group that met every morning to discuss our coverage of the Iraq issue'.[95] This committee, he explained in a private letter to Blair which was later made public,

> decided to prevent any senior editorial figures at the BBC from going on the anti-war march; it was that committee which insisted that we had to find a balanced audience for programmes like Question Time at a time when it was very hard to find supporters of the war willing to come on.
>
> And it was that same committee when faced with a massive bias against the war among phone-in callers, decided to increase the number of phone lines so that pro-war listeners had a better chance of getting through and getting onto the programmes.
>
> All this was done in an attempt to ensure our coverage was balanced.[96]

There is further evidence of efforts by the BBC leadership to 'balance' public hostility to the planned invasion. In a leaked email to senior editors, Sambrook expressed a 'growing concern' that the BBC was 'attracting some of the more extreme anti-war views' and reminded editors that it was 'important we have someone to articulate the Bush/Blair line'.[97] Sambrook acknowledged that a majority of the public were against the war, and the popular mobilisations certainly had some impact, for example, Dyke referred to the 'biggest ever public demonstration' in the aforementioned letter to Blair.[98] But it was certainly less significant from the perspective of the BBC than the apparent unease within the Establishment. Answering Campbell's charge that the BBC was anti-war, Sambrook replied that 'a number of BBC journalists who have close contact with both the military and the security services had reported that their contacts were concerned that intelligence reports were being exaggerated to strengthen the

case against Saddam Hussein'. He went on to list a number
of press reports which also suggested 'unease in the security services' and emphasised that it was 'in this context
that we judged that reporting the claim made by Andrew
Gilligan's source was in the public interest'.[99] Indeed, as
has been noted, the head of MI6 had briefed the editor of
the *Today* programme not long before the Gilligan report
was aired. Dyke has also since revealed that the MI6 officer
John Scarlett, who at that point chaired the JIC and who
would subsequently succeed Dearlove as head of MI6, had
similarly stated to a BBC journalist that he was uncomfortable with the case that was being made for war and the
interpretation put on the 'dodgy dossier', for which he had
been primarily responsible. That conversation, according
to Dyke, took place on a bench in the grounds of Ditchley
Park, one of a number of high-level private policy forums
used by the British foreign policy elite.[100]

Kevin Marsh also referred in an email to conversations
he was still having with 'the spooks' after Gilligan's report
was attacked by the government, and he recalls having
met with BBC Security Correspondent Frank Gardner,
who seems to have approached him and Mark Damazer
separately on behalf of his 'excellent' contacts in MI6.[101]
Marsh concludes from his conversation with Gardner that
MI6 wished to make clear that the reservations about the
intelligence were emanating from the Ministry of Defence
rather than 'rogue elements' in MI6, as had been suggested
in reporting, but at the same time did not seem to question
the scepticism that had been expressed.

The interactions between senior BBC personnel and
state officials over the Iraq invasion, which is detailed
in the documents that have become public as a result of
the various inquiries, as well as the accounts since provided by the main protagonists, illustrate the limitations

of conventional conceptions of the BBC and broadcast journalism more broadly. At first glance, the case of Iraq and the 'dodgy dossier' seems to be a perfect illustration of the BBC's commitment to independent, critical reporting. Indeed, Seaton cites it as an example of the 'determination of broadcasters not to be controlled', and writes that the BBC, in contrast to the US media, 'defied government pressure and insisted on critically scrutinizing the case for invading Iraq'.[102] This is an expression of the conventional take on the Gilligan affair, but is a serious misreading of what actually happened.

First, and most obviously, it overlooks what happened in the months after Gilligan's fateful report. As we have seen, a largely accurate story revealing an apparent abuse of power by the government of the day led to a very public conflict, only resolved with the resignation of the BBC's two most senior executives, an official apology to the government and the announcement of tighter editorial controls. Yes, the BBC questioned the government's case for war, but the price it paid for this intransigence was severe.

Second, while it is true that the BBC did belatedly scrutinise the case for invading Iraq, it had failed to give proper weight to anti-war opinion, and had focused overwhelmingly, as Kevin Marsh has readily admitted, on the views of politicians and officials rather than protestors. This was reflected in its output, which included a higher proportion of official sources than all its domestic rivals and which compares especially unfavourably with Channel 4 News.

Third, and finally, the Gilligan report itself is hardly suggestive of the BBC's independence from the centres of power. The reason the BBC felt confident running the story in the first place was down to the level of elite disquiet it had encountered. Opposition from the public certainly played some role, but elite opposition and misgivings appear to have been crucial. The question then is what sort of 'independence' is on display here? If the BBC's independence from the government of the day is contingent on an atmosphere of elite disquiet, then that is surely not adequate from a democratic perspective. And if such independence is contingent on enormous public mobilisations, then that suggests it could only be realised in quite exceptional circumstances.

Far from demonstrating the BBC's independence then, the Gilligan affair arguably illustrates the Corporation's embeddedness within the British state and the broader Establishment. Greg Dyke was, like BBC Chairman Gavin Davies, a multi-millionaire Labour Party donor, and Davies was especially close to New Labour. His wife, Sue Nye, was private secretary to Gordon Brown, and their children were bridesmaid and page boy at Brown's wedding. An investment banker, Davies had served as an unofficial economic advisor to Brown and to Blair, and throughout the conflict over the Gilligan report he maintained private contact with the latter, who hoped to minimise any fallout from the Hutton Inquiry.[103] Kenneth Bloomfield argues that the fact that Dyke and Davies were both well known to be close to the Blair government led them to adopt an overly defensive posture when the BBC came under attack.[104] He notes in particular an email from Davies to the Board of Governors, which stated that

> ... there could be an advantage for the BBC in reaching a settlement with No.10 ... However, I remain of the view that, in the big picture sense, it is absolutely critical for the BBC to emerge from this row without being seen to buckle in the face of Government pressure.[105]

Whether the fact that the personal reputation and integrity of the director general and the BBC chair were at stake influenced the course of the crisis remains a matter of speculation, but in any case Bloomfield's argument is predicated precisely on the fact that the most senior figures within the Corporation were not only Establishment figures but were closely tied to the most powerful figures in the British state. Moreover, as Davies noted while he was still BBC chair, Tessa Jowell in her role as culture secretary had by then appointed ten of the twelve BBC governors, including himself and his vice-chair.[106] The personnel who occupied the governing structures of the BBC at the time of the Gilligan affair, then, were not in the least antagonistic to the essential interests of the British state, even if by virtue of their institutional positions they followed a distinct set of interests to those of the government. Tensions and occasional bitter conflicts between the BBC and sections of the state – of which the Gilligan affair is an example – need to be understood in this context. Such a perspective allows us to recognise the Iraq episode not as a straightforward struggle between an 'independent' broadcaster and a bullying government, but rather as the most visible part of something of an imbroglio among the British elite, which played out within and between the institutions of the British state and manifested itself most publicly as a bitter dispute between the BBC and 10 Downing Street – a dispute which assumed the elevated importance it did precisely because it so publicly revealed tensions and misgivings. Such conflicts are especially common during and leading up to periods of armed conflict precisely because at such times the most powerful sections of the state, pursuing military and diplomatic agendas, will seek to manage news and limit even mildly critical voices, including Establishment voices, from being heard. An adequate conceptualisation of the role of the BBC in British society requires that we recognise the importance of such struggles without overstating the degree of 'independence' of which they are suggestive. Moreover, a fuller picture requires attention to evidence of collusion between BBC and state officials. This is a much-overlooked feature of periods of conflict and crisis, which are often imagined to be straightforward conflicts between the BBC and the state, but which on closer examination reveal a much more complex, and perhaps more disconcerting, picture of the patterns of power and influence in Britain.

CHAPTER 4

Politics, Power and Political Bias

In 2014, the BBC's economics editor Robert Peston was asked what he thought of claims that the BBC was biased to the left. He replied that on the contrary he had found the BBC to be 'completely obsessed with the agenda set by newspapers' – naming the *Telegraph* and the *Mail* in particular – adding that it 'quite often veers in what you might call a very pro-establishment, rather right-wing direction'. In short, he said, claims that the BBC is left-wing are 'bollocks really'.[1]

A facetious reply, perhaps, but an accurate one. Every reputable scholarly study suggests that the BBC's output has overwhelmingly reflected the interests and perspectives of powerful groups, and insofar as it has been perceived as biased by the public, it has tended to be regarded as a conservative, rather than a left-wing, organisation. Nevertheless, there is a prevalent myth in British politics, and among British political commentators, that the BBC is in some sense left wing.

Such claims date back to the earliest days of broadcasting. Even before its establishment as a public corporation, Conservatives complained of the BBC's 'Socialist leanings',[2] and even its blatant partisanship during the General Strike did not convince right-wingers of its loyalty. In 1931, the chairman of the Conservative Party complained to John Reith about what a fellow Tory peer called the 'perpetual anti-Conservative policy of the BBC',[3] and two years later, the director general joked during a luncheon speech that, whatever Labour MPs might think about the BBC's politics, 'Their views were comparatively mild compared with the views of the right wing of the Conservative Party.'[4]

In 1937, Reith attended a Conservative private members' committee to discuss alleged political bias in news and educational programmes, at which he agreed that BBC News was paying too much attention to the leaders of unofficial strike actions.[5] Such pressure continued during the Second World War, when left-leaning intellectuals were given greater access to the airwaves in an effort to win support for the war effort. In December 1941, Reith's successor as director general, Frederick Olgivie, wrote a confidential memo noting that the 'recurring allegation that the BBC is unduly leftward in its choice of speakers and programmes has recently taken on a new virulence' and asking that BBC controllers 'correct the balance'.[6] A year later, the then joint director general, Sir Cecil Graves, wrote a confidential memo to BBC controllers stating:

> There is a good deal of Parliamentary activity, notably the 1922 committee [a group of right-wing Tory backbenchers], about the BBC being all left. This is of course a hardy annual but cannot be disregarded ... until the matter is cleared up I should be grateful if you would keep off leftish speakers as much as possible.[7]

In 1947, Winston Churchill, who had recently been ousted as prime minister by Clement Atlee, instigated what seems to have been the first systematic attempt by the organised right to monitor BBC output for supposed political bias. The effort was led by the Conservative politician John

Profumo, later one of a number of backbench Tory MPs who campaigned for the establishment of commercial television, and who is most remembered for the sex scandal that bears his name. Having lost his seat in Labour's 1945 landslide election victory, Profumo was appointed the Conservative Party's first head of broadcasting and set up a unit at Conservative Central Office to monitor radio for signs of political bias. He recruited six monitors, who each week received instructions as to which programmes to monitor, which were selected at meetings at Conservative Central Office on the day the *Radio Times* was published. Profumo later told the author and journalist Michael Cockerell that 'as a result of our efforts we made a great deal of headway with the BBC – it had its effect'.[8]

For the Conservative Party, this was partly a question of seeking party-political advantage. But it was also an attempt at 'policing' a public space to marginalise the more radical politics on the fringes of the Labour Party and the broader left. Anxiety among elites about the threat of 'subversion' – the countering of which by the secret state and affiliated private political networks was justified by even the most loose affiliation to communists proper – increased markedly with the growth of radical and egalitarian social movements in the 1960s and '70s and the correlative surge in working-class militancy. Accusations of left-wing bias at the BBC then became ever more prevalent. Indeed, the critique of the media, and the BBC in particular, was a notable feature of the New Right, an umbrella term for the movement of right-wing activists, intellectuals, journalists and private propagandists who – supported by sections of big business and acting in concert with sections of the political elite – emerged in reaction to these developments, and more generally in opposition to the more egalitarian and democratic culture of the post-war settlement.

Attacks on the BBC were a notable feature of the inchoate moral conservative wing of the New Right, which cohered around the issue of sex and violence on television. Mary Whitehouse's Clean-Up TV campaign, launched in 1964 and renamed the National Viewers' and Listeners' Association a year later, initially focused on the BBC in particular, subsequently expanding its campaign to other media and to moral 'permissiveness' in general.[9] These were potent themes in British conservatism at the time. As the cultural theorist Stuart Hall and his colleagues detailed in their classic text *Policing the Crisis*, the cultural and social upheavals of the sixties and seventies – the changing sexual and gender norms, the rise in extra-parliamentary political activism, the eruption of political violence in Northern Ireland, the contemporary increase in levels of crime – and violent crime in particular – were met with a powerful conservative backlash which was moralistic and authoritarian in character. For Hall and his colleagues, Britain's economic crisis was experienced as a social crisis of 'law and order', wherein 'themes of protest, conflict, permissiveness and crime begin to run together into one great, undifferentiated "threat"'.[10] Mary Whitehouse, a conservative Christian and school teacher, was an important figure in this early conservative backlash, who along with the racist New Right trailblazer Enoch Powell anticipated the more pervasive 'authoritarian populism' (as Hall famously dubbed it) of the 1970s. Like Powell, Whitehouse adopted an anti-elitist political rhetoric, which she aimed at the 'small but powerful minority in the Broadcasting House' she believed was undermining traditional values through its promotion of liberal causes such as gay rights.[11]

Given her apparent remoteness from the centres of power, there is a tendency to see Mary Whitehouse as an old-fashioned but rather harmless figure; an admirably tenacious English eccentric, more prudish than political. This, however, does Mary Whitehouse a disservice. She led a powerful conservative movement which, though preoccupied with sex and violence on television, was driven by anxiety about 'moral decline' – a concept that on closer examination is revealed to be highly political. According to Durham, Whitehouse believed 'sexual anarchy will be followed by political anarchy and that in turn by "either dictatorship or destruction" unless we defend standards and "the family, the foundation-stone of civilised life".'[12] She was also something of a cold warrior, who believed that pornography was part of a secret communist plot to undermine the moral values of Western society.[13] For Whitehouse and those like her, the BBC was a vanguard-ist institution forcing dangerous social change from above through its high-minded liberalism. In her 1977 book, *Whatever Happened to Sex?*, Whitehouse wrote:

> If anyone were to ask me who, above all, was responsible for the moral collapse which characterized the sixties and seventies, I would unhesitatingly name Sir Hugh Carleton Greene, who was Director-General of the BBC from 1960 to 1969. He was in command of the most powerful medium ever to affect the thinking and behaviour of people – television.[14]

The claim that the BBC was biased to the left thus became part of a broader mobilising narrative adopted by the conservative movement, which claimed that a privileged, metropolitan elite was imposing its liberal values on the public. Whitehouse in her time championed and symbolised 'family values' in much the same way that one-time BBC presenter Jeremy Clarkson would 'common sense' a generation later. In 1974, her campaign was sanctioned by the then political leader of the New Right, Keith Joseph, who declared (in the notorious Edgbaston speech that would discredit him as a future Conservative leader):

> Let us take inspiration from that admirable woman, Mary Whitehouse ... Look at the scale of the opposing forces. On the one side, the whole of the new establishment, with their sharp words and sneers poised. Against them stood this one middle-aged woman. Today, her name is a household word, made famous by the very assaults on her by her enemies. She has mobilised and given fresh hearts to many who see where this current fashion is leading. Her book, *Who Does She Think She Is?* took its title from the outraged cry of an acolyte of the new hierarchy, who asked how an unknown woman dare speak up against the BBC, the educators and false shepherds.[15]

The political importance of the moral conservatives to Thatcherism is a matter of contention among scholars. But Thatcher, who herself is remembered for her 'free market' dogmatism, certainly sympathised with the moral conservatism of Mary Whitehouse. Douglas Hurd writes that

> the Prime Minister, though a free marketer, was no libertarian. She felt a strong sympathy for Mrs Whitehouse, then just past the peak of her campaign against violence and sex on television. Margaret Thatcher favoured a strong new law against obscenity. In particular she wanted to retain, or even strengthen, the existing regulations on the content of broadcasting.[16]

Indeed, the political inner core of early Thatcherites, with the possible exception of Nigel Lawson, were all committed to social conservatism as well as neoliberal reform. The latter, however, was the greater political priority. Recalling Joseph's Edgbaston speech in 1996, Thatcher commented that her political mentor

> was not only, or even primarily, interested in economics. It was simply that in the 1970s the economics had gone so devastatingly wrong that this was where any new analysis had to focus ... Reversing Britain's economic decline was such a huge and painful undertaking that, at least until the later years, the economy had to come first.[17]

Norman Tebbit – referred to by former BBC chairman Marmaduke Hussey as 'an enthusiastic scourge of the BBC'[18] – has insisted that although he, Thatcher and Joseph were often attacked 'for holding materialistic two-dimensional views', in fact '[n]one of us were simply economic liberals'.[19] Indeed, Thatcher herself exemplified the interweaving of neoliberal and socially conservative ideas that characterised the political movement to which she lent her name; a movement which in some ways developed a more sophisticated analysis of broadcasting than Whitehouse and her supporters, rooting the reactionary cultural attacks on 'permissiveness' in a neoliberal critique of the post-war political economy.

Thatcher regarded the BBC as a legacy of the 'authoritarian mood' of the interwar period and in her autobiography refers to broadcasting as 'one of a number of areas ... in which special pleading by powerful interest groups was disguised as high-minded commitment to some greater good'.[20] She saw an inherent link between the liberal culture that so incensed Whitehouse and the economic structures of broadcasting which were the target of the economistic critiques developed by Ronald Coase, Peter Jay, Alan

Peacock and others. One of Thatcher's many biographers, John Campbell, writes that she

> disliked the BBC on principle, long before she became Prime Minister, just because it was state-owned and publicly financed. She saw it as a nationalised industry, subsidised, anti-commercial and self-righteous: like the universities, she believed, it poisoned the national debate with woolly liberalism and moral permissiveness at taxpayers' expense.[21]

Paul Johnson, an influential intellectual of the New Right who criticised Thatcher for her alleged lack of progress on the BBC, considered that the Corporation's 'left-liberal slant' was 'inevitable in a nationalised industry financed by tax-payers' money.'[22]

The attacks on the supposed liberal or left-wing 'bias' of the BBC which emanated from the New Right, therefore, need to be understood as part and parcel of the broader contemporary attacks on the BBC over its funding and organisational structures. Perhaps the most infamous of the claims of political bias levied against the BBC in the Thatcher era came from Norman Tebbit, who played a significant part in an increasingly bitter conflict between the BBC and the government, which was only resolved by the forced resignation of the director general, Alasdair Milne. Shortly after announcing to the Conservative Party conference that he had established a media monitoring group at Conservative Central Office, Tebbit submitted a dossier to the BBC critiquing its coverage of the US bombing of Libya that April, for which the US military was controversially granted use of British air bases. He later described the document as a 'factual dossier comparing news bulletin by news bulletin, line by line, the reports broadcast by BBC and ITN'.[23] The BBC's *9 O'Clock News* was contrasted with ITV's *News at Ten*, the former said to be 'riddled with inaccuracy, innuendo and imbalance'.[24] It was claimed that

> *News at Ten* was able to preserve an impartial editorial stance, while the BBC took a number of editorial and journalistic decisions the effect of which was to enlist the sympathy of the audience to the Libyans and to antagonise them towards the Americans.[25]

The dossier was sent to the BBC on 30 October 1986 with a cover letter from Tebbit which read,

> In the light of our evidence, you may feel that the BBC news reporting, in this instance at least, fell short of the high standards which the Corporation espouses. Indeed, you may conclude that far from being balanced, fair and impartial, the coverage was a mixture of news, views, speculation, error and uncritical carriage of Libyan propaganda which does serious damage to the reputation of the BBC.[26]

Tebbit wrote in his autobiography that 'many reasonably minded people were uneasy, especially as they watched the misleading and unbalanced BBC coverage of the affair',[27] though years later he admitted: 'to tell the truth, I was probably as strident as I was partly because I had reservations (which I think were justified) about the Government process which led to our involvement, and some unease (which proved unjustified) about the policy itself.'[28]

Another key Thatcher aide who was especially hostile to the BBC was the journalist and former BBC reporter Woodrow Wyatt, who considered the Corporation 'hopelessly biased against private enterprise and the government because it is a loss-making nationalized industry which exists on public subsidies'.[29] Wyatt's famously indiscreet 'journals', which were published posthumously, are very revealing of the network of right-wing activists who plotted against the BBC in the Thatcher era. Among the consultations with former director general Ian Trethowen about political appointments and the regular discussions with the serving BBC chairman, Duke Hussey, are notes on meetings with the self-described 'counter-subversion propagandist' Julian Lewis.[30]

Lewis later became a Tory MP, but spent the early 1980s as the 'research director' of an anti-peace outfit called the Coalition for Peace Through Security, which was founded by the veteran counter-subversion propagandist Brian Crozier. Lewis is described by Wyatt as 'utterly charmless' but 'idealistic and determined', and is credited with having 'done marvellous work for the Tories, for the cause of curbing the trade unions, bias on the BBC and so forth'.[31] In 1995, Lewis was appointed to briefly head the revived Media Monitoring Unit at Conservative Central Office, the successor to Tebbit's operation. Woodrow Wyatt met with Lewis, Brian Crozier and two other conservative 'conspirators' in June 1986, and learned that they had been doing '[a] lot of work ... on bias in the media'. Wyatt was told that the conspirators would soon send him a report on political bias which would cover the BBC and ITV.[32] That document, which was launched in November 1986, took a year to produce and ran in 313 pages. It was written by a young libertarian activist named Simon Clark, who later worked as a tobacco lobbyist. Clark's efforts were financially supported by figures from the City of London,[33] and his report carried a foreword by the well-connected counter-subversion activist Lord Chalfont, who wrote,

> There is a widespread belief in political circles – although this is not necessarily shared by the general public – that

news and current affairs on television are neither objective
nor impartial; and that they are, in fact, persistently biased
in favour of the Left.[34]

This is precisely what this first report of the Media
Monitoring Group hoped to prove. Among its findings
were that the output of the BBC's flagship current affairs
television programme, *Panorama*, was 24.3 per cent biased
to the left, compared to only 8.1 per cent of output said to
be 'biased' to the right. If 'non-political' programming was
excluded, it was claimed, *Panorama* was overwhelmingly
(94.1 per cent) biased to the left.[35]

The launch of the Media Monitoring Group's report
was attended by senior figures from the BBC and ITN, and
over the course of the next five years the outfit produced
a number of similar reports, including one in 1990 commissioned by the *Daily Express* and promoted by Wyatt in
his *Daily Express* column, which claimed that the flagship
Radio 4 news and current affairs programme *Today* was
biased. That year, Wyatt, supported by his fellow peer Lord
Chalfont, proposed an amendment to the Broadcasting Bill
enshrining the requirement to maintain impartiality in law.
The amendment was opposed by the broadcasters and
their supporters in Parliament, and a less stringent amendment was tabled by the government that passed into law
under Section 6 of the Broadcasting Act.

How should we understand the impact and significance
of operations like Tebbit's and Lewis's monitoring groups?
It has been suggested that the former's campaign against
the BBC was part of Conservative Party electoral strategy.[36]
This is doubtless part of it; politicians certainly pressurise
journalists in the pursuit of electoral advantage. But even
though Tebbit's campaign was based at Conservative
Central Office, it should not be understood in such narrow

party-political terms. The network of elite actors who in the 1970s and '80s worked to institute a radical transformation in British society operated inside and outside the Conservative Party.

An elite social movement, they were spread across a variety of institutional locations beyond formal politics – think tanks, the private media, advertising and finance – and acted in concert, and occasionally in conflict, with sections of the British state. Getting Thatcher re-elected was of course crucial, but it was a means to the ends also pursued by extra-parliamentary political action, including campaigns against the BBC. Dossiers such as Tebbit's and Clark's, then, should be understood in the context of these networks and the political strategies they pursued. Like the reports produced by the Institute of Economic Affairs and other neoliberal think tanks, the dossiers were flimsy by scholarly standards. But such documents play an important role in constituting and consolidating such political networks, reinforcing their ideologies and focusing their political actions.

Considering the case of Tebbit's Libya dossier, the former Conservative minister Ian Gilmour writes that it was 'an inaccurate and trivial propagandist compilation which identified impartiality with what Conservative central office would like the BBC to have said'. The BBC, he writes, 'had no difficulty in shooting it to pieces'.[37] Indeed, the newly appointed BBC chairman, Duke Hussey, though he sympathised with some of Tebbit's claims, nevertheless defended the BBC. Gilmour argues, though, that while Tebbit's Libya dossier may have been a 'failure' in this respect, his 'general campaign of intimidation was, as he well realised, more successful'.[38] As for Tebbit's private counterparts in the Media Monitoring Group, Julian Lewis considers that the 'effective, regular and comprehensive reports' it produced led to a 'marked improvement in fairness shown by such programmes as *Panorama*'.[39] If true, this success was plainly not attributable to the veracity of the evidence presented, but rather to the power and influence of the political networks that mobilised around it and the broader movement of which they were a part.

Crucial to their success, of course, was the power which the Conservative Government wielded over the BBC. But another crucial element was the support of the reactionary press. While the BBC has been obliged to maintain 'due impartiality', the press have always been spared the same restrictions. The rationale for this more lax standard of regulation has been that the newspaper market produces a range of political perspectives, from which readers can freely choose. By the late 1970s, however, this justification had become rather hollow, as the market had become increasingly monopolised and scores of centre-left newspapers had been forced to close. The decline in Britain's left and centre-left press from the 1960s especially was not due to a lack of readership, or political support, but rather the inability of left-wing publications to compete in a market requiring high levels of capital investment and substantial advertising revenues.

In 1969, the *Sun*, which in a previous incarnation as the *Daily Herald* had been a popular centre-left working-class daily, came under the control of Rupert Murdoch, whose editor Larry Lamb transformed it into a populist right-wing tabloid. Murdoch's *Sun* joined the ranks of the traditional Tory press, shifting the market overwhelming to the right. In 1950, newspapers supporting the Conservative and Labour parties were split evenly in terms of circulation. By 1974, political support for the Conservatives and Labour had split to 71–32 per cent respectively – and by 1983 it was 78–22 per cent.[40] This had the effect of shifting political culture in the UK to the right. Crucially though, this shift was more due to changes in the political economy of the press than to public attitudes.[41] The BBC, meanwhile, like the public, and for a time parliamentary opinion, remained broadly tied to the social-democratic consensus, putting it at odds with the cultural shift in the private media and the simultaneous shift in elite opinion that was taking place in the business sector. The reactionary attacks on the politics of the BBC, enthusiastically supported by, or emanating from, the reactionary press, need to be understood in this context.

How was the BBC perceived by the public during this time? From the mid-1970s, the Independent Television Authority (later the Independent Television Commission) included in its annual surveys a question as to whether viewers perceived any party-political bias on different television channels. While the majority of respondents consistently perceived no party-political bias on the BBC, of those that did, the proportion perceiving it as pro-Conservative was always significantly higher than those perceiving a pro-Labour bias. This finding holds from the Labour Government of the 1970s right up to the election of Tony Blair in 1997. Importantly, perception of party-political bias on ITN was, meanwhile, fairly evenly split between the two main parties under Thatcher and Major, while the proportion perceiving a pro-Labour bias was higher under the Labour governments of the 1970s and the early years of New Labour.

By comparison, the percentage perceiving a pro-Tory bias on the BBC also declined dramatically in 1997, falling below the proportions perceiving a pro-Labour bias for the first time ever. But it then rose again the following year, again outnumbering those perceiving a pro-Labour bias. What this data suggests, then, is that while viewers have generally regarded the BBC as non-partisan, if anything it is viewed as a right-wing organisation, a perception which is not merely attributable to the politics of the party in power, as would seem to be the case for the BBC's main domestic rival during that period.[42] The right, therefore, was attacking the BBC as left wing at a time when the public, if anything, viewed it as a conservative organisation, a fact which made the attacks seem overwrought, even deluded.

But behind the trivial propaganda and hysterical rhetoric was a fairly coherent political strategy. The BBC was rightly understood by the New Right to have institutionalised the values of social democracy and to some limited extent – and to the chagrin of Mary Whitehouse – the liberal culture of the 1960s. Norman Tebbit's contempt for the BBC, for example, was certainly linked to the impact that the social movements of that decade had had on its institutional culture. He described it as the 'insufferable, smug, sanctimonious, naive, guilt-ridden, wet, pink orthodoxy of that sunset home of that third-rate decade, the 1960s'.[43] Ian Gilmour remarked of this vitriol that it 'was the sort of thing Senator Joe McCarthy used to say about the US State Department', and this is an insightful remark.[44] Tebbit and others hoped to shift elite opinion and political institutions further to the right, and he and his comrades' attacks on the BBC were one part of that strategy.

The 'War on Terror' in the 2000s saw a revival of conservative movements, and of organised attacks on the BBC. In 2004, the then editor of the *Today* programme, Kevin Marsh, wrote,

> probably dating from September 11 and the declaration of the so-called War on Terror – a new charge of systematic

bias [at the BBC] has become much more evident. It is not
a charge of deliberate partisanship, but of an unconscious
and systematically left-leaning mind-set.'[45]

Marsh noted in particular the *Daily Telegraph*'s 'Beebwatch'
column and John Lloyd's 2004 book *What the Media are
Doing to Our Politics*. Lloyd's book argues that a hyper-
critical media has undermined faith in democracy – a
line of argument that was later repeated by Tony Blair in
a June 2007 speech in which he likened the media to a
'feral beast'. Lloyd was one of the group of former leftists
who supported the 2003 Iraq War. His writing though has
always been characterised by a certain hostility to popular
movements. In *The Miners' Strike*, for example, he and his
co-author criticised the miners for being undemocratic,
an accusation he later made of the anti-corporate movement in the 1990s in his 2001 book, *The Protest Ethic:
How the Anti-Globalisation Movement Challenges Social
Democracy*.

The second example cited by Marsh, the *Daily Telegraph*'s
Beebwatch column, ran three times a week for two months
in late 2003. The Telegraph Group was at the time still
controlled by the Canadian-born conservative businessman Conrad Black, who would later be convicted in the
US for fraud and obstruction of justice. Black was a passionate supporter of the New Right. Earlier, in 1990, when
the then editor of the *Telegraph*, Max Hastings, moved to
distance the paper from Julian Lewis's propaganda operations, Black intervened at the request of Woodrow Wyatt,
arranging a lunch with a *Telegraph* journalist to work with
Lewis on what Wyatt called the 'flow of good pro-Tory
anti-Militant and anti-Labour stories'.[46]

A total of twenty-six Beebwatch articles were published by the *Telegraph* between early September and early

November 2003, each claiming to show evidence of a left-wing bias in the BBC's output. The Beebwatch column was introduced in an article by Max Hastings's successor, Charles Moore, the official biographer of Margaret Thatcher and an influential figure in post-Thatcherite British conservatism. While conceding that the BBC was probably not biased against the Conservative Party, Moore argued that its 'mental assumptions are those of the fairly soft Left':

> They are that American power is a bad thing, whereas the UN is good, that the Palestinians are in the right and Israel isn't, that the war in Iraq was wrong, that the European Union is a good thing and that people who criticise it are 'xenophobic', that racism is the worst of all sins, that abortion is good and capital punishment is bad, that too many people are in prison, that a preference for heterosexual marriage over other arrangements is 'judgmental', that environmentalists are public-spirited and 'big business' is not.[47]

Moore went on to explain how the Beebwatch column would 'offer brief reports culled from the airwaves' and would be 'helped in gathering information by Minotaur, a media monitoring unit that will study all relevant bits of the BBC output, television, radio and electronic'. Minotaur Media Tracking was established with the backing of Lord Pearson, a neoconservative Tory peer who later defected to the UK Independence Party. Its founders, Kathy Gyngell and David Keighley, were former employees, and the second wife and close friend respectively, of the late Bruce Gyngell, an Australian television executive who was prominent in Britain during the Thatcher era.[48] As head of the ITV franchise TV-am, Gyngell had impressed Thatcher with his ruthless handling of a 1987 industrial dispute and was subsequently invited to 10 Downing Street with his young wife, Kathy. Gyngell later employed Thatcher's daughter, Carol, and the two families met socially on a number of occasions.[49] The loss of the franchise in 1991, which Thatcher said left her 'heartbroken', led to Gyngell's departure from public life in Britain, but his wife would later emerge as a conservative activist.[50] Having spent a period in Australia, Kathy Gyngell co-founded the Full Time Mothers Association on her return to London, before setting up Minotaur Media Tracking with Keighley in July 1999.

The outfit didn't only provide research for Beebwatch. Along with its successor, Newswatch, it produced a number of reports for the Eurosceptic think tank Global Britain and the Centre for Policy Studies, the neoliberal think tank founded by Thatcher and Keith Joseph where Gyngell later became a research fellow. The great majority of reports published by Minotaur and Newswatch alleged a bias in favour of EU integration and several alleged a broader bias against right-wing politics and the Conservative Party. As was the case with the earlier right-wing media monitoring groups, the press proved an invaluable outlet, while direct lobbying of the BBC was also utilised. The Global Britain reports, for example, were followed up with correspondence between the BBC and Tory peers who supported the organisation, notably Lord Pearson.

As Robin Aitken, a former BBC journalist and right-wing critic of the Corporation notes, the 'huge time and energy' Newswatch and their allies devoted to their campaign over the BBC's coverage of the EU 'eventually bore fruit with the Wilson Report'.[51] This was an independent report produced by a panel set up by the Board of Governors to examine the BBC's coverage of the EU, which was headed by the former senior civil servant and Sky executive director Richard Wilson. Among the questions the panel was asked to consider was whether the BBC was 'systematically europhile', or whether 'anti-EU, pro-withdrawal voices have been excluded from BBC coverage'. The Board of Governors also commissioned a content analysis from a private company, Morrison Media Consultants, which looked in particular detail at four news stories, comparing the BBC's coverage to that of the press and the other broadcasters. The conclusions of this analysis were tentative and mixed. The report criticised *Newsnight*, for example, for not 'signalling clearly in advance' that a report by the *Guardian* journalist George Monbiot was 'not a piece of impartial reporting, but a personal view'.[52] On the question of immigration from the EU, it found 'striking similarities between BBC and press coverage, both in broad structure and in detail', and noted that the Labour Government, the Conservative Party and the anti-immigrant pressure group, Migration Watch UK, were all well represented, though it noted that the 'concerns' about immigration expressed by *The Times* and the *Daily Mail* 'were not reflected by the BBC'.[53] The content analysis was in any case not referenced in the Wilson Report, which appears to have relied instead upon the views of the groups it consulted.

The panel found 'no evidence of deliberate bias', but noted 'a widespread perception that [the BBC's coverage of Europe] suffers from certain forms of cultural and unintentional bias'.[54] In response to the recommendations, the BBC created a new European editor post and introduced mandatory training on the EU. It strengthened the existing 'monitoring system' it had established three years earlier, requiring programme staff to log the positions of key interviewees on EU-related issues, and agreed to develop qualitative monitoring of 'tone and approach'.[55]

Behind this particular campaign – which eventually led to institutional changes at the Corporation – was a faction of Britain's elite which was pursuing a particular position on the European Union and the prospect of a single currency. The five-person Wilson Panel included a representative of this faction, the businessman and Conservative peer Rodney Leach, chair of the main anti-Euro pressure group, Business for Sterling, as well as Sir Stephen Wall, a former senior civil servant and a board member of the corporate-funded pro-European outfit, Britain in Europe. The latter organisation could claim the support of key figures from New Labour, the Liberal Democrats and the pro-European wing of the Conservative Party, while the former also enjoyed significant business support and was led by figures from the Conservative Party. As the makeup of these campaigning groups illustrates, the issue of the European Union is one which has split the British elite.

The struggles over Britain's relationship with the EU are recounted in a 2011 pamphlet published by the Centre for Policy Studies. *Guilty Men*, as the pamphlet was called, was co-authored by the conservative journalist Peter Oborne with a foreword by the BBC's former economics editor Peter Jay. Drawing on research conducted by Minotaur, it claims that 'the BBC lost all objectivity and became aligned to a partisan propaganda operation', allying itself 'with the left/liberal élite'.[56] The authors write that

> in the nine weeks between 22 May and 21 July 2000, the Today programme on Radio 4 featured 121 speakers on this topic: 87 were pro-Euro compared to 34 euro-sceptics. These euro-sceptics provided 34 interviews and 21 soundbites, whilst the pro-Euro camp provided 72 interviews and 40 soundbites. The case for the Euro was represented by

twice as many figures, interviews and soundbites than the case against.[57]

Oborne and his co-author attribute this apparent partiality on Europe to the political culture of the BBC, suggesting that it is unlikely to have 'reflected any kind of conscious decision or arrangement', but rather the fact that 'the high-minded attitudes of BBC producers and reporters meshed only too easily with those of the pro-Euro pressure groups.'[58]

In a footnote, the authors of *Guilty Men* also quote claims about liberal/left bias made by former BBC newsreaders Peter Sissons and Michael Buerk.[59] Sissons and Buerk are just two of a good number of current and former BBC journalists and executives who have blown the whistle on its supposed left-wing bias. Sissons, in his book *When One Door Closes*, writes

> In my view, 'bias' is too blunt a word to describe the subtleties of the pervading culture. The better word is a 'mindset'. At the core of the BBC, in its very DNA, is a way of thinking that is firmly of the Left.

Reviewing the book for the neoconservative *Standpoint* magazine, another former newsreader, Michael Buerk, suggests that Sissons doesn't 'quite skewer the complicated issue of the BBC's supposed institutional bias', but his analysis of BBC culture is broadly similar:

> What the BBC regards as normal and abnormal, what is moderate or extreme, where the centre of gravity of an issue lies, are conditioned by the common set of assumptions held by the people who work for it. These are uniformly middle class, well-educated, living in north London, or maybe its

Manchester equivalent. Urban, bright thirty-somethings with a pleasing record of achievement in a series of institutions, school, university, BBC, with little experience of – and perhaps not very well disguised contempt for – business, industry, the countryside, localness, traditions and politicians. The *Guardian* is their bible and political correctness their creed.[60]

A similar argument has been advanced by the former BBC executive Roger Mosey, a less well-known figure who was responsible for recruiting the future Conservative minister Michael Gove to BBC TV's *On the Record*. Mosey spoke at a 2006 seminar on impartiality hosted by the BBC governors, saying he had 'some sympathy' with claims by the *Telegraph* journalist Janet Daley, who had been invited by the BBC to discuss what Mosey called its 'liberal/pinko agenda'.[61] Mosey argued that, while the BBC is scrupulously non-partisan in its political coverage, it nevertheless exhibits a 'groupthink' on certain issues, meaning that although its journalists and editors are not consciously bias, they accept certain taken-for-granted assumptions. Like many right-wing critics of the BBC, Mosey focuses on Europe and immigration. He writes that he 'went into battle in the summer of 2003 with the BBC's Editorial Policy team' after it criticised the conflation of the issues of immigration and terrorism in television news, which it had rightly noted was 'being led by an angry tabloid agenda and extreme right-wing groups'. Mosey attacked the 'liberal-defensive response' adopted by the Editorial Policy team and he shared the correspondence with Jeff Randall, an outspoken right-winger brought in as the BBC's business editor by Greg Dyke to push the BBC in a more pro-business direction. Randall responded:

> Does anyone in the BBC's Policy Unit/Thought Police read [the right-wing columnist] Richard Littlejohn? They should. He reflects popular opinion far more accurately than the views of those whose idea of a good night out is reading the Indy over a vegetarian meal in a Somali restaurant.

Randall's views on the BBC are not dissimilar to those of another former BBC journalist, Robin Aitken, who in his book *Can We Trust the BBC?* writes,

> To succeed at the BBC it is necessary to sign up to – or, at the very least, not publicly dissent from – a range of attitudes and opinions. Collectively the tribe's values might be termed 'liberal' – but liberal in this context doesn't mean tolerant, merely the opposite of 'conservative'. So for instance, there is strong emphasis on 'non-discriminatory' attitudes; 'sexism' and 'homophobia' are deadly sins. 'Judgemental' attitudes are disapproved of; within BBC circles it would, for instance, be frowned upon to disapprove of unmarried mothers.[62]

Anecdotal claims such as these have been useful currency for the BBC's right-wing critics. Another Newswatch report, for example, produced for the right-wing think tank Civitas in April 2014, quoted claims about anti-EU bias at the BBC made by Mark Thompson, Nick Robinson, John Humphrys and the former *Today* editor Rod Liddle.[63] But what exactly is being claimed by these many critics about the 'bias' on display at the BBC? As the above quoted remarks illustrate, the BBC's right-wing critics often allude, in pseudo-sociological language, to an institutional culture which reproduces certain unconscious collective assumptions. This is all well and good. But what is often less clear is from where exactly this liberal bias comes, or how it is perpetuated. A typical explanation is provided by the BBC presenter and former political editor Andrew Marr, one of the best-known BBC figures to have alluded to the Corporation's supposed liberal-left bias. Marr made the following remarks on 'cultural bias' at the aforementioned 2006 impartiality seminar:

> The BBC is a publicly funded urban organisation with an abnormally large proportion of younger people, of people in ethnic minorities and almost certainly of gay people than the population at large. It depends on the state's approval at least for its funding mechanism and all this creates an innate liberal bias inside the BBC.[64]

The reference to state funding here is slightly unusual in this context, and perhaps made a little more sense in the context of the more centrist Labour administration which was in power at the time. The notion of an unconscious liberal cultural bias stemming from the makeup of the Corporation's personnel and its metropolitan location though is much more typical. The evidence on this point, however, is hardly compelling.

Take for example the ethnic diversity of the BBC's staff. The 2011 Census for England and Wales found that white and non-white people made up 85.9 per cent and 14.1 per cent of the population respectively, while figures released by the BBC that same year reported that its staff were 87.7 per cent white and 12.3 per cent BME.[65] Incorporating the data for Scotland and Northern Ireland would obviously adjust the picture somewhat, given that both regions are overwhelmingly white. But equally, the BBC's own 2011 figures include its international staff, around half of whom are non-white.[66] That year the BBC launched a four-year diversity strategy, and its latest figures at the time of writing suggest a modest increase in BME representation. Black and minority ethnic people now make up around 13 per cent of staff, although in a number of divisions the proportions are much lower. In Television and Radio for example, BME people make up just 10.6 per cent and 10.5 per cent of staff respectively. Moreover, at the senior level, representation for BME people is much lower than for the BBC as a whole. Though ethnic minorities are well represented in the Director General's Office, the Creative Director's Office and in Editorial Standards and Policy (all of which are defined as one 'division' by the BBC), in all other domestic divisions of the BBC, BME people are seriously underrepresented at the senior level, with proportions ranging from zero per cent within the BBC Trust and in BBC Northern Ireland to 8.8 per cent in the Finance and Business Division.[67]

The evidence on the representation of minorities at the BBC, then, is that it is broadly in keeping with the ethnic makeup of the UK as a whole, but still slightly unrepresentative of England and Wales, and certainly of Greater London, which is much more diverse than most other regions of the UK. This being the case, comments like Marr's really only make sense if they are assumed to be an implicit criticism of the fact that the BBC, by virtue of employing non-white people, is somehow unrepresentative of the white population of the United Kingdom, or perhaps of the less diverse regions of the UK where negative attitudes towards ethnic minorities tend to be more prevalent. The policy implications of this – that a national broadcaster paid for by ethnic minority citizens either should avoid employing non-white people or should act as a vehicle for racist views – are so plainly unjust that they could not be openly advocated. But these are the logical implications of the reactionary attacks on the BBC's diversity policies as 'liberal' or 'politically correct'. That an influential BBC journalist like Andrew Marr could have so casually expressed such a view in 2006 reflects a reactionary drift in British political culture which followed New Labour's first term. With the hegemonic faction of the Labour Party having renounced any pretence of socialism and explicitly aligned itself with Britain's financial elite, an effective taboo had taken hold around any discussion of class. In such circumstances, the only opposition to neoliberalism permissible in British public life was opposition to liberalism as such. The 'white working class' in these circumstances came to be seen as a repository of reactionary common sense in opposition to the middle-class liberalism of New Labour, and was increasingly invoked as currency in elite political struggles, especially over immigration and the European Union. Closely tied to the world of Westminster and Whitehall and with its senior staff disproportionately drawn from the private school–educated upper middle classes,[68] the BBC has had no answer to its tenacious right-wing critics. In these circumstances, it is easy to see why the BBC, wedded as it is to an increasingly remote political elite, has felt vulnerable to the charge of liberal elitism and under the leadership of Mark Thompson began to shift editorial policy rightward in a clumsy attempt to engage politically with its audience.

The underlying problem with the political debates which underlined that rightward shift was that, like so many debates the politics of the BBC, it lacked any sense that politics is not merely about different cultural values, but also about power. Implicit in the polemical attacks on the BBC's liberal culture has been the notion that the Corporation and its staff are more sympathetic to the left wing of the political Establishment, as represented by the *The Guardian* and the Labour Party, than to its right wing represented by *The Times*, the *Daily Telegraph*, the *Mail* and the Conservative Party. As we have seen, the BBC's right-wing critics claim that it has supported European integration and take this as evidence of left-wing bias. The trouble with attributing the patterns of reporting which Minotaur and Newswatch claim to have uncovered to a left-wing institutional culture, though, is starkly revealed, albeit unintentionally, in the aforementioned *Guilty Men* pamphlet. The authors of that report acknowledge that the pro-European position they claim to have identified was not unique to the BBC, arguing that its 'coverage should be seen as part of a wider and more significant national pattern'.[69] Along with the BBC, they also name and shame two other institutional 'villains' in their story: the CBI and the *Financial Times*. The former, they note, was by the mid-1990s controlled by large corporations and headed by big business's favoured director general, Adair Turner, while the latter is significant for serving as 'the acknowledged voice of the City of London and the business community'.[70] In other words, the BBC's reporting on this particular issue was in step with organised political opinion among Britain's corporate elite.

What is even more remarkable about the whole issue is that, even within such a narrow conceptualisation of political 'bias', there is no substantive evidence to support such claims. On the contrary, the evidence points in the opposite direction. One of the most extensive scholarly investigations of BBC political reporting in recent years has been carried out for the BBC Trust by a team of researchers at Cardiff University. The 'Breadth of Opinion Review' they conducted included an examination of the BBC's coverage of the EU and immigration in 2007 and 2012, as well as the range of opinion on the BBC as compared with its competitors. The researchers found that 'Eurosceptic views were regularly featured, while those arguing for the benefits of EU membership were less prominent'.[71] Indeed, one author of the study, Mike Berry, notes that 'business lobbyists provided much of what little pro-EU opinion was available'.[72]

In terms of political balance between the major parties, the respective ruling party in each year dominated both sample periods, but the dominance of the Conservatives in 2012 was 'by a notably larger margin than Labour dominance in 2007'.[73] Indeed, a separate strand of the research, which compared the BBC's output with other broadcasters, found that Conservative politicians were featured over 50 per cent more than Labour politicians on the BBC's *News at Six* across the two sample periods, a pattern not evident in the output of the BBC's rivals.[74] One of the major findings of the study was the dominance of Westminster sources and perspectives in BBC political reporting. BBC news, the researchers noted,

> reflects a relatively narrow range of sources – primarily political leaders, with the Prime Minister remaining the most newsworthy and widely quoted individual source, and other government figures just behind him. This, in turn, is closely connected to another striking tendency, particularly apparent in our samples of stories on the UK's relationship to Europe and on immigration: the stories on these topics which topped the news agenda largely dealt with tensions and fights between the main Westminster parties, rather than the broader issues associated with the societal impact of the EU and immigration.[75]

Political sources were especially dominant in the BBC's coverage of the EU, accounting for as much as 65 per cent of source appearances in 2007 and 79.2 per cent in 2012.[76] The coverage of the negotiations over the EU budget in

2012, it was noted, 'frequently focused on the parliamentary machinations over the issue rather than opinions on the subject', and this 'focus on political sparring meant that much of the information about the actual substance of the budget, as well as the pros and cons of EU investment policy, tended to be lost'.[77] Though the BBC's reporting on immigration included 'a more diverse range of sources', coverage still 'reflected the overall pattern of dominance by political sources' and 'frequently focused on political infighting'. Moreover, the qualitative analysis the researchers conducted found that debates over immigration on the BBC 'were usually framed by politicians, whose statements were often presented as "facts"'. The domination of BBC News by Westminster politicians, and the analysis of political issues through the machinations of Westminster politics, the researchers concluded, suggests an understanding of political impartiality based on 'a balance between the two main Westminster parties'.[78]

This sort of coverage reflects the extent to which BBC journalists, and the BBC itself, are embedded in the world of formal politics. This was candidly admitted in 2015 by the BBC's Nick Robinson during his series of programmes on British democracy: 'I live in Islington and I work in Westminster. Oh dear, I'm in the coterie!', he joked in conversation with a voter. 'Yes, like it or not, I am a small cog in what many now see as the nation's creaky and outdated political machine.'[79] Robinson, who has since moved to the *Today* programme, was then the BBC's political editor, a position described in a 2009 intelligence briefing for Barack Obama as 'the most important job in British political journalism'.[80] His approach – which was very much in keeping with BBC tradition – was informed by a sincere, even passionate, commitment to a particular conception of politics and a particular type of political journalism.

For Robinson, politics is, in short, what politicians say and do, and the task of the political correspondent, meanwhile, is to effectively communicate and explain this, as well as the formal political process, to viewers and listeners. His job as political editor, he declared during a stretch at ITN in the same role, was 'to report what those in power were doing or thinking' – or, as he later wrote in his book *Live From Downing Street*, to expose 'publicly what many know to exist privately: tension between colleagues, policy contradictions or a failure to have thought through a policy clearly'.[81] Robinson has undertaken this task with gusto, describing with great clarity and inordinate enthusiasm the personalities, cliques and machinations of Westminster politics. His own background made him well suited to this task. He grew up in a Conservative family in 'a wealthy, leafy Cheshire village', attended private school, and from a young age was close friends with the son of Brian Redhead, the then co-presenter of the *Today* programme. Redhead – a household name regarded by the Thatcherites as a left-winger but who considered himself a Tory moderate – inspired the young Robinson to become a broadcast journalist and would later serve as a mentor.[82] While Redhead had attended Cambridge University, his protégé, like many other senior BBC figures, chose Oxford. The student union debating society was Robinson's 'university playground', and at the height of Thatcherism he was appointed president of the university's Conservative Association. He read Politics, Philosophy and Economics (PPE), a prestigious degree tailored to Britain's political elite-in-waiting very common among senior BBC journalists. All this imbued Robinson with an almost instinctive understanding of the workings of the Westminster-Whitehall system and a natural ease among its inhabitants, making him particularly adept at embedded political reporting.

At best, the sort of approach Robinson exemplifies makes for accomplished insider journalism, offering a window on the insular world of high politics, bringing greater transparency and thereby enhancing democracy. The reality, though, has been far less satisfying. The approach tends to foster an elitist, 'insider' perspective on politics, encouraging viewers to see it as a strategic game between its leading players – with whom viewers are encouraged to identify – rather than a system of public deliberation over social policy or contestation over the distribution of wealth and power. Greg Dyke has said that during his time as director general he attempted to address the excessive Westminster focus of BBC journalism, but that his efforts were thwarted by 'the political journalists at the BBC' and the 'politicos on the Board of Governors'.[83] Dyke specifically named the former economics journalist Baroness Hogg, who was a BBC governor from 2000 to 2004. Another Oxford PPE graduate, Hogg served as the head of John Major's Policy Unit from 1990 to 1995, has served on numerous corporate boards, and is married to the Old Etonian Conservative politician Douglas Hogg, the Viscount Hailsham. Speaking about what he called a 'Westminster conspiracy', Dyke told the media scholar David McQueen,

> It's a village and that village includes the politicians, it includes the civil servants, it includes the journalists, it includes the lobbyists and they have increasingly become one group and everyone else has become another.[84]

Dyke suggested that this led to a culture in which Westminster politics is over-reported and journalists adopt a less-questioning attitude. This is certainly a serious problem. With the opportunities that proximity to power brings – access to sources, insider information and 'scoops' –

comes the loss of critical distance. Andrew Marr wrote of this problem in his book *My Trade*:

> If you really talk with a politician about their in tray, and the problems of rival departments, or of dodgy past initiatives, it is hard to avoid seeing things their way. The same perspective that gives you insight, also blunts your hostility. So is it better to stand outside, defiantly ignorant, making judgments that the crowd will applaud? There is no final answer. If you don't form close understandings with senior politicians so that you can hear them think aloud honestly in a relaxed way then you are unlikely to understand much of what is really going on. Yet if you do then you drift closer to them emotionally and may very well flinch from putting the boot in when they have failed in some way.[85]

Ten years later, Marr's first novel, a political thriller, was launched at a reception at 10 Downing Street.

The problem of proximity to power is not merely a professional dilemma inherent to journalism, it is also a particular feature of the neoliberal transformation of British society. One of the new spaces the BBC moved into in the 1990s was the privately owned Millbank Studios opposite Parliament, where the BBC 'became the founding tenant' in 1993.[86] Just as the recently shut studios, Lime Grove, had embodied the journalistic ethos of the 'old guard', so to its critics symbolised the craven journalism that displaced it – its geographical proximity to Westminster mirrored by its journalists' incestuous relationships with politicians and their spin doctors, whose agenda of news management dovetailed with the neoliberal director general John Birt's suspicion of adversarial journalism and his centralisation of editorial authority.[87]

Since that time, there has been something of a revolving

door between the BBC and Westminster. A number of Blairite ministers were former BBC employees. Chris Bryant was briefly head of European Affairs at the BBC, from 1998 to 2000, before becoming an MP in 2001. Ben Bradshaw, who was the secretary of state for culture, media and sport from 2009 to 2010, is a former BBC Radio reporter. Bradshaw's predecessor in that office was James Purnell, who now receives £295,000 a year as the BBC's director of Strategy and Digital, and was previously the BBC's head of Corporate Planning in the mid-1990s, before his appointment as special advisor to Tony Blair. BBC political reporters Don Brind and Lorraine Davidson both took political communications posts and Bill Bush, once the BBC's head of Political Research, joined Blair's strategic communications unit.[88]

Robin Aitken notes a number of other 'revolving door' connections in his effort to paint the BBC as left wing, but the same pattern has been evident since the return to power of the Conservatives. As has been noted, Michael Gove once worked as a BBC reporter. George Osborne's special advisor, Thea Rogers, is a former BBC producer who once worked with Nick Robinson. David Cameron recruited Craig Oliver from the BBC after the former *News of the World* journalist Andy Coulson was forced to resign. The former London mayor Boris Johnson similarly hired Guto Harri, a former BBC chief political correspondent, as his director of communications, who himself was later succeeded by Will Walden, formerly the BBC's Westminster news editor, who had previously worked closely with both Nick Robinson and Andrew Marr. Robbie Gibb, currently editor of BBC Live Political Programmes, is a former chief of staff to the influential Conservative politician Francis Maude and is the brother of the Tory minister Nicholas Gibb.

What we see here is the circulation of a particular subset of the 'political class' with experience and expertise in media and political communications, and marketable connections in the intertwined world of media and politics. As political consultants and PRs, they are representative of a trend towards greater professionalisation in political life and members of a broader industry specialising in political and corporate communications. A few of these types will be political partisans. But by virtue of the waters they swim in, they overwhelmingly share a realism – if not cynicism – about politics and the post-Thatcherite corporate-dominated political consensus of which they are both products and reproducers. The circulation of such figures back and forth between the BBC and pro-business factions in both major parties mirrors, at a lower level, the circulation of elites at the apex of the BBC hierarchy, which has been a feature of the Corporation since its establishment. This illustrates that the BBC, whatever liberals would like to imagine, does not stand apart from the world of politics and power and the corporate interests which predominate there. Rather, it is an important part of those complex networks of power and influence. It further shows that, insofar as the BBC can be said to exhibit any political bias, it is not based in political partisanship, but rather in an orientation towards those networks of power and their shared interests – interests which, it should be noted, are not necessarily self-evident or immutable, but are worked out in and through these networks, and in and through key political institutions like the BBC.

CHAPTER 5

The Making of a Neoliberal Bureaucracy

'There is a corporate myth which is carefully, assiduously, propagated, and there is the reality. And they bear little relation to each other,' announced the American economist J. K. Galbraith on BBC TV in 1977. The myth, he calmly explained, was that the consumer is sovereign and the corporation responds to his or her preferences, efficiently allocating society's resources. In reality, Galbraith continued: 'Corporations influence government, influence the consumer. Only the textbooks hold otherwise.'[1] These remarks introduced a programme entitled 'The Big Corporation', the ninth episode in a documentary series written and presented by Galbraith and co-produced by the BBC with several other public service broadcasters around the world. *The Age of Uncertainty* was an ambitious thirteen-part series, which examined the 'rise and crisis of industrial society' and included episodes not only interrogating the role of corporations in society, but examining the limitations of capitalism and the ideas of Karl Marx and John Maynard Keynes. An erudite public intellectual close to the US Democratic Party, J. K. Galbraith was a disciple of Keynes. He was no radical. In fact, he identified as a conservative. But like many of his generation, he was a measured critic of neoclassical economics and corporate power. He championed, even exemplified, a tradition of American liberalism that by the time *The Age of Uncertainty* was broadcast in 1977 was in crisis and, so it has transpired, had fallen into terminal decline.

Galbraith had been approached four years earlier by Adrian Malone, the producer of the acclaimed BBC series *The Ascent of Man*, which broadcast that same year. Malone, an independent-minded producer who was close to the BBC executive Huw Wheldon and to the national security state, had approached Galbraith with his idea for a documentary series on economic thought without having sought the approval of the BBC hierarchy. The BBC leadership were reportedly 'furious', but reluctantly allowed Malone to proceed with the project.[2] When the series finally aired in 1977, each hour-long episode was subtitled 'a personal view'; the series received considerable criticism from the right and generally unfavourable reviews, and the BBC leadership ordered that it never be repeated.[3]

The tirade of criticism *The Age of Uncertainty* received was, in part, an orchestrated counterattack from a network of politicians, businessmen, journalists, academics and pamphleteers that were rising to prominence. The neoliberal faction within the Conservative Party got wind of the project in early 1976 when it was brought to the attention of Keith Joseph, the party's head of policy. Joseph swiftly wrote to his colleagues, expressing alarm that the BBC had invited 'an open advocate of socialism' to present a programme on economics. Galbraith, he wrote, was 'about the most dangerous intellectual opponent that we have on the economic front', and he suggested they should 'put [the BBC] on warning ... lead[ing] them [perhaps] to inviting someone like McFadzean [the chairman of Shell and a former president of the Federation of British Industry] to give an equivalent series'.[4] In a subsequent letter, Joseph complained,

Galbraith is socialist, interventionalist, anti-enterprise, and totally indifferent to the realities of life ... [H]e could do the country and us as a party immense damage if he is given the pedestal which the BBC proposes.[5]

Fellow Thatcherite Geoffrey Howe said he shared Joseph's anxiety about 'so plausible an advocate of the wrong approach' being given so prominent a platform, and thought that the 'proper balance to Galbraith might be provided by a series of talks from Hayek or Friedman'[6] – however, the former, Howe later conceded, was 'perhaps now too old'.[7] Friedman, by contrast, was a formidable and increasingly influential figure, who was already a friend and sparring partner of Galbraith's, much as Hayek had been for Keynes.

Galbraith later recalled that to pre-empt the broadcasting of *The Age of Uncertainty*, 'a high convocation of British conservatives imported Professor Milton Friedman all the way from the University of Chicago to lecture adversely on my economic views'.[8] The doyen of monetarism gave two lectures to journalists, politicians and businessmen that were arranged by the seminal neoliberal think tank the Institute of Economic Affairs, presumably to arm their sympathisers with ammunition for their counterattack.[9] Meanwhile, the Centre for Policy Studies – the think tank co-founded by Thatcher and Joseph to promote neoliberalism within the Conservative Party – commissioned a pamphlet by McFadzean, who had previously given a series of lectures attacking Galbraith.[10] In the United States, where *The Age of Uncertainty* was due to be broadcast by PBS, a parallel political campaign was launched against the Galbraith series. Under pressure from critics, an executive at the American public broadcaster wrote to Friedman saying they were 'anxious [to] discuss with you at greater length the possibility of putting together some form of commentary or critical analysis or even "counter programming" *vis-a-vis* the Galbraith series'.[11]

The plan for 'counter programming' by Friedman began in early 1977 when the Chicago economist was approached by Robert Chitester, an American public service television executive. Chitester had read Friedman's *Capitalism and Freedom*, developing an 'absolute faith' in the market, and he was keen to popularise Friedman's radical views in a television series.[12] Seeking a producer for their film, they initially approached Malone, who declined, according to Friedman, because of 'his lack of sympathy with our philosophy'.[13] Having approached a number of producers in the US, their search for a sympathetic collaborator took them back to the UK, where Ralph Harris of the Institute of Economic Affairs arranged a number of meetings for Chitester to discuss with the BBC its interest in acquiring the broadcast rights for the planned series. Chitester met with Sam Brittan, a former student of Friedman's who was an important proponent of monetarism in the UK at the *Financial Times*. But his most important meeting was with a former BBC producer, Antony Jay – now best known as the co-creator of the wry political satire *Yes Minister*, which aired on the BBC in the early 1980s. Jay was by this point a long-standing 'convert to market economics' and a 'Friedmanite'.[14] He had joined the BBC after attending English public school and Cambridge University, and left to work as an independent writer and television producer before becoming a right-wing pamphleteer.[15] At the time he was introduced to Chitester, Jay had recently set up a production company, Video Arts Television, with Michael Peacock, a one-time Controller of BBC 2 and another former BBC producer.

Jay and his partners, Friedman later recalled, 'were

sympathetic to our philosophy and enthusiastic about producing a documentary to present it'.[16] 'Interesting', Friedman remarked, 'that Britain, the fatherland of the welfare state and the home of a major avowedly socialist party, should be where we would find producers sympathetic to free markets.'[17] In the United States, the project was easily able to raise ample funding from corporations and conservative foundations keen to support a film which, as Nigel Lawson explained to Thatcher, would 'expound the virtues of the market economy'.[18] BBC bought the rights to six episodes of *Free to Choose*, as the series was called, which were broadcast on Saturday nights in early 1980.[19] It arranged studio discussions with Friedman, chaired by the monetarist journalist Peter Jay, featuring among others the Thatcherite ministers Geoffrey Howe and Nigel Lawson. After Friedman's visit to London for these studio recordings, Thatcher wrote thanking him for visiting her in 10 Downing Street, adding a handwritten note: 'We are all enjoying your TV performances.'[20]

The broadcasting of *Age of Uncertainty* and the organised counterattack that led to the airing of Friedman's *Free to Choose* was one episode in a much broader struggle over the direction of capitalist democracy in Britain and the United States. The year before *Age of Uncertainty* was broadcast, 1976, was a key turning point.[21] Thatcher had recently been appointed as leader of the Conservative Party, and the Labour right-winger James Callaghan, who had succeeded Harold Wilson as prime minister that year, declared to the Labour Party conference that 'spend[ing] your way out of a recession' was no longer an option. By the time *Free to Choose* was aired in 1980, Thatcher had come to power, and her government would, in time, dismantle many of the key institutions of the post-war consensus. The Establishment, of which the BBC has always been a part, was reconstituted, its personnel won over to neoliberal ideas and practices, and its non-market components evermore subjected to the logic of the market and the values and interests of the corporate elite. The transformation of the BBC and the broader 'industry' of which it is part was an important part of this process. As these events illustrate, the Corporation is not an independent sphere, standing apart from politics and society. Rather, it is itself an arena of conflict and contestation between different groups, especially rival factions of the elite. This struggle, though, has not been limited to competing efforts to gain access to programmes or to influence content through pressuring programme makers. The neoliberals and the other factions of the New Right sought not only to wage a successful 'battle of ideas', but more profoundly to reconstitute the terrain on which such battles took place. They recognised broadcasting, and the BBC in particular, as a crucial component of the British Establishment, which had to some extent institutionalised the more egalitarian and democratic settlement, and which therefore needed to be either demolished or radically reformed.

Margaret Thatcher's antipathy to the BBC was well known. Ian Trethowan recalls in his memoirs that Thatcher visited Broadcasting House a year before her election as prime minster with 'all guns firing', showing 'scant interest in, let alone tolerance of the editors' problems'.[22] In September 1979, just months into her premiership, members of the Board of Governors joked about an interviewer for the BBC's annual survey of the public attitudes knocking on the door of 10 Downing Street and asking the new occupant what she thought of the Corporation.[23]

But whatever her personal feelings, the BBC's relations with the government during Thatcher's first term were for the most part amicable, and conditions for the BBC were perhaps more favourable than they had been under the Labour Government, which had imposed a number of harsh and short-term licence fee settlements.[24] This relatively untroubled period for the BBC reflected the cautious approach taken by the first Thatcher Government in many areas. Crucial for the BBC during this period was the appointment of William Whitelaw as home secretary, whose favoured approach to broadcasting policy was more in step with the traditional pragmatism of the Home Office than the radicalism of many of his Cabinet colleagues.[25] In her autobiography, Thatcher writes that, 'Unfortunately, in the Home Office the broadcasters often found a ready advocate.'[26] Whitelaw, despite his closeness and loyalty to Thatcher, was not a neoliberal and did not share their natural antipathy to publicly funded institutions. Neither did he share the perception common among the members of the New Right that the BBC was left wing. He noted in his memoirs that, 'on broadcasting matters', he and Thatcher were 'never quite eye to eye. In particular we tended to have different views on the bias of BBC programmes':[27]

> My experience and so perhaps inevitably my views were very different from those of the Prime Minister and the overwhelming majority of my colleagues. And so when there were controversies over different television or radio programmes, I tended to come out as a defender of the BBC ... This led to spirited discussions on occasions.[28]

During his period as home secretary (1979–83), Whitelaw oversaw the renewal of the BBC Charter and licence fee settlement and the establishment of Channel 4. The latter illustrates well the elements of pragmatism and moderation that characterised the first Thatcher Government. Though in some ways Channel 4 was congruous with the rhetorical emphasis that neoliberals placed on entrepreneurialism, it also represented a considerable victory for those who had campaigned for a more inclusive broadcasting system during the 1970s, while its explicitly 'alternative' cultural and political orientation was plainly at odds with the more reactionary elements of the New Right.

This period of relative calm between 1979 and 1983, however, was subsequently broken by a great storm of political action as Thatcherism moved into its more radical phase. From 1984, a coalition of forces – including prominent figures in the Conservative Government, most of all the prime minister herself – launched a seemingly unrelenting assault on the BBC that seemed to threaten its very survival. This network of interconnected individuals, companies and private advocacy groups came from a variety of backgrounds, as noted by Tom O'Malley:

> Some, like Murdoch or the Saatchis, were by occupation capitalists. Others – such as those associated with the Adam Smith Institute and the Institute of Economic Affairs – are best understood as ideologues driven by the desire to promote the virtues of capitalism. Still others were politicians with close links to both industry and the ideologues. Some of these politicians like Young and Tebbit were in government. These networks acted as an informal coalition interest on the issue of broadcasting, a coalition which operated inside and outside the formal state system linking the world of business to the world of policy-making.[29]

A focal point for policy debates was the Committee on Financing the BBC, which was headed by the neoliberal economist Alan Peacock. An 'Anti-Establishment' advocate of 'free market' ideas and a pioneer in 'cultural economics', Peacock was a trustee of the seminal neoliberal think tank the Institute of Economic Affairs (IEA) and served as the first vice chancellor of the University of Buckingham, the UK's first private university.[30] Another member of the Peacock Committee was Sam Brittan. Committee members were advised by Cento Veljanovski, who later joined the IEA, and informally by Peter Jay, the former economics editor at *The Times*, who had been converted to monetarism following a trip to the United States during which he became good friends with Milton Friedman.[31] The Peacock Committee was widely expected to abolish the licence fee and recommend that the Corporation take advertising, as Thatcher had hoped. But the final report rejected this option, recommending instead that, 'The British broadcasting system should move towards a sophisticated market system based on consumer sovereignty.'[32] A key recommendation of the committee was the introduction of an independent production quota obliging the BBC to commission output from the private sector.

While the Peacock Committee deliberated, there were a series of forceful attacks on the BBC's programming. Probably the most vituperative of these related to a BBC *Real Lives* documentary, 'On the Edge of the Union', which featured an interview with Sinn Fein's Martin McGuinness. Looking back on the programme twenty years later, its producer Paul Hamann remarked that he thought McGuinness and his DUP counterpart Gregory Campbell were 'ruthless bigots', and said the intention of the programme had been to expose 'the futility of their positions'.[33] Assistant Director General Alan Protheroe, a member of the Territorial Army and an all-round military enthusiast, told the Board of Governors that the programme 'demonstrated the deep divide between extremists in both communities' and stressed that although the programme had not been through the appropriate referral procedures, filming 'had been cleared at all points with security officials in the province'.[34]

Home Secretary Leon Brittan, however, saw things differently, and so, it transpired, did the increasingly politicised Board of Governors. Brittan hadn't actually seen the programme, but nevertheless complained in a letter to BBC Chairman Stuart Young that if the documentary were broadcast, the BBC would be 'materially assist[ing] the terrorist cause' by 'giving an immensely valuable platform to those who have evinced an ability, readiness and intention to murder indiscriminately its own viewers'.[35] In response, the governors took the unprecedented step of previewing the programme and advised the home secretary that they had concluded 'it would be unwise for this programme ... to be transmitted in its present form', since its 'intention would continue to be misread and misinterpreted'.[36]

The Board of Governors' decision to cancel the already-trailed broadcast under pressure from the government – and, as Deputy Director General Michael Checkland noted, the Murdoch press[37] – led to a one-day strike by BBC staff. A bitter conflict between the BBC management and the governors followed, with the latter demanding to know how the BBC 'controlled its journalists' and threatening to fire Director General Alasdair Milne if, as was planned, he announced that the documentary would be broadcast at a later date.[38]

'On the Edge of the Union' was eventually broadcast in October 1985, with some minor amendments. The media scholar Steven Barnett has argued that the *Real Lives* controversy illustrates the independence of the BBC. The crucial point, for Barnett, is that the controversy 'did not weaken the BBC, or the resolve of its journalists, or its sense of professional journalistic pride, or its determination to pursue independent and non-partisan journalism even where it became uncomfortable for a powerful government'.[39] This celebratory assessment, however, completely misses the long-term significance of this and similar events. Without having an immediate impact on output, such moments can have an enduring impact on the BBC's culture and policies. In this case, it led to a rift between the Board of Management and the Board of Governors, sections of which, according to Seaton, now resolved to unseat Alasdair Milne.[40]

In October 1986, a year after the *Real Lives* controversy, the Conservative Party chairman Norman Tebbit – who during the Falklands conflict had been enraged by what he later referred to as the 'unctuous "impartiality" of the BBC's editorialising' and its 'elaborate even-handedness'[41] – announced to the Conservative Party conference that he had set up a unit at Conservative Central Office to monitor BBC programming. That same month saw the appointment of a new BBC chairman. Thatcher had been advised by the former director general Ian Trethowan (via her confidant Woodrow Wyatt) that it was not necessary to impose a new constitution or organisational structure to discipline the BBC. The Board of Governors were 'all powerful' and subject to political appointment. All that was needed, he suggested, was a strong chairman.[42] The man appointed on the death of Stuart Young (himself the brother of the Thatcherite minister and former director of the neoliberal Centre for Policy Studies, David Young) was the former *Times* executive Marmaduke Hussey, an old friend of Trethowan's.[43] Thatcher consulted with Rupert Murdoch before the appointment, and Hussey was reportedly given a brief from Tebbit's office to 'get in there and sort it out'.[44]

On his arrival, Hussey settled a pending libel case concerning a *Panorama* programme broadcast in January 1984 called 'Maggie's Militant Tendency'[45] – another controversial programme, which alleged far-right infiltration of the Conservative Party and made allegations against several right-wing Tory MPs. The libel case, brought by MPs Neil Hamilton and Gerald Howarth, was supported by a fighting fund of around £100,000 raised by Ralph Harris, the chairman of the Institute of Economic Affairs, with the help of the right-wing financier James Goldsmith.[46]

Over the next few months, Duke Hussey, with the assistance of his deputy, Joel Barnett, planned and orchestrated the forced resignation of Alasdair Milne. Hussey had first consulted with former BBC chairman Michael Swann, who was supportive of the plan. He and Barnett then agreed on a date and resolved, as Hussey later wrote, to 'do it quickly and brutally'.[47] Milne was summarily removed from his post on 29 January 1987, with the execution timed so that it would not be raised at Prime Minister's Question Time that afternoon. Ambushed on his way to lunch, Milne was ushered into the chairman's room by BBC Secretary Patricia Hodgson, a Thatcherite who would later head the media regulator Ofcom. Hussey, sitting alongside Barnett, according to Milne's account, told him, lip trembling, that it was the unanimous decision of the Board of Governors that Milne should 'leave immediately'. He was threatened with the loss of his pension and asked to resign 'for personal reasons'.[48] Hussey and Barnett, in the words of former BBC governor Ken Bloomfield, had acted against Milne with 'decisive brutality'.[49] In his autobiography, the sacked director general describes his shock and humiliation at 'being discarded by such people without a word of explanation or discussion' and refers to a letter he received from an unnamed 'distinguished British broadcaster':

'What has happened to you is something that will stand high in the annals of broadcasting infamy.'[50]

In her official history, Seaton explains that Milne had been 'misleading the governors' over *Maggie's Militant Tendency* and that the Board of Governors had planned his dismissal long before Hussey's appointment.[51] However, she cites no documentary evidence for either claim, and her major source appears to be Patricia Hodgson, an accomplice in Hussey's coup. More importantly though, the evidence she presents calls into question her interpretation. She writes, for instance, that Hussey and Barnett 'wanted evidence of professional incompetence to avoid the charge that their move to sack Milne was politically motivated', but notably makes no reference to any such evidence as having emerged. She also notes that Alwyn Roberts, a supporter of Milne on the Board of Governors whose retirement dinner was held the night before Milne's forced dismissal, had no knowledge of the coup planned for the following day. All this undermines her spin on the episode as being a resolution to a long-standing breakdown in trust between a haughty and evasive editor-in-chief and the reformist trustees of the public interest on the Board of Governors. Conversely, it supports the dominant interpretation at the time: that this was a demonstrative decapitation of the BBC management by a politicised, and of course politically appointed, Board of Governors.

Milne was certainly no radical. He was educated at Oxford and Winchester College, one of the traditional public schools at the heart of the Establishment,[52] and once described the claim by Tony Benn that the BBC was right-wing as an 'absurdity'. But having spent almost his whole working life at the BBC, including on seminal programmes like *Tonight* and *That Was the Week that Was*, he personified the institutional changes that the BBC had undergone in recent decades. His career had witnessed the rise of anti-war and anti-racist movements, and the broader sixties counterculture; he had been involved in the emergence of political satire and more class-conscious documentaries and dramas, and helped form an institution which was more independent and more distanced from the Establishment than before.[53] Milne was therefore committed to a more substantive notion of broadcasting independence than had traditionally been upheld by the BBC leadership. Perhaps most importantly though, as Hendy suggests, he was 'a man [the Board of Governors] suspect[ed] of being temperamentally unable to introduce the internal changes needed after Peacock'.[54] In other words, he was not trusted by the right-wing governors to institute the neoliberal and authoritarian overhaul of the BBC they had planned.

Jean Seaton concludes her account of the 1987 coup by celebrating Milne as something of a martyr, who through his professional death allowed the Corporation to be reborn under the leadership of 'strategically accomplished' reformers, the men and women who would 'save' the BBC. This remarkably sanguine assessment is in keeping with Seaton's earlier analysis of the transformation of the BBC that began in the wake of Milne's removal. The BBC's survival 'despite the most determined onslaught it has ever faced', was, for Seaton, the outcome of a project first 'to save the Corporation from the government' and then 'to re-engineer the BBC from within'.[55] What this fails to recognise, however, is that this re-engineering was not only carried out under political pressure, but was part of the same project of social and political transformation which Thatcher had begun. While the BBC survived what were doubtless existential threats, its survival would come at the price of ever greater accommodation with the emerging neoliberal order.

Milne's successor, Michael Checkland, was appointed on the condition that 'he brought in a deputy who could successfully undertake the much needed overhaul of news and current affairs'.[56] That deputy would be John Birt, who was 'strongly recommended' to Hussey by ITN Chairman Paul Fox and by Peter Jay, whom Hussey knew from his time at Times Newspapers.[57] As director of programmes at London Weekend Television (LWT), Birt had headed the highbrow current affairs programme *Weekend World*, 'a key centre of economic debate in the UK in the 1970s'.[58] Peter Jay hosted the show and brought in like-minded monetarists such as Sam Brittan and the London Business School economists Alan Budd and Terry Burns. The latter became close friends with Birt, who recalls how Burns 'patiently explained the significance of different monetary measures'.[59] Birt also met with the leading Conservative Party neoliberal Keith Joseph 'many times in the 1970s, often lunching alone with him',[60] and attended seminars at the Institute of Economic Affairs, where he saw Milton Friedman speak.[61] Brian Walden, Peter Jay's successor as presenter on *Weekend World*, was also a regular at the Institute of Economic Affairs. Its director, Ralph Harris, later remarked that Walden 'became a scalp that we treasured' and 'would often have our chaps on his television programmes'.[62]

Through these professional relationships and personal friendships, Birt, who by his own account left university a politically naive, faintly left-wing libertarian, became a committed neoliberal. He summarises his political development as follows:

> I had become a convert to free-market mechanisms. I was
> deeply sceptical that the state could run business. I abhorred
> the increasingly ugly abuse of power by the trade unions,

not least in my own industry. I could see that my unthinking conviction in the 1960s that the state could solve every problem, that public spending could rise and rise, was ill founded.[63]

By the time of his appointment as the BBC's deputy director general in 1987, Birt was a long-standing 'convert to the value of markets'. Moreover, he was 'hostile to vested interests' and had 'experience [from LWT] of the difficulties of driving change against heavy resistance'.[64]

He arrived with a political remit for, and personal commitment to, radical reform, and was determined to impose his version of good journalism and good management on the Corporation. Influenced by Peter Jay, Birt had attacked journalism for its lack of analytical rigour, claiming that it drew attention to the symptoms of political and economic problems without providing any analysis of their root causes – a fact that had exacerbated the political and economic crisis of the 1970s. Television had no political bias, as had been claimed by other critics; rather, it was guilty of a 'bias against understanding'.[66] The proposed solution, according to Birt and Jay, was to dispense with the distinction between News and Current Affairs, to introduce more context and analysis into the latter, and to recruit specialist journalists to provide informed analysis of political and economic problems.[66]

This was in essence the philosophy that underpinned the changes that Birt would introduce as deputy director general. Two months after his arrival, he summoned all the BBC's senior managers to a four-day conference at a hotel in Surrey and set out his plans for a unified news and current affairs directorate, which would produce 'authoritative and analytical journalism' delivered by journalists with specialist expertise.[67] To Birt's disappointment, his proposed changes were not welcomed by staff, who, he recalls, 'feared I had been imposed from the outside to neuter the BBC's journalism'.[68] James Long, who left the Corporation shortly after Birt's arrival, explains,

> One of the things that really bothered people was an increasing move towards script approval. Until then, as a correspondent, if I was in some God-forsaken part of the world and I called in with a story, it was expected that as a correspondent I was almost self-scheduling and it was almost up to me to decide which stories I did and where I was, according to budgets. But if I said, 'This is the story', nobody was going to turn round and say, 'We know better.' After that, I stayed in touch with Kate Adie and Martin Bell and lots of people after I left and they were finding it extremely frustrating that you would get to the point where you'd called the desk from somewhere and before you'd started talking they'd say, 'Now by the way, the way we see this story is …', and tell you what your story ought to say when you were out there actually at the story. That sounds like a joke, but that is the way it became. And it became that way out of a sort of slightly centralising, control-freaky thing that was going on around the new bureaucracy.[69]

In his own account, Birt describes carrying out his task despite 'the stifling conservatism and inertia of the organisation, its civil service culture, its hostility to change'. 'I had battled on many fronts', Birt recalls, 'against bone-headed baronialism and obstructionism'.[70] Sidestepping the usual recruitment procedures, he assembled a senior management team by direct appointment. Meanwhile, he warned the Board of Governors that there would be 'blood on the wall', as his cabal 'fought battle after battle with the forces of resistance among BBC journalists'.[71] Birt's belligerence is matched only by his self-pity. He complains that he pursued his thankless task in a state of 'friendless-ness', comforted only by his 'soulmates at work', Howell James and Patricia Hodgson, and Chairman Hussey, who stood by him as 'solid as a rock'.[72] Indeed, so dispirited was Birt that in December 1987 a group of his 'chums' organised a 'Cheer-Up-John-Birt Dinner' with the intention, in the words of Channel 4's Liz Horgan, to 'rescue John from the cruel and unusual punishment that seems to attach to his new job'.[73]

Birt was highly unpopular, but with the backing of Hussey and the rest of the Board of Governors, he was indeed 'all powerful' and was able to impose his vision on a sceptical and demoralised workforce. His author-ity was imposed through the promotion of ambitious staff members and consolidated through an influx of new personnel not socialised into the old 'institutionalised ide-ologies'. A former News and Current Affairs executive told Born: 'In 1987 when Birt arrived, there was a night of the long knives when most of the senior people in News and Current Affairs were booted out. It was brutal, a coup.'[74] Birt and his lieutenants then embarked on a 'vast recruitment and deployment exercise', bringing in 'eighty specialist journalists' from the private sector, prompting 'a flock of early retirements' from existing staff.[75] Among the recruits was Peter Jay, who in 1990 was appointed the BBC's economics and business editor.

Birt's vision of good journalism was institutionalised not just through the expansion of editorial control and the recruitment of new personnel, but also through changes in the physical spaces in which BBC journalism was prac-tised. A particular bugbear of Birt's was the Lime Grove studios. Physically remote and architecturally complex, the cluster of buildings was anathema to the bureaucratic rationalisation Birt was determined to impose. Bewildering to the outsider, their arcane structure and relative isolation fostered insular self-regulated enclaves and symbolised, indeed embodied, the uncontrolled and allegedly superficial journalism that Birt sort to eradicate. In his autobiography, Birt describes Lime Grove as

> Plonked unnaturally in a residential street in the Hammersmith/Shepherds Bush area of London, the centre was British broadcasting's Gormenghast – a labyrinthine building of bewildering complexity, run-down and ram-shackle, unsuitable for modern programme-making, a festering rabbit warren sheltering hidden cliques.[76]

Birt later contrasts the 'many shabby premises' that once hosted BBC News and Current Affairs with the 'modern, purpose built, technically advanced complex at Television Centre' and the privately owned Millbank Studios opposite Parliament.[77] White City One, another BBC building of this era that housed much of the Corporation's current affairs programming, is referred to by one former BBC journalist as a 'ghastly silver building which only an engineer could possibly commission' and as having been a 'manifest[ation]' of Birt's management style.[78] Widely unpopular with staff, the business-like complex was designed for flexibility, allowing for glass partition panels to be put up at minimum cost, meaning it could house workers for short periods and at short notice.[79]

Having restructured BBC journalism, Birt turned his attention to the question of finance and administration, seeking to transform the Corporation, as he put it, into the 'best managed public sector organisation in the world'.[80] During the course of 1990, Birt headed the Television Resources Review, 'the place where the real motor of BBC reforms was invented'.[81] The 'review' was a cost-cutting exercise conducted in anticipation of the reduction in BBC production expected to follow the implementation of the independent production quota recommended by Peacock. Birt brought together a 'core of people' to investigate the BBC 'machine', including a team of accountants assembled by a senior economist at Coopers and Lybrand.[82]

Birt claims to have been 'offended and appalled' by the group's findings and presented a 'radical' proposal: the introduction of an internal market. The 'fundamental' motivation behind the recommendation, Birt writes, was 'to sweep away the command economy that had produced such boundless waste'.[83] The initiative was called 'Producer Choice' to distinguish it from the 'internal market' then being introduced in the National Health Service (NHS). According to Seaton, the term was developed after 'a public relations alarm bell rang, and a special brainstorming session was set up'.[84]

In July 1991, Producer Choice was approved by the Board of Governors,[85] who a week later also designated Birt as Checkland's successor. This appointment represented a final breakthrough for the cabal of radical reformers at the top of the BBC. Birt recalls: 'I had been put into power by a coup, led by Hussey, designed to overthrow for the first time the established interests and power structures of the BBC.'[86]

Producer Choice was to reorganise the BBC into financially autonomous units which could 'buy' or 'sell' services, creating a system of trading that would make its finances directly comparable with the private sector. The BBC was to be split into separate 'units', of which some would be involved in producing programmes, while others would sell programme-making resources. The latter were termed 'Resource Business Units' and the former 'Production

Business Units'. Central to the system was the requirement that these separate units be financially autonomous and would 'breakeven', as was explained in one BBC document: 'This means that individual managers have more to do than manage their spend within a budget – they now have to *earn income to cover their costs*.'[87]

Significantly though, Resource Business Units would do so in competition with external providers, with whom they would compete on cost, while at the same time not being permitted to offer their services to outside providers, except to cover 'spare marginal capacity'.[88] Production Units were not only required to break even, they were also permitted, indeed encouraged, to purchase their services from external providers. This exposed the BBC for the first time to *cost-based* competition with private companies. This, it was claimed, would create a 'sharp business edge' and encourage staff 'to seek the most efficient and cost effective ways of making programmes'.[89]

The realisation of this ambitious scheme required the construction of a vast new bureaucratic machinery. Producer Choice 'Implementation Groups' were established to cover Television, the Regions, Network Radio, News and Current Affairs, Central Directorates Education, and Finance, each – with the exception of the Finance Group – staffed with a private consultant.[90] New budgeting and planning systems were developed, along with new 'commercial ground rules' for contractual bidding and pricing processes. The value of everything within the Corporation, animal or mineral, had to be quantified, since in order for the system to work on 'a fully costed basis' it was necessary not just to develop a price system for internal trading but, as the project director for Producer Choice, Michael Starks, noted, to 'charge both production resource departments and programme makers for their overheads, accommodation and capital'.[91] Asset registers were examined for the allocation of capital, and the Producer Choice Steering Group created a Property Group headed by externally recruited property professionals.[92] All BBC real estate had to be identified and valued at market rate so as to establish the costs to be borne by Business Units with which it was to be matched. This, Starks explained, would allow the new system to 'charge all users a rent for the space they occupy', rent which would be 'a function of the volume of space and the market value of the property concerned'.[93]

Producer Choice was launched on 1 April 1993. In the lead-up to the changeover, Birt also set up 'an immense programme of training and mentoring'.[94] Seminars and training sessions were designed 'to accustom BBC buyers and BBC sellers to the new relationship they will need to have with one another', a relationship which would shape 'the future ethos of the organisation'.[95] Starks was tasked with developing an 'inventory of training needs' and designing a 'culture change programme'.[96] The BBC management decided to 'kick-start the process' by recruiting the London Business School to run workshops entitled 'Living in the Market'.[97] A 'Training Needs Analysis' concluded that there was a need to 'build understanding of, and commitment to, the changes implicit in Producer Choice' and, more ambitiously, to 'support and equip senior managers to become "Champions"'.

The culture change programme was strategically targeted. Though only 6 per cent of total staff participated in the one- and two-day training courses; the plan was to then 'cascade' this training 'to the wider staff population as appropriate'.[98] The whole initiative, while emphasising freedom from bureaucratic strictures, was implemented through the existing system of managerial control. Identifying compliant managers was an early priority and

Implementation Groups for each BBC Directorate were given a month to identify heads for every proposed business unit.[99] Managerial support – or compliance – was to be encouraged through a system of rewards and incentives which, it was hoped, would shape individual behaviour, just as the quasi-market incentives would shape the structure and practices of 'business units' as a whole.

The Producer Choice Steering Group was made responsible for developing a 'philosophy and structure' for 'rewards and incentives'[100] and recommended that 'existing systems of salary administration and bonus awards ... should be used to deliver rewards and incentives under Producer Choice'. This included 'lump sum unconsolidated bonuses to recognise the achievement of defined targets', as well as 'salary adjustments to reflect the degree of success with which the overall role is being undertaken'.[101] Following these recommendations, a system of 'financial rewards for individual and team performances' was developed which was 'handled through base salary and incentive reviews'.[102]

The Producer Choice system took effect in April 1993 and 'for the first time in its history', Birt declares triumphantly, 'the BBC became a trading institution, and ceased to be a command economy'. The casualisation of labour was key to the new bureaucratic design. Whereas the BBC had been a potent symbol of life-long job security, under Birt it moved towards what is euphemistically referred to as a 'flexible labour market'. Increasingly precarious conditions of employment not only impacted negatively on individual workers, but also threatened to undermine the public service ethos which the BBC was felt to embody. The 'cradle-to-grave expectation of security', maligned by Birt as a cause of waste and inefficiency,[103] engendered great loyalty to the BBC and commitment to notions of public service broadcasting, and arguably encouraged greater creativity and risk-taking in programme making. All this was seen to be under threat from Birtism.[104] There was also a strong opposition to the commercialisation of the Corporation. Though the BBC leadership emphasised the continued importance of public service broadcasting, staff considered that 'the role and status of the public service ethos' was unclear 'in a system where price appears to be everything'.[105]

These were the bitter ironies in Birt's reforms, not least because the fact that such a strong emphasis had been placed on freedom and devolution. In reality, however, the reforms resulted in an increase and centralisation of managerial and editorial authority. Indeed, Birt's leadership was unashamedly authoritarian. At the time, the veteran television executive and former ally Michael Grade charged that Birt's BBC was a place of 'iron discipline' where staff were 'afraid to speak publicly', and one former BBC producer remarks that Birt 'made himself a dictator and somehow sapped the confidence of those underneath him'.[106] Such claims are supported by evidence provided to the Producer Choice Evaluation Study. One member of staff referred to 'diktat with little consultation' and 'rule by fear'.[107]

Furthermore, despite the strong emphasis on efficiency, Producer Choice resulted in a proliferation, rather than a reduction, in administration, since it required the construction of a new and complex layer of bureaucracy that, Birt acknowledges, necessitated 'a vast influx of skilled outside recruits from the finance sector'.[108] Under the new regime, critics complained, 'creative staff [were] usurped by legions of lawyers, accountants, business affairs executives, and policy unit apparatchiks'.[109]

In July 1993, BBC Director of Finance and Technology Rodney Baker-Bates wrote of a 'concern that life under Producer Choice is characterised (at least by anecdotal comment) by paper overload, bureaucracy, needless volumes of transactions and undue complexity'.[110] The Evaluation Study similarly noted that 'increased workload (including reporting, administration, negotiating and contracting) was widely reported'.[111] Another document noted the 'increase in paper work' and the 'unanimous view that there had been a huge increase in the volume of transactions to the point of unmanageability'.[112]

The maddening managerialism of Birt's BBC was maligned in the press across the political spectrum. The assessment of the conservative humorist Quentin Letts – who gives Birt the dubious honour of being ranked number six in his *50 People Who Buggered Up Britain* – is scathing in tone, though quite typical. Birt was 'obsessed with systems and procedures and power diagrams and channels of accountability' and 'turned the BBC into a bean-counting Babel'.[113] For Letts, the fact that bureaucracy increased under Birt (he notes that 'overheads' rose by over 60 per cent during his leadership) is the final proof that far from being an 'agent of free-market rationalisation', Birt was in fact 'a state megalith-maker'.[114] This argument, though, assumes that neoliberalism has generally delivered on its promises to 'cut red tape' and bring cost savings and efficiencies. Not only has it not, but it has been characterized by the very opposite outcome.[115] Whether in markets or quasi-markets, financial bureaucrats tend to proliferate, and if you look past the rhetoric of neoliberalism it is not difficult to see why. Making markets requires the development of complex calculative processes, as well as mechanisms of accountability and control, whether in the shape of regulatory oversight, auditing, or internal monitoring and reporting. In this respect, the ironies of Birtism simply reflected the ironies of the neoliberal revolution. Producer Choice did not deliver efficiency. But it did erode the public service ethos of the BBC, institute a business-like ethos and further integrate its operations into the private sector. It thereby augmented and accelerated a process of *neoliberalisation* that had begun under Michael Checkland. Before Birt's radical reform programme was launched, the BBC had already 'embraced' the independent production quota and had contracted out 'ancillary support services'. Producer Choice, Michael Starks noted, gave 'a further push to these developments ... carrying further processes initiated in the late 1980s'.[116] Coupled with the 25 per cent independent production quota, it entailed a significant integration of the BBC into the capitalist market.

The whole process of programme making and commissioning became intertwined with the private sector, which attracted BBC personnel able to capitalise on their skills and connections by selling back programming or resources to the Corporation. The BBC itself, meanwhile, stepped up its commercial operations to compensate for the reduction in licence fee income, which now flowed outwards to private landlords, companies providing catering, cleaning, security and other services, independent producers who now provided a quarter of BBC programming, and other private sector providers, who under Producer Choice could compete with the BBC's Resource Business Units.[117] This marketisation was consolidated by a further structural reorganisation imposed by Birt in 1996. Under the advice of McKinsey, the BBC was split down the middle into separate bodies, BBC Production and BBC Broadcast, with the former providing programming to the latter in competition with the private sector. Just as money and personnel flowed to and from the private sector, so its commercial ethos and working practices worked their way inwards to the BBC, with very concrete impacts on its organisational structure and working culture. The outcome has been detailed by the anthropologist Georgina Born, who describes 'the installation throughout the BBC ... of a new culture of entrepreneurialism'. The Birt-era reforms, Born concludes, 'generated a new value system', and the BBC became 'infatuated with markets'.[118] These reforms are not merely historical. While to some extent lessened under the leadership of Birt's successor, Greg Dyke,[119] they set in place the basic organisational architecture of the contemporary BBC. Despite the deep scepticism of BBC staff, Producer Choice, Birt writes, 'changed the BBC's culture fundamentally – for ever'.[120]

CHAPTER 6

Public Service Broadcasting and Private Power

Weeks before the 1979 general election that swept Margaret Thatcher to power, the chairman of the London Stock Exchange, Nicholas Goodison, appeared as a special guest at the BBC News and Current Affairs meeting. Appointed in 1976, Goodison was the quintessential gentleman capitalist. A member of the Athenæum Club in Pall Mall, known for the intellectual calibre of its members, he had attended English public school and studied classics at Cambridge before joining the stockbroking firm originally founded by his grandfather.

Goodison opened the congenial discussion with an account of the history of the London Stock Exchange. He stressed its great importance for government borrowing and therefore for the health of the 'free economy'. The country's success depended on trade and industry, without which, he said, it was impossible to provide public services. Having outlined the great importance of finance to public life, Goodison expressed concern over conditions for business in Britain, referring to the 'long-standing anti-business ethos' in the country. What was needed, he argued, was lower government borrowing, tax cuts and fiscal incentives to encourage private investment. He was apparently optimistic about the long-term prospects for business in Britain, despite what he took to be the prevailing public mood. According to the meeting's minutes, he said,

He now detected a swing against ... the corporate state, but it would take a long time, perhaps fifteen years for the public to understand that a high level of profits should lead to more jobs and that the country was not at present making the most efficient use of its resources.[1]

Goodison was also courting the higher levels of the BBC hierarchy. At around the same time he went for dinner in the City of London with Director General Ian Trethowan and BBC Governor Roy Fuller. Later relaying this to the Board of Governors, Fuller, a poet who said Goodison had approached him because he was interested in 'his verses', suggested that the chairman of the exchange be invited to the BBC for lunch. The director general, meanwhile, endorsed Fuller's 'good opinion' of Goodison, noting with approval his interest in 'furniture, clocks, barometers and ormolu'.[2]

A man of great culture and good taste, no doubt, but Goodison is best known not for these traits, but for his central role in a set of institutional and organisational reforms to the London Stock Exchange in October 1986. These reforms, known as 'Big Bang', modernised the exchange's technological infrastructure, abolished minimum commission charges and opened the exchange up to new institutions, especially powerful American investment banks.

Big Bang is sometimes imagined as part of a Thatcherite assault on antiquated vested interests which, through introducing competition, shook up an insular and elitist world – the 'closed system' of the City, dominated by a public school–educated elite. The reality though is rather different. Sir Nicholas himself has remarked that 'the real cause of the Big Bang was not all the things that the journalists say, or indeed the books say'.[3] While the reforms certainly transformed the culture and constitution of the City of London, and there were members of the exchange more opposed to reform, 'modernisation' was lobbied for by City interests through men like Goodison, who hoped to break free of the institutional constraints of the post-war regulatory regime and re-establish the City as a financial centre for global capital. The change began in the mid-1970s, but the most significant step was the Thatcher Government's abolition of exchange controls in 1979, which laid the path to Big Bang.[4]

The 1986 reform of the London Stock Exchange, in combination with other dramatic events of the Thatcher era and more subtle processes of social change, would over time transform the BBC's economics reporting beyond recognition. The long process of change was complex, contested and uneven. But the overall direction is clear. There was a turn away from industrial reporting and a remarkable growth in business and economics journalism at the BBC. Although the interests and perspective of workers had long been marginalised in the BBC's output, what we conventionally refer to as 'the economy' – an abstraction of aggregate practices relating to production, consumption and investment – was increasingly reported from the perspective of business, a small section of society which assumed ever greater power in the neoliberal period.

Business news was traditionally the joint responsibility of the BBC's economics correspondents and its industrial, or labour, correspondents. While the former were charged with reporting on macro-economic policies and indicators, the latter, though nominally responsible for covering business and industry, in practice largely reported on actual and potential industrial actions, a pattern which continued well into the 1980s. Mark Damazer, later a powerful editorial and managerial figure at the BBC, recalls,

In my early career the economic-industrial patch was dominated by relations between the government and the trade
unions; most evidenced by industrial actions. So there was
a lot of focus on strikes [and] manoeuvres before strikes.[5]

The industrial and labour correspondents, who were eventually to disappear altogether, had been central to the news
agenda in the 1970s and early 1980s and were prominent
not only in broadcasting, but equally in the press. Indeed,
most of the BBC's industrial and labour correspondents
were former newspaper journalists. Their status relied
upon their knowledge of, and contacts in, the trade union
movement, which was then still capable of exerting significant disruptive power, as well as exercising a greater degree
of political influence via the Labour Party. At the BBC,
labour and industrial correspondents did some reporting
on business. 'We went out of our way to make sure that
we had our contacts with both sides [of industry],' recalls
John Fryer, who was labour correspondent and then editor
at the *Sunday Times* before joining the BBC as industrial
correspondent in 1982. Nevertheless, reporting, Fryer says,
was 'very heavily weighted towards union stuff ... We were
sort of the strikes correspondents really.'[6]

This pattern of reporting – which reflected the prevailing 'news values' and a particular allocation of resources
and division of labour – did not entail a partiality towards
the interests and perspectives of organised labour. On
the contrary, sections of the press that shared this structure of reporting were vehemently anti-union. Moreover,
the output of the BBC barely featured the perspectives
of workers themselves, largely adopting the perspectives
of the owners and managers of industry, even if the attention was overwhelmingly on the actions of workers and
trade unions.

The widespread misrepresentation of industrial conflict, and the implication in much reporting that the unions were to blame for Britain's relatively poor economic performance, led to significant criticisms of the BBC's reporting in the 1970s. This fed into the Annan Committee on the Future of Broadcasting, which was set up by the Labour Government. It referred in its 1977 report to the evidence of systemic anti-union bias in news programmes submitted by academics, and its muted criticisms led to a modest increase in the resources the BBC allocated to its reporting of business and industry, and the recruitment of new reporters. Annan's specific recommendations on the 'reporting of industrial and commercial affairs', however, did not focus on the representation of industrial conflict but on what it described as 'a more fundamental shortcoming', namely that 'other aspects of industry or commerce and the world of work as a whole are inadequately covered'.[7] The BBC and ITV's coverage of business and industry was described as 'dingy and unimaginative' and Annan recommended that the broadcasters better represent 'the vigorous competitive life at all levels in industry … and the fascinating social structures and manufacturing processes that go to make industry work'.[8] This criticism tallied with the dominant approach that had been taken by the BBC's Consultative Group on Industrial and Business Affairs, which had been set up in response to Annan, and which won the committee's approval.

Though the world of business and industry was thought by Annan to be poorly served by broadcasting, there were exceptions. One programme specifically commended was BBC Two's *The Money Programme*, which was first broadcast in 1966 and during the '70s and '80s would enjoy relatively high ratings by virtue of being less tedious than mandatory religious programming. Another singled out for praise was Radio 4's *The Financial World Tonight*. Peter Day, who worked on the programme, recalls that it 'covered stuff that … the BBC hadn't considered: stocks, share prices and things like that, company reporting'.[9] Tom Maddocks, a former presenter, describes it as a 'sort of radio equivalent of the City pages of the papers'.[10] Founded in 1971 by Vincent Duggleby, then deputy editor of *The World Tonight*,[11] the programme responded, Maddocks explains, to 'the requirement for more business and financial coverage'[12] in a context of industrial unrest and economic volatility. The BBC, Peter Day says, 'were just beginning to wake up to the fact that business was a really interesting subject because the City was getting more and more important'.[13] The establishment of *The Financial World Tonight* was followed three years later by the setting up of the Financial Unit within BBC Radio, supported by funds previously paid to Reuters and Exchange Telegraph for stock exchange reports produced for the World Service. Ed Mitchell, who joined the unit in 1978, recalls,

> Increasingly, headline news was being made by business and financial news – oil prices, sterling crisis, financial scandals, big takeover bids and so on. In response to this the BBC formed the Financial Unit, a small team of economic 'experts' who would provide the rest of the corporation with output and advice. There were already specialist programmes such as *Moneybox* and *The Financial World Tonight*, but the unit was more like wholesale news for any takers – a sort of money sausage factory.[14]

Another precursor to the Financial Unit was a news service provided to the BBC by staff of *The City Press* weekly, who filled a regular five-minute slot on the *PM* programme from a remote studio in the Guildhall, the heart of the City of London.[15] The Financial Unit's main output was a ten-minute 'summary of the main stock, bond, currency and commodity markets' for international commodity traders for the World Service, but it also provided a regular financial report broadcast on the *Six O'Clock News*.[16] Though still a small operation compared to the BBC's later business output, the Financial Unit slowly expanded in the early-to mid-1980s. Mitchell, who headed the news side of the unit while Vincent Duggleby headed programmes, writes that: 'Business and financial news was increasingly topping the news bulletins' in the early 1980s and 'the Financial Unit was asked to supply a daily three-minute business slot on lunchtime television'.[17] It was assigned two chief sub-editors and two senior producers in 1984 and two more producers the following year.[18] This was part of a long process whereby the BBC integrated and expanded its coverage of business, while the influence of its labour journalists began to decline. In 1982, Martin Adeney was promoted from his position as labour relations correspondent to become BBC TV's first industrial editor. Adeney recalls,

> The then editor of BBC TV News, Peter Woon, asked me to become the BBC's first industrial editor with the aim of running a collegiate team of three correspondents to cover economics, business, industry and labour in an integrated way. We went out of our way to encourage business to talk about itself, not always with success.[19]

Business programming was also expanded. In February 1983, BBC Radio began broadcasting *In Business*. According to its long-standing presenter, Peter Day, 'the first series [of the programme] was commissioned by Radio 4 after BBC governors were badgered at a "Meet

the BBC" meeting to recognise that there was a lot more
to business than the City'.[20] Another significant initiative
that year was the appointment as economics editor of
Newsnight of Will Hutton, a director and producer on the
Money Programme. Hutton remembers his appointment as
having been regarded as a significant development at the
time: '*Newsnight* having an economics editor in 1982 was
a really big step. Gosh, you know, that's innovative, that's
path breaking.'[21] Hutton had originally joined the BBC in
1977, having spent the previous seven years at the London
stockbrokers Phillips and Drew, a firm which was later
subsumed by UBS and which at that time also employed
one Paul Neils, who according to former BBC Governor
Richard Tait was 'the first sort of television economist'.[22]

While the BBC had already made some important
changes to its reporting, the upheavals of the Thatcher
period were to have a much more dramatic impact. A
number of key events loom large in BBC business journalism of the 1980s. The miners' strike of 1984–5 was one,
after which trade union power, and with it industrial and
labour reporting, went into a steady decline. In an internal review of its coverage of the year-long strike, the BBC
noted that the dispute had 'received more coverage than any
other [industrial dispute] in the history of broadcasting'.[23]
Though of an unprecedented magnitude, the nature of the
BBC's reporting was comparable with that of the major
industrial conflicts of the previous decade. Compared to
a private press that was overwhelmingly hostile towards
the striking miners, it undoubtedly presented a more balanced picture. But its reporting nevertheless remained
overwhelmingly favourable to the perspectives of the
Conservative Government and the National Coal Board.

The BBC's television news reporting of the strike has
received the most criticism, particularly the coverage of

the events of 18 June 1984, when police violently suppressed a mass picket at a coking plant in Orgreave, South Yorkshire. At a News and Current Affairs meeting the following day, Assistant Director General Alan Protheroe said he had a feeling that the BBC's early evening news coverage of Orgreave 'might not have been wholly impartial'. Peter Woon, head of Television News, admitted that there may have been a 'marginal imbalance' in the reporting, though not, he claimed, enough to 'justify the NUM's view that the BBC was biased'. The News and Current Affairs editors went on to discuss 'how neutral one could be as between law-breakers and the police' and to what extent 'the BBC's coverage must show the extent to which the miners were to blame'.[24]

What was not discussed at that meeting was the fact that the BBC's television news bulletin had altered the sequence of events that day to make it appear that the miners had provoked the police. This came to the attention of senior editors several months later when Protheroe referred in a News and Current Affairs meeting to 'an extraordinary complaint from a miner alleging that the BBC had reversed sequences in a film so as to suggest that missile throwing by pickets had been followed by a police baton charge when in reality the police had moved first'. It was not until 1991 that the BBC finally admitted that the sequence of events had indeed been reversed, claiming that this had been done 'inadvertently' in 'the haste of putting the news together'.[25]

It has been alleged that such distortion was undertaken at the behest of the Conservative Government. Writing in the *British Journalism Review* in 2009, the late Geoffrey Goodman, the *Daily Mirror*'s industrial editor during the strike, claimed to have confirmed from an unnamed 'impeccable source' that there were 'specific instructions from the highest level of Government to the BBC to ensure that

TV camera crews filming the conflict between miners and the police focused their shots on miners' violence, but not on the police smashing heads'.[26] To date, no evidence has come to light to support this claim. But whatever the truth of the matter, contemporary academic research supports the criticism that television reporting tended to focus on violence on the picket line, and to marginalise the miners' perspective of the strike. A study of how people responded to this reporting found that people from all classes questioned, to different degrees, the focus on violence, but that the reporting still strongly influenced perceptions of the strike, even among those sympathetic to the miners, and sceptical of the reporting. A majority believed that picketing was mostly violent, and the media was overwhelmingly cited as the source of this belief.[27]

Radio is generally thought to have presented a more nuanced picture of the strike. In its own review of its coverage, the BBC commended its labour correspondent for radio news, Nicholas Jones, for his 'grip on the central and sensitive aspects of the story that was second to none'.[28] Indeed, Jones was named industrial journalist of the year by the Industrial Society for his reporting. One former colleague recalls,

> I remember him coming up indefatigably every day and offering packages ... which we'd accept and put out. I mean every day for months and months. I think the newsroom gave him a special award at the end of it out of their own pockets as a thank you because he'd done such a fantastic job.[29]

Nevertheless, Jones himself admits in retrospect that his reporting on the strike inadvertently buttressed the Conservative Government's political strategy:

I have to admit that in the end I got ensnared by the seeming inevitability of the Thatcherite story that the mine workers had to be defeated in order to smash trade union militancy ... While I would contend that broadcasters like myself tried valiantly to represent both sides of the dispute, we did have to work within what had become an all powerful narrative: the country could not afford to continue subsidising uneconomic coal mines, devastating though that might be for their communities; the strike itself was a denial of democracy because there had been no pit head ballot and the violence on the miners' picket lines, by challenging the rule of law, constituted a threat to the democratic government of the country.[30]

Towards the end of the strike, Jones acknowledges,

the balance of coverage tipped almost completely in the management's favour ... Attention was focused on the 'new faces' who were going back to work. For the newspapers these men were heroes; television pictures, filmed from behind the police lines, showed them being bussed into their pits, braving the pickets.[31]

The subsequent defeat of the print workers in the Wapping dispute of 1986–7, during which the Thatcher Government, the Murdoch press and the police again united in opposition to organised labour, was a further victory for those same interests.[32] Though not as deeply engrained in political memory, the Wapping dispute was especially significant as it radically diminished the influence of organised labour in the media industry, and conversely augmented the power of News International in particular, and the large media corporations in general.

The outcome of both strikes was deeply demoralising

for the labour movement and signalled their weakening as a political force. This resulted in a definite shift in journalistic practices at the BBC (and beyond). John Fryer recalls,

> Covering stories from a strike perspective quite obviously fell away. ... I think even more than the miners' strike the Wapping dispute changed things hugely. We had two people really who were covering a beat that was declining.[33]

As the power of the trade unions declined, so the power of finance increased markedly, with City interests assuming an ever more dominant role within policy making. Having successfully lobbied for a degree of deregulation under Edward Heath, and an immediate end to exchange controls in the early months of the first Thatcher Government, what scholars have termed the City–Bank–Treasury nexus[34] oversaw the restructuring of London's financial markets. In preparation for Big Bang, the Bank of England and the BBC arranged for an exchange of staff between them for six-month secondments. This resulted in the BBC sending the head of its Financial Unit, Ed Mitchell, to the Bank of England (which in the event did not reciprocate). Mitchell writes,

> In the mid-eighties the City of London was on the verge of profound changes in its structures and regulations. It seems the Chairman of the BBC and the Governor of the Bank of England had met for lunch and, presumably over brandy and cigars, decided that it would be a jolly good idea for the two institutions to get to know each other better.[35]

Mitchell's arrival at the Bank of England was on the very day that the regulatory reforms took effect: 27 October

1986. In his account of his time at the Bank, Mitchell makes no effort to disguise how thrilling he found being at the heart of Britain's corporate-state power structure:

> It was absolutely riveting to be at the Bank at that time. I was given an office of my own just down the corridor from the Governor, Robin Leigh-Pemberton. I also had my own peg in the toilet, a hand towel with my name embroidered on it and shoe-cleaning equipment – only black polish, naturally.
>
> The deal was that I had access to everyone, everywhere and every meeting on condition that I did not report on anything. For a journalist, this was unprecedented.
>
> I was invited to sit in on all the Bank's committees that regulated the markets in commodities, precious metals, bonds and money ... For a financial journalist it was pulse-quickening to watch the Bank's dealers intervene in the market ... I was also invited into the Holy of Holies, known as 'Books' – the 11am meeting between the Governor, the Executive Directors and the department heads in the ornate, panelled Court Room. ... I could go down to the vaults and stare at several hundred million pounds worth of gold bullion.[36]

While BBC Radio's financial news editor was busy at the Bank of England staring at gold, other major social changes were afoot which, in combination with Big Bang, would fundamentally reshape the BBC's economics and business reporting. By the time of Big Bang the Thatcher Government had already privatised Cable & Wireless, British Telecom, British Aerospace and British Gas, the latter of which was the largest share issue ever – famously promoted by the 'Tell Sid' campaign. With the re-election of the Conservative Party in June 1987, the privatisation programme continued apace. The privatisations were central to the perception that the Conservative Government had ushered in a new era of popular capitalism, transforming Britain into a shareholder democracy.

Nick Jones recalls a feeling of 'buoyancy' in newsrooms at the BBC: 'there was a sense that the country was on the move and that we wanted to reflect this'.[37] Similarly, Peter Day describes 'an awakening feeling': 'Things like privatisation pushed company and economic news more and more into prominence.'[38] 'After the Big Bang in the City,' another BBC business journalist recalls, 'there was just much more interest in share prices and economic stories and things like that. So it was an expanding area.'[39]

The 'explosion' in financial reporting in the late 1980s coincided with the arrival at the BBC of John Birt. 'The men in suits were coming,' Ed Mitchell writes, 'the era of the accountants, "management" and "Birtism" was dawning.'[40] Former BBC reporter Richard Quest considers that this was more important than the wider changes that were taking place: 'The big change came not with Thatcher or with the "Big Bang" but with John Birt ... Birt and Ian Hargreaves came in and changed everything.'[41] Birt, as we have seen, was a committed neoliberal who would radically reshape the organisational structure and culture of the BBC. Following his appointment as deputy director general, business journalism became a much greater priority. 'It was exciting', recalls one former BBC business journalist. 'Partly because it was growing and people were coming in from outside and so I suppose it did have a slightly different culture in that it was bringing people in from where ever – Thames TV, Reuters, stuff like that.'[42]

Birt's deputy Ian Hargreaves (himself recruited from the *Financial Times*) appointed Daniel Jeffreys, chief economist at the stockbrokers Cazenove, to serve as the BBC's first economics and business editor.[43] The title of 'editor' at the BBC would usually have implied a role on a specific programme, but this new post, by contrast, was one of four senior reporting positions, the incumbents of which were expected to provide 'leadership' to those below them in the editorial hierarchy by setting the tone of the journalism rather than providing managerial oversight.[44]

'The editors', John Fryer recalls, 'were elevated to a strata that we never had before. We never had editors like that before.'[45] The creation of these new senior posts was part of a broader organisational rationalisation and centralisation of editorial control. In business and economics journalism, a key aspect of this was the creation of the Economics Unit which was set up in 1989 'under the keen eye of John Birt'.[46] It incorporated all the television correspondents covering business, economics and labour (and peculiarly also transport), as well as staff from the Financial Unit, BBC Radio's economics editor, labour correspondent, industry and business correspondent, and a New York business correspondent to cover the US financial markets – a post proposed by Richard Quest, later a well-known business presenter on CNN.[47] By 1992, the Economics Unit housed a news editor, a senior producer, an economics editor, an organiser, a finance and city correspondent, five economics correspondents, a business correspondent, two business and industry correspondents, four reporters, six business journalists, two transport correspondents and a single labour relations correspondent.

Daniel Jeffreys, who joined the BBC in January 1988, served only for a relatively short period before becoming New York correspondent.[48] This meant that in late 1989 the former economics editor of *Newsnight*, Will Hutton, having spent a period working on the European Business Channel in Zurich, was 'in the frame' to succeed him.

Hutton, who had made a name for himself on *Newsnight* as a Keynesian critic of Thatcherism, describes himself as having been 'a casualty of Birt's arrival':

> I was a sceptic about privatisation. I was a sceptic about house price sales, about council houses. I was concerned about de-industrialisation. I was worried about the financialisation of the business sector – [that it] was actually advancing short-termism. You know, those were the kind of pieces I did at my career at *Newsnight*. But actually it wasn't ... It was seen, you know: 'It would be much better if Will's talents were deployed less obviously behind camera than in front of camera.' I mean that was, I think, what the nabobs of the BBC thought after Thatcher's [1987] election victory. So my going to set up the European Business Channel was part pushed ... I'd done what I could do at the BBC and portions of it were going to get more and more problematic.[49]

Perhaps unsurprisingly given the circumstances of his departure, Hutton was not appointed the new economics and business editor. The post went instead to Birt's old friend, Peter Jay. In the 1970s he had played a key role popularising monetarism as economics editor at *The Times* and had acted as an intellectual mentor to John Birt, bringing him into the orbit of the neoliberal movement. Both his parents were influential Labour figures and his first marriage was to the daughter of the Labour leader James Callaghan, whose government appointed him ambassador to the United States (where he regularly played tennis with the heads of the CIA and the FBI).[50] Jay was also responsible for Callaghan's famous speech in 1976 declaring 'that you could [not] spend your way out of a recession', a speech in which he had originally included a section, subsequently cut, declaring that 'the way forward for socialists is ... to change the role of labour so it becomes entrepreneurial', and a further passage which pronounced that 'Keynesianism has no future'.[51]

Jay officially took up his new post at the BBC on 1 January 1990. Despite his seniority, he was employed by the BBC as a freelancer, initially offered approximately £70,000 a year on the understanding that the position would not be full-time and that the 'loss of earnings' he incurred could be compensated by outside writing and speaking.[52] This included receiving substantial sums from leading financial institutions. In 1992 he was offered £4,000 by Barclays, plus travel and accommodation, to speak at a dinner hosted by the bank. In March 1999 the investment bank Lehman Brothers invited him to speak at a Country Club dinner, offering him £2,000 in return for delivering a twenty-minute talk and apologising for the low sum.[53] Part of Jay's job, he recalls, was 'to report on air, radio, television, on the agenda of economics and business across the BBC's news and current affairs'.[54] His reporting, though, was not well regarded. Although a formidable intellectual, Jay did not have much of a talent for communication and his unabashed elitism was well known. He notoriously once told a sub-editor on *The Times* that an article he had written was 'not intended to be understood by people like you', and that it was written for 'three people, two of whom are in the Treasury and one of whom is in the Bank of England'.[55]

At the BBC Jay drew on his high-level connections by introducing special lunches where a government minister or a top banker was invited to address the twenty or thirty members of the Economics Unit over wine and a formal meal.[56] These off the record meetings still take place. In September 2014 the then editor of the BBC's Business and Economics Centre referred to fortnightly meetings attended by corporate elites and occasionally 'people from the political sphere as well'. These meetings, it was explained, 'just really help our understanding' and 'shape the language and all that kind of thing around the coverage that we put together':

> People will come in, off the record, and talk to us about the issues they are facing [and] allow us to ask questions ... We work out what areas of mutual interests we have whereby they might be developing something which we think we'd be interested in covering, or whatever the angles of the story would be. But it's a particularly useful way in for people ... I'd say invariably it does lead to a subsequent broadcasting appearance.[57]

Most of Jay's colleagues felt alienated by his elitism, and found him to be a remote figure. Rory Cellan-Jones remembers him as being 'like an emeritus professor', whose 'only real influence there was in recruiting people in his image'.[58] One influential figure Jay recruited in his image was Evan Davis, who later succeeded him as economics editor. Davis, who joined the BBC in 1993 as a radio economics correspondent, already had media experience from his appearances as an economics pundit for the Institute of Fiscal Studies, an influential think tank from where he had been seconded to the Thatcher Government to work on the 'poll tax'.[59] Davis considers Jay a 'mentor' and says his economics broadcasting in the 1970s 'fired me up to study economics'.[60] It was at the level of senior journalists like Davis that Jay appears to have had an editorial influence. Jay, Davis recalls, 'had very demanding standards of economics correspondents at the BBC and believed they needed to have studied economics at quite a high level ... Economics was the big thing ... Adversarialism didn't enter into it. The value system was "mission to explain" journalism.'[61]

Economic news became much more prominent in the 1990s, during which it was firmly tied to the routine reporting and analysis of macroeconomic indicators such as growth, unemployment and inflation, and was led by figures (like Peter Jay and Evan Davis) who were thoroughly committed to orthodox economic theory. BBC reporting was based largely around routine statistical releases from government departments and the Bank of England, but occasionally from private sector sources such as building societies and retail consortiums. Business news, meanwhile, was, and remains, shaped largely around the quarterly and annual results of public limited companies, product launches, takeovers and mergers, new procurement contracts and so on. Former BBC Industrial Editor Martin Adeney, interviewed by Aeron Davis in 1998, estimated that business news 'was 85 or even 90 per cent driven by formal announcements or events', with very little independent investigation.[62] Central to shaping the routine and elite-orientated economics news agenda established in the 1990s was the news diary maintained by the Economics Unit. Speaking in 2012, the BBC's then chief economics correspondent, Hugh Pym, confirmed this is still the case: 'We are quite diary driven, you know, we have the employment figures, inflation every month, we have GDP every quarter.'[63] Rory Cellan-Jones describes the reporting in the 1990s as having been 'very reactive' and 'not very ambitious'.[64] The 'humdrum coverage' was well suited to the post-ideological elite consensus of the 1990s, as was the technocratic bent of the 'mission to explain' values system. The output, however, also reflected Peter Jay's scepticism about business reporting, which was increasingly prevalent in the wider media. Jay believed economics was the more proper perspective for a public service broadcaster to adopt, since it represented the 'economic life of the nation', while business was just one section of the economy. This view, however, 'did not prevail'. According to Jay, the then director of News and Current Affairs Tony Hall, later director general, considered that 'as a matter of high strategy' the BBC should 'develop something which in his mind he called "business"'.[65]

Populist business programming, which contrasted sharply with the high-minded, analytical approach favoured by Peter Jay, was developed by different sections of the BBC – 'baronies' as the cliché goes. In Broadcasting House, the home of BBC Radio, the 'business programmes people' worked separately from the correspondents like Evan Davis, who contributed to radio news and current affairs programmes such as *Today*, *PM* or the *Six O'Clock News*. Another particularly influential group worked at Television Centre under a 'baron' called Paul Gibbs. Gibbs was recruited by Tony Hall from the European Business Channel, where he had worked with his close friend Will Hutton. John Birt, Gibbs recalled in 2013, 'certainly wanted a business show and I have the herogram from him still [saying], "Well done." He liked it. He liked all business stuff.' Gibbs was given a brief from Hall 'not to do too much economics; to just concentrate on the micro'. This, according to Gibbs, meant 'gearing' the output towards 'entrepreneurship and investment and work':

> I just ended up telling stories. And it was a rich vein for business then because I thought it had not been told properly. So we did *Business Breakfast*, which we knew was probably a professional City-type audience getting up, wanting a briefing in the morning, getting to work ... And we also had a lot of features, lots of which ran in news during the

day – I mean they were picked up as news stories by some of the other bulletins.[66]

Gibbs's 'business programmes' unit was established in 1990, initially with an editor, deputy editor, two senior producers and two reporters. It oversaw newer output like *Business Breakfast* and *Working Lunch*, as well as more established programmes like *Money Box* and the *Money Programme*.[67] *Business Breakfast*, which was particularly significant, was first broadcast in 1989 as part of *BBC Breakfast News*, but in 1993 was spun off as an hour-long programme in its own right. Gibbs's 'empire' expanded during the 1990s to meet the greater demand for business content from other parts of the BBC, especially World News which was now competing with CNN.[68] In 1994, the BBC launched *Working Lunch*, which, according to Gibbs, was 'really downmarket' and launched the career of the chummy presenter Adrian Chiles. The tone and imagined audience of the programme tallied strongly with the Thatcherite rhetoric of a shareholding democracy. A former senior BBC editor recalls,

> *Working Lunch* was created, which I think had two objectives. One was certainly to see how cheaply you could make such a programme. I mean honestly that was one objective ... And also it was playing to this kind of shareholder democracy thing, you know ... There was an implication that people would be somehow tuning into *Working Lunch* at half past twelve, on a lunchtime on BBC2, shift workers when they got home, or retired people would turn on the television and see how their share portfolio was doing.[69]

Other developments in this period similarly broke with the more formal Oxbridge tone which had been traditional at the BBC. Radio 5 Live was also important in this respect. Its launch in 1994 gave 'a lot of programming time to fill in and part of the mix for Five Live was the commitment to financial and business news'.[70] In particular, it presented considerable opportunities to more junior reporters to develop business expertise, and as an outlet allowed for the more populist style that had been developed in business programmes.

As business became increasingly prominent in BBC programming, so business values became increasingly prevalent, and neoclassical economics came to dominate news reporting. Organised labour, meanwhile, all but disappeared from routine reporting. In 1991, Nick Jones, the BBC labour correspondent from 1978 to 1988, lamented that

> Labour correspondents once held prominent positions in the journalist hierarchy of most news organisations. Now they find they are being displaced by city analysts who, in their striped shirts, can be seen regularly on television making pronouncements which frequently go unchecked and unchallenged. Union affairs rarely impinge on the work of the new generation of business reporters. Even when major industrial developments involve substantial job losses, the implications are invariably assessed by specialists and advisers employed by stockbrokers, banks and city finance houses.[71]

The division of labour within the BBC was such that business and economics journalists generally did not consider trade unions to fall within their remit, while labour and industrial correspondents found little or no demand for their skills and expertise among programme editors. The decline of the labour journalists was consolidated in 1993 with a cull by management of what Richard Quest calls 'a lot of old lag correspondents'.⁷² Another former business journalist recalls,

> There was a sort of 'day of the long knives' where we all came in one morning and Dominick [Harrod] wasn't there, Peter Smith wasn't there … They had gone. And we were sitting there thinking, 'Oh, where's Dominick gone? And Peter?' And they'd been kicked out. And then Chris Kramer came over from TV – he was head of news I think at telly and later went on to CNN. And the myth was he kept the engine running on his limousine outside Broadcasting House. And he came up, it was kind of 11:55 so we were all working on bulletins for 12:00 and this kind of stuff. He walked in, didn't seem to be aware that we might actually need to keep working and said, 'Right, announcement to make. As you can see, we've made some changes. Dominick and Peter have gone. We clearly weren't meeting the requirements of the output and that's what we've done. Any questions?' And … Sam Jaffa said, 'In what way were we not meeting the requirements of the output?' And Chris Kramer said, 'Wrong question Sam. Any more questions?' And strangely there were no more questions and then he went away again … It was quite a watershed, them shaking off the … But that was probably happening across the Corporation I guess.⁷³

This sudden departure of 'old lag correspondents' consolidated a shift in news values that can be traced to the end of the miners' strike, privatisation, Big Bang and the arrival of John Birt as deputy director general in 1987. A certain social democratic paradigm that had been institutionalised in BBC business and economics reporting had been displaced. 'I think the way in which the news stories in particular were framed', Richard Tait comments, 'changed from on the one hand the union says that and on the other hand the management say that, to a rather different series of considerations.'[74] Another interviewee remarks, 'We maybe previously would have thought of labour and business as being two areas ... And then it became business and economics.'[75]

At the end of the Birt era, Tony Hall oversaw the merging of the various rival 'baronies' producing economics and business output into a new silo, the Business and Economics Centre. Daniel Dodd, who had worked on the relocation of the News Department to Birt's 'modern, purpose built, technically advanced' News Centre,[76] was appointed to head the new hub of BBC business journalism.[77] The initiative was very much in the spirit of the earlier rationalisations of the Birt era, incorporating formerly (relatively) autonomous units into one space and under one organisational structure.

The new Business and Economics Centre not only pitched business stories to news editors, it was also allocated particular slots for business reporting.[78] These included the 6.15–6.30 a.m. slot on BBC Radio 4's prestigious *Today* programme, *Wake Up to Money* on 5 Live and business slots on News24, BBC World and the World Service. The former BBC news analyst Stephen Coulter recalls,

> What they did was they started to, rather than having a one-hour slot for business programmes, they'd have a five- or ten-minute slot you see now, with business coverage on breakfast news for instance. And also on the main bulletins, on the 6 or the 9, or 10 as it is now, they'd start having their own proper business sections as well. So the idea was to take business coverage out of the sort of ghetto at six in the morning and make it a bit more mainstream.[79]

Such slots were not necessarily imposed against the will of programme editors. According to Martin Greig, who appeared regularly on the *Today* programme in the 2000s, its then editor Kevin Marsh

> was very, very tuned in to the new business agenda and very quickly said, 'Look, I want to expand the business output on the *Today* programme.' So at the time we did a six- or seven-minute slot at 6.15 in the morning and then we did another one at 8.30. Kevin was very clear and he said, 'No, I want to expand the 6.15 slot, I want to make it very much just a dedicated business slot so people wanting to hear business news on the *Today* programme know that they are going to get it at 6.15.' So that expanded to a fifteen-minute slot. But he also introduced a specific slot at 7.20. He wanted to hear specifically from the chief executives, the movers and shakers in the business world. And so he specifically went out and devised a slot that would attract them onto the radio at that time of the day. And that was at 7 a.m. … could be companies and their corporate announcements to the stock exchange, could be results, could be whatever. And we very much used that 7.20 slot as a platform for them to come on and say, you know, 'We've just announced a billion pounds profit', or whatever.[80]

Shortly after the establishment of the BBC's Business and Economics Centre, John Birt was succeeded as director general by the millionaire businessman Greg Dyke. Dyke, who in the early 1990s had advocated the creation of an internal market at the BBC, was a former colleague of Birt's at LWT where he succeeded him as director of programmes. Dyke then served in a number of executive roles in the private broadcasting sector and at the time of his appointment to the BBC was chief executive of Pearson Television, an executive director of its parent company Pearson plc, as well as chairman of Channel 5.[81] He brought this private sector perspective with him to the BBC, where his enthusiasm for business seems to have been broadly shared by the existing management. As Mark Damazer puts it, the senior management considered that 'the BBC wasn't taking business very seriously' and wasn't 'intellectually sympathetic, in its broadest sense of the word, to an understanding of the problems of wealth generation and its importance'.[82] Dyke appointed Damazer, one of Birt's 'young lions', to review the BBC's business coverage.[83] 'I had gone to Wharton Business School for a six-week management top-up and came back not a hugely changed person', Damazer recalls. 'But Greg asked me to have a look at business journalism and change it a bit.' Damazer concluded that the 'understanding of what the main issues were in corporate Britain was too small and the level of sophistication of the discussion was too thin'.[84] While it was felt that the BBC's existing coverage of economics was strong – as represented by the presence of Peter Jay and Evan Davis – the view was that business reporting, as opposed to business programming, was lacking. Three criticisms seem to have been central. The first, Evan Davis recalls, was that 'business, when it was covered at the BBC, was too much from the point of view of the consumer rather than the point of view of the employer'.[85] The second was that company news focused too much on the impact which investments and divestments had on employees, without enough attention to the motives of the company involved or the interests of shareholders. Speaking to *Sunday Business* in July 2000, Damazer emphasised that the BBC must of course consider the impact companies have on employment, but 'must, must, must make the effort to … to understand the forces affecting a company and which stakeholders are affected

[by] … We must never lose sight of the fact that companies are entitled to make profits.' The third was that the BBC was not giving adequate attention to mergers and acquisitions, which, despite having little impact on viewers and listeners, were nevertheless major developments in the corporate world.[86] Dyke says he

> used to joke with a lot of the guys there and say, 'Look, you still report business as if it's 1968 really. That somehow business is bad, profit is bad and non-profit is good really.' I mean, I always joked that they saw profit as stealing from the consumer. Now if you worked in business you knew quite the opposite.[87]

The BBC, one former senior editor claims, 'wasn't really reflecting the significance of shareholders and … it wasn't reflective of the broader range of shareholders'. But under Dyke it would endeavour to reflect the 'value of globalisation' and provide a 'really good explanation for what was going on in the business world' – which apparently involved 'raising public consciousness about the importance of business'.[88] Evan Davis, who considers that 'business came into its own under Greg Dyke', recalls the mood of the time:

> [The feeling was] we mustn't be hostile to business, we need to explain business. We mustn't take a side in a kind of pro-business, anti-business debate, we're just there, explaining it and interpreting it. But above all we are there with it. I mean, we are reporting on it rather than ignoring it, because it's very important and increasingly so. And so we need to get stories and we need those stories to be well reported and well explained. And we need more people to do that and we need more space on our bulletins to cover that.[89]

On 6 November 2000, Dyke gave a speech to the annual conference of the Confederation of British Industry (CBI). 'I am here this morning', he told delegates, 'to persuade you that the BBC under my leadership will take business more seriously than we have ever done before.'[90] He praised *Working Lunch* in particular as an 'innovative' programme, but claimed that mainstream news and current affairs programmes had 'ignored or failed to understand the real business agenda'[91] and had too often assumed that 'profits are easy to achieve and are automatically against the consumer's interests'.[92] 'At times,' Dyke said, 'we treated it as an old-fashioned industrial relations story – we even dragged Red Robbo out of retirement for his views.'[93] Announcing a series of changes to the BBC's business journalism, he said he was committed to 'taking business centre stage in the BBC'.[94] The editorial team responsible for the BBC's online business coverage would be doubled, BBC News 24's business output would be expanded, *Working Lunch* would be extended to one hour and a specialist business reporter would be appointed to *Newsnight*.[95] The headline-grabbing measure in Dyke's speech, though, was the appointment of the right-wing business journalist Jeff Randall to the new post of business editor.

Randall's background was in the right-wing press. He studied economics at university and lectured for a short time before becoming a financial journalist. He was City correspondent on *The Sunday Telegraph* during Big Bang and joined *The Sunday Times* in 1988. After holding several roles in business journalism at the paper, he became City and business editor in 1994 as well as a director of Times Newspapers. At the time of his appointment to the BBC, Randall was the editor of *Sunday Business*, a title which he was recruited to launch for the multi-millionaire Barclay brothers,[96] later owners of the Telegraph Group and *The Spectator*. Randall was reportedly given the job as BBC business editor as a result of a highly critical article he authored for the *Sunday Business* in May 2000, in which he complained that:

> Business is rarely covered in Radio 4 news bulletins, unless it is a story about a beastly multinational making workers redundant or fat-cat directors collecting outrageous salaries. It is as if this country's executive class, whose taxes underpin the BBC's funding, does not exist.
>
> The BBC's new Director-General, Greg Dyke, made a personal fortune from business. It's about time he looked at the corporation's institutionalised bias against free-enterprise wealth-creators – and did something about it.[97]

Dyke, according to Randall, then telephoned him and said: 'You can be one of those geezers sitting on the sidelines carping, bitching and whinging, or you can come here and do something about it. Have you got the balls to do that?'[98]

As an outspoken critic of the BBC, Randall was a provocative appointment and one that symbolised the determination of the new director general to institute a pro-business agenda at the BBC. With the appointment of Jeff Randall, Peter Jay's remit was narrowed from economics and business to just economics, and within months Jay had announced his retirement. This followed a six-week review of the BBC's business and economics journalism by Randall and the deputy head of newsgathering, Vin Ray. The results were announced along with a series of initiatives, including the creation of twenty new business and economics posts and a £2 million investment in the Business and Economics Centre.[99]

Jay's departure had been anticipated when his contract with the BBC was renewed in January 2000. He had been

offered a salary of £160,000 a year, well over double his
salary when he joined the BBC nine years earlier, and was
asked to continue as economics editor for two years, in
the second year helping the BBC identify a successor.[100]
Jay suggested his protégé Evan Davis, then economics
editor on *Newsnight*. Richard Sambrook wrote to Jay
on 4 December 2001, remarking, 'I hope you agree that,
with Evan, your legacy is in safe hands'.[101] Davis developed a much stronger on-screen presence than Jay and was
well liked by editors. He remarked in an email to Jay in
September 2002, 'The [News at] Ten folks now trust me,
and in fairness to them, more or less let me dictate what I
do with a minimal amount of interference.'[102]

Jeff Randall, meanwhile, had arrived in March 2001
with a reported salary of £250,000 and a brief to oversee
'attitudinal change in the Corporation'.[103] 'I was there to
rattle cages and, if necessary, make myself unpopular to
force business up the news agenda,' Randall later recalled.
'When I started, Greg Dyke warned me, "don't go native;
be an agent of change".'[104] Asked in 2014 how you change
culture at the BBC, Greg Dyke replied, perhaps only half
joking, that: 'You have a heavyweight like Jeff Randall
who's a bit of a thug. And he insists.'[105] The experiences
of BBC journalists working under Randall varied. Some
emphasise the freedom they still enjoyed in their reporting;
others say that he was strongly interventionist. One business journalist says that he 'set the tone [and] if you didn't
do what Jeff Randall did you got negative vibes coming at
you through the management system'.[106] Another recalls
that Randall would

> come to our morning meetings and more or less harangue
> us about being anti-business and saying we all need to be
> more pro-business … There wasn't anyone handing down

editorial lines [previously]. The first time that ever happened was when Jeff Randall arrived. And Jeff Randall arrived and did it in quite a brutal way ... He would say, I don't want to hear anybody saying *this*, or being anti-business on *this*, or just portraying British Gas results as bad news for consumers.[107]

This same journalist, however, also acknowledged that the pro-business agenda associated with Randall's arrival was advantageous, since his presence increased the status of business reporting and opened up greater opportunities. He 'came with the blessing of the director general'[108] and acted not only as an 'ambassador on the most significant news outlets', but also as 'someone within the organisation who would stand up and say, "this is what we need to focus on"'.[109] Another BBC journalist remarks that 'the reason for bringing the big hitters in was to tell the managers of the other parts of the BBC that they had to pay attention'.[110] Rory Cellan-Jones remarks,

> I think we, in general, having feared what the impact would be ... actually he was pretty good for all of us because he raised our profile. He had the ability to go down and say, 'You ought to run this on the *Nine O'Clock News*,' and people who would have a few years back never run those kind of stories would say, 'Yes sir,' and jump to it.[111]

John Fryer considers that there was a definite shift in editorial culture in the 2000s, but emphasises that Jeff Randall should be understood more as a symbol than the agent of this change: 'It wasn't ... that Jeff was sitting there imposing any views of his own on us, because that's not the way the BBC works. The programme editors decide what goes in the programmes.'[112] This is of course true, but editors also defer to the upper echelons of the BBC hierarchy. The BBC, Dyke remarks, is

> an amazingly top-down organisation. If you are the direc-
> tor general and you say, 'I want more of this,' actually you
> tend to get more of this. They don't ignore you. And the
> news guys knew we were interested in business, that I was
> interested in business.[113]

And it was at the level of the editors, the BBC's gatekeepers, that the most important shift took place. Asked if their atti-tudes changed, one senior figure replied: 'Did editors wake up and smell the coffee in 2001? Yes they did.'[114] Gradually, the new editorial agenda became more entrenched, and by the time of the 2008 global financial crisis it was particu-larly marked. Just days before the bankruptcy of Lehmann Brothers in September 2008, Randall's successor as busi-ness editor, Robert Peston, told *The Guardian*,

> When I arrived at the BBC I didn't think it gave enough
> weight to stories that were pretty important and it was
> harder to get stuff on air … But now the instinctive reaction
> of the BBC on a quiet news day is to turn to the business
> and economics department for a lead in a way that would
> have been unthinkable two or three years ago.[115]

Remarkably, there were at that time still voices claiming that the BBC was anti-business. In 2006, the BBC Board of Governors, which became the BBC Trust at the beginning of 2007, appointed the neoliberal economist Alan Budd to chair an independent panel tasked with 'assess[ing] whether the BBC portrays a fair and balanced picture of the world of business and of its impact on society more generally'.[116] According to then BBC governor Richard Tait, one of the reasons the review was set up was 'a sense that the BBC was still quite hostile to business'.[117] The Budd Report concluded that 'there is no doubt that the BBC takes business as a genre seriously – in terms of both the amount of coverage and the resources devoted to it'.[118] Indeed, the content analysis it commissioned found that the BBC's evening news gave almost twice the amount of airtime to business stories compared with ITN, while BBC News 24 devoted almost five times the amount of airtime compared with the same evening hour of broadcasting on Sky News.[119] Surveying the 'resources available to the generation and production of business news' at the BBC compared with its rivals, the author of the content analysis remarked, 'when it comes to broadcast business news reporting there is only one 500-pound gorilla in the room'.[120] This was the outcome of an extraordinary growth of BBC business reporting over the previous two decades or so. Although in the early- to mid-1980s, BBC TV's industrial editor headed a team of three correspondents, while their radio equivalents worked alongside just half a dozen or so specialist staff who made up the Financial Unit, by 2007 the BBC could boast a '24-hour, tri-media operation of around 160 journalists and support staff producing 11 hours of business programming every weekday'.[121]

The Budd Report made some familiar criticisms of the BBC's reporting, claiming that there was evidence of occasional 'unconsciously partial and unbalanced' reporting, resulting 'mainly from a lack of awareness of the commercial world' and 'a lack of specialist knowledge and perhaps a lack of interest on the part of some mainstream programme editors'. It was argued that 'a preoccupation with taking the consumer perspective' had marginalised the perspective of 'direct and indirect shareholders' and meant 'much business coverage is seen as a battle between "unscrupulous" company bosses and their "exploited" customers'.[126] Significantly though, the panel readily acknowledged the remarkable extent to which the perspective of workers had been marginalised in the BBC's output. The section of the report detailing this is worth quoting at length:

> 3.1 Around 29 million people work for a living in the UK and spend a large proportion of their waking hours in the workplace. However, little of this important part of UK life is reflected in the BBC's business coverage. As noted above, the audiences are served in their identity as consumers. But they are not that well served in their role as workers.
>
> 3.2 Unions in Britain represent around 6.5 million people and deal with a wide range of issues affecting the rights of workers. Yet union witnesses told us that the union perspective is often narrowly defined by the BBC and is only raised in the case of employment disputes. The T and G [Transport and General Workers Union] pointed out in its written evidence that it believes there is a lack of engagement in labour affairs issues.
>
> [...]
>
> 3.4 Unions believe that there are relatively few stories about important issues such as equal pay, workplace safety/ occupational health and equal opportunity. They believe that their views are not sought on wider employment issues and the role of workers in society. They note that there are programmes on consumers' rights but not the equivalent on workers' rights. In short, their view is that the world of work does not really feature on the BBC – and even when it does it is without the workers.
>
> 3.5 From our own viewing and listening there are times when the union and employee perspective is missing. One reason may be because the importance of these issues in a modern society may not be widely recognised by BBC

journalists. We believe this stems in part from what wit-
nesses describe as a lack of knowledge and interest.

3.6 We note that the BBC currently only has one labour
affairs correspondent and although very experienced and
knowledgeable he rarely appears on television.[123]

The Budd Report thus represented a curious mix of arguments. While it found no evidence of the anti-business bias
it had been set up to investigate, it argued nevertheless
that a dominant consumerist perspective at the BBC had
eclipsed the perspective of both owners and workers. This
hardly seems plausible in light of the considerable resources
the BBC had dedicated to promoting the perspective of
business in its reporting. A more convincing conclusion
might have been that BBC business reporting had adopted
a strong consumerist focus as part of a strategic adapta-
tion to neoliberalism, an orientation which occasionally
conflicted with its commitment to sympathetic coverage of
the business world, and which had at the same time more
or less completely displaced the notion of the audience as
workers and citizens.

Another interesting aspect of the Budd investigation was
audience research it commissioned to assess public interest
in business reporting. Although this research was 'skewed
towards those who were pre-disposed to business news', it
found that 'business news registered a below average mean
score of 5.5 out of 10 in comparison to other subjects such
as Politics (6), Environment (7) and Current Affairs (7.6)'.
Those most interested in business news, according to this
research, were middle-aged men in 'AB social class', while
those declaring a low interest 'were more likely to be young
(18–24 years), female (26 per cent not interested) and
C1C2 (25 per cent not interested)'.[124] In other words, interest in business reporting was found to be low compared

with other areas of reporting and was most marked among the more privileged sectors of the population.

That same year, Ofcom published details of a survey which found that when asked 'Which types of news are you personally interested in?', 'city, business and financial issues' received the second-lowest level of interest out of 15 'types of news' – the only less interesting topic being 'celebrity behaviour'.[125] These findings are significant, since they undermine the prevalent belief among senior editors and business journalists at the BBC that the growth in business reporting responded to a public interest in, and enthusiasm for, business. In 2014, the head of the Economics and Business Centre, Jon Zilkha, would remark that persuading BBC editors to run business stories was 'pushing at a bit of an open door', since 'each of those programmes will know that their audience at the moment is hyper interested in anything to do with finance, economics, business'.[126]

But this 'open door', as we have seen, was not a result of public interest in business reporting, but rather the outcome of a long process of institutional change that the BBC underwent from the Thatcher period onwards; and in no small part, this was the result of explicitly pro-business initiatives by the neoliberal leadership of the BBC.

Other factors, though, certainly require a mention. The neoliberal turn of the Labour Party under Blair was of course crucial in terms of constitutionally justifying this shift. Indeed, the most unambiguously pro-business shift took place under the joint leadership of Greg Dyke and former Goldman Sachs banker Gavyn Davies, who were extremely close to New Labour prior to the Hutton Report debacle. Connected to that shift was a much broader corporate consolidation of British public life. This was evident in the media and cultural industries in which the BBC operated, which were increasingly commodified and dominated by large multinationals; the privatisation of public utilities; the neoliberal reform of public services; and the shift in the British political economy away from a wage-based growth model to one based increasingly on debt and asset price inflation.

None of this was ever very popular with the public, and insofar as it can claim some support, it can mainly be found in the more affluent sections of society, who have benefited materially from the neoliberal project, and perhaps in the realist acquiescence that inevitably began to take hold. To return to Zilkha's remark about the 'hyper interest' of the BBC's audience in finance, economics and business, what in fact had happened was that public interest in these issues grew enormously after 2007, not because the public suddenly embraced business values in the way that the BBC had, but because people suddenly felt insecure about their futures, which had been tied to the future of the financial markets. By this point, however, economics and business reporting had become hopelessly conflated as 'the economic life of the nation' was covered ever more from the viewpoint of the corporate elite. While the interests and perspective of workers had long been marginalised in the BBC's reporting, those of business had become ever more deeply embedded within the working practices and professional ideologies of BBC journalists.

'Business' had become a word identified less with a distinct (and powerful) socio-economic group, or a particular mode of social organisation, and ever more a catch-all term incorporating all facets of economic life. Indeed, this is one of the strange ironies of the financial collapse of 2008. Whereas it might have been expected to have led to a more heterodox approach to economic issues, it largely appears to have strengthened the influence of neoliberalism and big business at the BBC. Content analysis commissioned by the BBC Trust found that in 2007 business representatives were more than five times more prevalent than representatives of labour, and by 2012 the former outnumbered the latter almost twenty times.[127] Mike Berry, one of the co-authors of that study, also conducted a content analysis of BBC Radio 4's flagship news and current affairs programme *Today*, which found that during six weeks of the 2008 financial crisis, representatives from financial services made up the single largest group of sources, 35.1 per cent of all 'source appearances', while organised labour made up only 0.4 per cent.[128]

Berry's subsequent examination of discussions of the post-crash budget deficit on *BBC News at Ten* in 2009 pointed to a similar domination of elite, pro-business sources in the BBC's output. After politicians and the Institute for Fiscal Studies, which were by far the most prominent sources, the most prevalent were the Bank of England and City analysts, which appeared in a quarter of the coverage. They were followed by business-friendly institutions like the IMF, the OECD and the CBI. Such institutions, Berry notes, 'sometimes operate[d] as news hooks that structure coverage' in a way that alternative sources do not, and their perspectives were 'echoed by reporters and frame the contours of debate within which policy is discussed'.[129]

The strongest alternative voice in Berry's study was the Work Foundation, which had for several years been headed by the former BBC journalist Will Hutton, who as we have seen was essentially pushed from his role as a prominent Keynesian critic of Thatcherism on *Newsnight*. Even Hutton's continued prominence, however, powerfully illustrates the orientation of BBC reporting. Hutton is candid about his elite credentials: 'Though I'm seen as kind of a liberal-left person ... I have lifelong friends in the

Bank of England and the Treasury and many friends at the top of British business. I mean genuine friends, you know, who you'd go on holiday with. That was true in the eighties, and of course it's even more true now.'[130]

Democracy and the Future
of Broadcasting

'It's my job to leave my personal views and prejudices at the door when I report on TV or radio or online', the BBC's Nick Robinson remarked in the run-up to the 2015 general election. 'I am not, though, required to be impartial between democracy and the alternatives.'[1] This was a somewhat disingenuous remark. For it was precisely the undemocratic nature of the political-economic system which had driven the anti-political sentiments and movements which Robinson was decrying.

The surprise majority that general election delivered to the Conservative Party would to some extent obscure the context of these remarks. Political commentators quickly forgot the constitutional uncertainties which had marred the campaign and the unabated feelings of anger, alienation and cynicism with which so many people still viewed politicians and formal politics. A profound distrust of politicians, and disengagement from politics, has been a longstanding feature of the post-Thatcherite political settlement in the UK, and has been a cause of growing unease not only among politicians, but among the broader Establishment, the BBC included. Delivering a lecture at Oxford University in 2006, Nick Robinson had argued that politicians and journalists – who he likened to a quarrelsome married couple – shared a problem: 'cynicism and disinterest in politics are bad for journalists', he said, 'just as much as they are bad for politics'.[2]

The problem was only exacerbated by the 2008 financial crisis, which the Conservatives were largely successful in portraying as somehow stemming from the mismanagement of public finances, and the parliamentary expenses scandal of 2009, which was itself a symptom of the increasing gulf between politicians and the public – as Robinson noted, MPs had been encouraged by whips and by parliamentary officials to use the expenses system to bring their salaries closer to the level of other elites, ironically out of a concern about how the public might view a 'political class' generously remunerating itself.

In the years leading up to 2015, 'cynicism and disinterest' had developed into anger and discontent, with anti-political mobilisations on the left and the right. A radical student movement emerged, though it was quickly suppressed by heavy-handed policing. Influential actions by outfits like UK Uncut and Occupy successfully challenged mainstream political consensus, without seeking power, and in formal politics – more the BBC's purview – previously marginal parties such as UKIP, the Greens and, most spectacularly, the SNP in Scotland, challenged the domination of the traditional parties of government. In retrospect, these movements all prefigured the remarkable rise of Jeremy Corbyn as Labour leader following the election. For Nick Robinson though, the dissidents, naysayers, populists and demagogues – especially those who rebuffed the ballot box as an effective means of political action – were critics not of a corrupt politico-economic system, but of democracy itself.

Robinson's remarks stemmed most directly from his 'beef', as he called it, with Russell Brand. The comedian and comic actor turned anti-capitalist activist had famously declared in an interview on BBC *Newsnight* that he had never voted and never would. Not out of 'apathy', he stressed, but 'absolute indifference and weariness and exhaustion from the lies, treachery and deceit of the political class'. Brand's full-frontal assault on the electoral system was later abandoned during the 2015 general election with an awkward endorsement of Ed Miliband. Before then though, his all-too-public dismissal of the electoral process had been met with moral outrage, not least from Nick Robinson, who in the course of making a programme about the 'fracturing' of 'traditional democracy' in Britain had hoped to interview Brand as a representative of the new radical anti-politics. When Brand apparently declined, Robinson was reported to have angrily denounced him as a 'sanctimonious twat'. Recalling the incident in the *Radio Times*, and invoking memories of communism and fascism, Robinson berated Brand's position on voting, referring to himself as 'an unapologetic believer in elections'.[3]

Robinson's remarks were not merely another example of hopelessly impoverished political analysis. They were also a classic statement of the basic political orientation of the BBC: a declaration of loyalty not in fact to democracy, as Robinson would have it, but to the political institutions of the British state.

John Reith had made much of the democratic potential of the BBC. The 'extension of the scope of broadcasting', he argued, would mean 'a more intelligent and enlightened electorate'. The BBC, he thought, could serve as 'an integrator for democracy'.[4] This language of integration is revealing. The BBC was established at a time when formerly disenfranchised groups were being integrated into formal politics, while elites – anxious about the impact on the existing social and political order – attempted to manage this process. The medium of broadcasting was thought to hold great potential in this regard. Radio, Reith believed, would help create 'an informed and reasoned public opinion as an essential part of the political process in a mass democracy'.[5] Similar sentiments were expressed by Hilda Matheson, the cultured former MI5 officer who became the BBC's first Head of Talks. Broadcasting, she wrote in 1933, 'is ultimately a persuasive art' which 'can help to make the modern state work'.[6] Liberal media scholars have often emphasised the democratising function, or at least potential, of broadcasting. Scannell and Cardiff, for example, describe radio as an 'unprecedented means of helping to shape a more unified and egalitarian society':

> The fundamentally democratic thrust of broadcasting – of which Reith was well aware – lay in the new access to virtually the whole spectrum of public life that radio opened up for everyone. Broadcasting equalized public life through the principle of common access for all.[7]

There is an unavoidable problem with this argument, however. While public service broadcasting is certainly 'egalitarian' in the sense that it creates a universal audience, the same could be said of the use of the same communicative technologies in even the most repressive societies. To be democratic in any meaningful sense, the medium must surely afford not only universal access to politics and culture, but also universal opportunities for the contribution towards, and contention of, political and cultural life. Yet as Scannell concedes, broadcasting has not afforded opportunities for the 'interaction that is the basis of any properly communicative situation', and the BBC's output has been dominated by 'politicians, businessmen, authorities, experts, media reporters and commentators', with others rarely 'entitled to newsworthy opinions'.[8]

In considering the democratic potential of broadcasting, it is revealing to examine Reith's personal attitudes to democracy. In May 1933, the BBC's first director general told an audience at Manchester University that in his view: 'A man may be as good a democrat as any other and yet reject, in the light of philosophy, history or experience, democratic process.'[9] Two years later, he made a similar remark, praising Mussolini for his pursuit of 'high democratic purpose by means which though not democratic, were the only possible ones'.[10] His fascist sympathies did not end there. Like many other British elites of that period, Reith was quite open about his admiration for Hitler, and according to his daughter, Marista Leishman, having been effectively ousted from the BBC, he came to believe that his personal calling was for dictatorship.[11] Reith's comments show that for him 'democracy' was not a process, or even an administrative system for collective decision making, but rather was synonymous with what was then called mass society.

Indeed, Reith had little time for democracy in the more substantive sense. A notorious authoritarian, he did not expect or desire that the public should participate in broadcasting, or even influence it much. He was famously condescending towards popular tastes, and envisaged the audience merely as passive receivers of the BBC's output. He once remarked that there was 'no electoral process anywhere in the BBC constitution and procedure', and considered this a model 'for other public bodies from Parliament down'. Any 'body vested with authority and responsibility', he thought, should be similarly 'autocratic'.[12] Reith then was not really a democrat at all, but rather a liberal nationalist who like many of his contemporaries, saw broadcasting as potentially playing an important role in resolving class conflict. This is perhaps why he developed an otherwise surprising sympathy with the goals of fascism, if not the means. While fascists and other ultra-nationalists responded to the apparent contradictions of modernisation and industrial society through violence and repression, Reith hoped to achieve the same goal with appeals to middle-class culture, the 'constitution', and the symbols and institutions of the nation and the Empire.

Through the BBC, Reith wrote in his broadcasting manifesto, *Broadcast over Britain*, 'the clock which beats time over the Houses of Parliament, in the centre of the Empire, is heard echoing in the loneliest cottage in the land'. Radio, he wrote, was capable of 'making the nation as one man'.[13] Scannell and Cardiff note that the Victorian public service ideal which so animated Reith 'did nothing to change the balance of power in society, and maintained the dominance of the middle classes over the lower ranks', and that for Matthew Arnold culture 'was a means of incorporating the working classes within the existing social and political order, and thus preventing the threat of revolt from below'.[14] Broadcasting would seem to follow in this same pattern. Reith, Scannell notes, believed that broadcasting could 'prove to be a powerful means of promoting social unity particularly through the live relay of ... national ceremonies and functions'.[15]

This has been an ongoing feature of the BBC's small-'c' conservatism ever since. In 1977, the report of the Committee on the Future of Broadcasting referred to the BBC as 'arguably the most important single cultural institution in the nation' and referred approvingly to BBC Chair Michael Swann's evidence to the Committee that an enormous amount of the BBC's work was in fact social cement of one sort or another. Royal occasions, religious services, sports coverage, and police series, all reinforced the sense of belonging to our country, being involved in its celebrations, and accepting what it stands for.[16]

Precisely what the nation stood for, though, was not as clear then as it had once seemed. The upheavals of the 1960s only increased in the 1970s, as the supposed consensus politics of the post-war era seemed to further disintegrate in the midst of an acutely felt political and economic crisis. Tied to the imperilled social-democratic state and drawing on the liberal anti-communism which had come to define its orientation, the BBC appealed, just as Nick Robinson would in 2015, to the democratic character of the British state. In 1973, with the crisis at its nadir, the BBC's editor of News and Current Affairs reassured members of the BBC's General Advisory Council that the Corporation's 'News Staff are not impartial in the least, although they say they are. They are greatly in favour of parliamentary democracy.'[17] These words were later approvingly quoted by the then Director General Charles Curran in an article in *The Listener* – it was a comment he said he 'cherished'.

Such appeals were quite common at that time. An internal BBC discussion paper from 1975 entitled 'How Should We Broadcast News and Current Affairs?', for example, was typical when it stated: 'Of course the BBC totally accepts the need to support and maintain Parliamentary democracy.'[18] Another document held that 'the parliamentary democracy evolved in this country is a work of national genius to be upheld and preserved', linking it to the BBC's 'primary constitutional role' as 'a supplier of news'.[19] Another stated that 'responsible journalism rests on the belief that society will, through the institutions of Parliament, cure itself of ills which are brought to its attention'.[20]

These almost sentimental tributes to the democratic character of the British state were at least more plausible then than they are now. A number of social forces and historical factors – principal among them working-class organisation and agitation, total war, capitalist crisis and the threat of Soviet communism – had converged in such a way as to create, for a relatively short period, more democratic and egalitarian social formations in Britain, as it had in the other advanced capitalist societies of the Global North. Indeed, in retrospect, this was a high-water mark for democracy in Britain. Three decades later, neoliberalism had thoroughly transformed British society and, far from democratising culture and public life as had been claimed, in public proclamations at least, had hollowed out the social democratic state, concentrating power ever more among a financial and corporate elite.[21] As we have seen, the BBC itself underwent a gradual process of institutional transformation in much the same way as other social institutions. The changes mirrored those of the wider society. Power became more centralised, professional decision making became more marketised and working conditions were made more precarious. Meanwhile, as most found their freedom curtailed by neoliberal bureaucracy, a largely Oxbridge-educated elite retained its decision-making powers and the salaries of those at the top sky-rocketed. As for the enduring question of its independence from government, the BBC today still maintains a precarious existence, reliant in the long term on the trust and affection of its audience for its legitimacy, but dependent more immediately on the support of political elites, who hold not only the 'purse strings', but also the constitutional power of life and death. This was a difficult-enough balancing act for the BBC in the social-democratic period, when its ties to the 'Establishment' could feasibly be squared with its commitments to public service. But as politicians and the class interests they represent pull further and further away politically, economically and socially from the people they purport to represent, the BBC will inevitably find itself facing the sort of legitimacy crisis which has engulfed other institutions of power in Britain.

The central problem with the BBC throughout its history has been the extent to which powerful interests have been able to influence its institutional culture and its output. While the early BBC, as Scannell and Cardiff note, 'rejected the profit motive as the basis of its institutional existence', during the 1930s pressure from politicians and state officials, combined with 'well-orchestrated campaigns in the right-wing national press', were effectively able to stifle the medium's democratic potential.[22] Whatever view one has on the nature and extent of the BBC's independence in the 'golden age' of broadcasting, or to what extent it has ever delivered on its promise of independence and impartiality, it is very clear that the contemporary BBC is no more free from the powerful interests which now dominate British society than it was in the 1930s, the last time Britain was as unequal as it is today. The current BBC is not just part of the Establishment, as it always has been, it is part of the neoliberal, business-dominated Establishment, a central institution of Britain's post-democratic settlement. Tied as it is to the neoliberal state, the BBC, even as it faced with being hung, drawn and quartered by political elites and their allies in the corporate media, seems constitutionally unable to resist, let alone to articulate a notion of the public interest which is out of step with the imperatives of the corporate-state elite. Today many on the left still support the

BBC as an institution which, despite all its faults, remains a trustworthy source of news in an 'industry' dominated by private interests and corporate propaganda. Perhaps the BBC remains broadly defensible on those grounds. Its wholesale privatisation, or the removal of the requirement for all broadcasters to maintain impartiality, could only worsen matters. But the BBC has been on the defensive now for three decades, and things have only got slowly worse.

Were some sort of public service–based reform of the BBC possible, its long history points to some obvious ways in which its 'governance' could be effectively overhauled. It would have to be placed on a permanent constitutional footing. Political control over senior appointments and its finances would have to be abolished and replaced with a more democratic system of public accountability. Recruitment practices would have to be made more fully representative of the audience in terms of class, race, gender, geography and so on. Reporting practices would have to be effectively decoupled from the communicative infrastructure of the British state, the corporate media, and the much broader corporate communications industry which has built up around them. Centralised editorial controls would have to be dismantled, with editorial standards still maintained. It would also be necessary to develop ways of democratising editorial power, such as the model of 'public commissioning' advocated by Dan Hind.[23]

Such a programme of radical reform would mean radically transforming the structure of the BBC, and its culture, tearing it away from the state and the corporate sector and placing it firmly in the sphere of 'civil society'. In other words, it would mean transforming it into the authentically independent and democratic institution it has always claimed to be. Were such a transformation to be realised, the BBC would not only have the potential to significantly democratise British society, but also to enrich its culture. One of the greatest fallacies of our contemporary period has been the association between precarity and creativity, entrepreneurialism with innovation – and Birt's BBC was a great case study in this regard. Capital, in reality, has never created anything; it has only capitalised on people's creativity and expertise, and directed their activities towards profitable ends. Unsurprisingly then, modelling institutions around capitalist principles, as the BBC was in the 1990s, only leads to a concentration of cultural production in a narrower section of the population and reduces the sorts of creative freedom on which cultural work depends. The outcome is depressing to watch.

While the focus of this book has been on the politics of broadcasting, many of its political limitations are built into the technology itself. As a 'one way' system of communication utilising expensive equipment, radio – and especially television – was always going to be heavily production based, hence why the projects for media reform in the 1970s emphasised decentralisation and mutualisation, and initiated experiments with 'open access'. These were all ways of 'opening up' the broadcasting system, and they were to some extent institutionalised with the creation of Channel 4 and other contemporary initiatives.

Neoliberals at that time seemed to advocate a similar, perhaps even more effective 'opening up' of the broadcasting system based around the idea of consumer sovereignty, and the technology then seemed to be on their side. In his 1981 MacTaggart lecture, Peter Jay argued that with the disappearance of 'spectrum scarcity' – the original rationale for the public regulation of broadcasting and the establishment of the BBC – 'there will be no technically based grounds for government interference in electronic publishing'. Jay was of course right to recognise the transformative potential of emergent technologies, which now allow us to choose what we view and when. Over time, the internet will make the old system of broadcasting obsolete, much as Jay predicted.

The neoliberals, however, failed to foresee the full implications of new technologies. The real consequence of the rapid technological changes in communicative technology in the last few decades has been that it is increasingly difficult for corporations to monetise cultural products, and journalism especially, which can now be replicated and redistributed without cost. Corporations have responded by attempting to restrict access by introducing pay walls and by lobbying states to introduce protectionist intellectual property laws. In the cultural sphere, subscription services of the type advocated by the Peacock Committee do appear to be taking hold. But it is doubtful that such services can sustain the sort of journalism widely recognised to be a necessity for democratic societies. Ironically, we have now reached a stage where the most efficient system of journalistic and cultural production would be publicly funded at the point of production, and freely available to all. Indeed, the BBC's website and the development of the iPlayer are both huge successes from an otherwise rather lamentable period in the Corporation's history, and the website in particular has been attacked by the private sector precisely because of its popularity. Such successes point to the sort of role a strong, independent, publicly funded BBC might play in a post-broadcasting future, which presents opportunities for much more authentically democratic arrangements than were possible when radical media reform was last on the agenda in the 1970s. We have reached a peculiar juncture though, where such a programme of radical reform is readily achievable in technical terms, yet seems, for now at least, unimaginable politically.

Notes

Introduction

1   BBC Media Centre, 'BBC's combined global audience revealed at 308 million', 21 May 2015, bbc.co.uk.
2   BBC, BBC Audience Information Data Tables (document 1), April–June 2015, bbc.co.uk.
3   BBC Media Centre, 'BBC's combined global audience revealed at 308 million'; ITN and Sky, the next most popular sources, have nothing like the same audiences, while the *Daily Mail*, the UK newspaper group with the largest readership, is used by less than one in six of us. Ofcom, *News consumption in the UK: research report*, 15 December 2015, Stakeholders.ofcom.org.uk.
4   Ofcom, *News consumption in the UK: research report*.
5   Owen Jones, *The Establishment: And how they get away with it*, London: Penguin 2015, 118.
6   Georgina Born, *Uncertain Vision: Birt, Dyke and the Reinvention of the BBC*, London: Random House, 2004, 178.
7   Michael Svennevig, *BBC Coverage of Business in the UK: A Content Analysis of Business News Coverage,* Leeds: Institute of Communications Studies, University of Leeds, 2007, 29.
8   Quoted in David McQueen, 'BBC's Panorama, war coverage and the "Westminster consensus"', *Westminster Papers in Culture and Communication* 5:3, 2008, 47–68.
9   Asa Briggs, *History of Broadcasting in the United Kingdom: Volume I: The Birth of Broadcasting*, London: Oxford University Press, 1961, 123.
10   Charles Curran, 'Broadcasting and society', speech, Edinburgh Broadcasting Conference, 23 March 1971.

11 Hugh Greene, *The Third Floor Front: A View of Broadcasting in the Sixties,* London: Bodley Head, 1969, 125.

12 James Curran and Jean Seaton, *Power Without Responsibility: The Press and Broadcasting in Britain,* 5th edition, London and New York: Routledge, 1997, 363.

13 Stuart Hood, *On Television,* London: Pluto Press, 1987, 49.

14 *Report of the Committee on the Future of Broadcasting,* London: HM Stationery Office, 1977, 14.

15 James Curran recalls the 'mood of dissatisfaction with the "middle-brow", Oxbridge, male elites' and the 'cosy, complacent, condescending, establishment of broadcasting'. He relayed the following anecdote which illustrates the BBC leadership's alienation from post-sixties British society: 'I remember – one forgets the dates – I had dinner with a very nice man, who was Alastair Milne – this is later right, the early eighties ... So I invited him to come to Goldsmiths. And I felt kind of responsible because I had behaved badly at the dinner party, so I said, "Come along" ... And of course my students behaved really badly. The place was absolutely packed and the time came for questions and I said, "Has anyone got any questions?" And that went on for about half an hour. Like: "Why is it you only have Oxbridge people?" "Why are they only white?" "Why are they only men?" "How can you claim to represent the nation?" In the end, in desperation, I turned to a person at the back who was wearing a suit and I thought, "At last! He will ask a question on something else." ... Alistair Milne had brought with him a whole praetorian guard of senior broadcasters. It was like an away day and they were going to bask in the approval of people admiring the way they were defending broadcasting independence against a right-wing government. And they had no idea that this was the kind of reception they were going to get.' (Interview with James Curran, 2 March 2011.)

16 BBC Written Archives Centre, News and Current Affairs Minutes, 13 March 1979.

17 Although the proportion of former barristers in the Commons has declined in recent decades, it remains a common occupational background for MPs after business and professional politics. House of Commons Library, 'Social background of MPs', 14 December 2010, researchbriefings.files.parliament.uk.

18 John Birt, *The Harder Path: The Autobiography*, London: Time Warner, 2002, 254.

19 Ibid., 283.

1. Under the Shadow of Power

1 John Reith, 'Forsan', *Parliamentary Affairs* 17:1, 1963, 25.

2 Ibid., 29.

3 John Reith, Charles Stuart (ed.), *The Reith Diaries*, London: Collins, 1975, 97.

4 Cited in Ian McIntyre, *The Expense of Glory*, London: Harper-Collins, 1994, 146.

5 Reith, 'Forsan', 23–30.

6 Quoted in Philip M. Taylor, *British propaganda in the 20th century: Selling Democracy*, Edinburgh: Edinburgh University Press, 1999, 92.

7 J. C. C. Davidson, Letter to Edward Wood, Lord Irwin (later Lord Halifax), 14 June 1926.

8 Ibid.

9 Asa Briggs, *The History of Broadcasting in the United Kingdom, Volume 1: The Birth of Broadcasting*, Oxford University Press, 1961, 363.

10 Christopher Farman, *The General Strike 1926*, London: Granada, 1972, 125.

11 Davidson, Letter to Edward Wood.

12 Briggs, *The History of Broadcasting in the United Kingdom*.

13 Andrew Marr, *The Making of Modern Britain: From Queen Victoria to VE Day*, London: Pan Books, 2010, 275.

14 Reith, 'Forsan', 29.

15 Quoted in McIntyre, *The Expense of Glory*, 146.

16 John Reith, Letter to the senior staff of the BBC, 15 May 1926, quoted in Briggs, *The History of Broadcasting in the United Kingdom*, 364–6.

17 John Reith, *Into the Wind*, London: Hodder and Stoughton, 1949, 113.

18 Ibid.

19 Reith, 'Forsan', 23–30.

20 John Reith, Letter to the senior staff of the BBC, *The History of Broadcasts in the United Kingdom* in Briggs, 368.

21 National Archives, HO 45/12431. *General Strike, 1926: Report of Deputy Chief Civil Commissioner*, 24 June 1926, 9.

22 Reith, *Into the Wind*, 109–10.

23 See Peter Putnis, 'British government control of Reuters during World War I', *Media History* 14:2, August 2008, 141–165; and Reith, *Into the Wind*, 109–10.

24 Peter Eckersley, *The Power Behind the Microphone*, London: Jonathan Cape, 1941, 157.

25 The exception is the engaging biography of Reith by his daughter Marista Leishman, who lifts the quote from Ian McIntyre's biography. Marista Leishman, *Reith of the BBC: My Father*, Edinburgh: St Andrew Press, 2008, 66; McIntyre, *The Expense of Glory*, 146.

26 Briggs, *The History of Broadcasting in the United Kingdom*, 360.

27 James Curran and Jean Seaton, *Power Without Responsibility: Press, Broadcasting and the Internet in Britain*, 7th edition, Abingdon and New York: Routledge, 2010, 113

28 National Archives, HO 45/12431. *General Strike, 1926: Report of Deputy Chief Civil Commissioner*, 24 June 1926, 1.

29 Quoted in Michael Tracey, 'BBC and the reporting of the General Strike. Introduction to the microfilm edition. Microform Academic Publisher, 2003, 15.

30 BBC Written Archives Caversham, R34/325, undated. Quoted in Paddy Scannell and David Cardiff, *A Social History of Broadcasting: Volume One 1922-1939, Serving the Nation*, Oxford: Basil Blackwell, 1991, 87–8.

31 See Curran and Seaton, *Power Without Responsibility*, 227; and Anthony McNicholas and Jean Seaton, 'The BBC and the British State: a Curious Example of the Advantages of an Unwritten Constitution', RIPE: Re-Visionary Interpretations of the Public Enterprise, 2006, Ripeat.org.

32 Briggs, *The History of Broadcasting in the United Kingdom*, 236.

33 Ralph Miliband, *The State in Capitalist Society: The Analysis of the Western System of Power*, London: Quartet, 1973, 46; 50; 47; 209–10.

34 Tom Burns, *The BBC: Public Institution and Private World*, London and Basingstoke: MacMillan, 1977, 195; 192.

35 Georgina Born, *Uncertain Vision: Birt, Dyke and the Reinvention of the BBC*, London: Random House, 2004, 33.

36   Hugh Greene, 'The World Image of BBC', *Financial Times*, 24 August 1964, 2.

37   Schlesinger, *Putting 'Reality' Together*, London: Methuen, 1987, 167–8.

38   John Reith, quoted in Andrew Boyle, *Only the Wind Will Listen: Reith of the BBC*, London: Hutchinson, 1972, 238.

39   Quoted in Ralph Miliband, *Capitalist Democracy in Britain*, Oxford University Press, 1982, 81.

40   John Birt and Peter Jay, 'Why television news is in danger of becoming an anti-social force', *The Times*, 3 September 1976, 6.

41   Meirion Jones, 'The BBC, Savile and investigations', Open Democracy, 22 January 2016, Opendemocracy.net.

42   John Naughton, 'Diary', *London Review of Books* 14:24, 17 December 1992, 21.

43   Ian Trethown, 'Broadcasting and Politics', speech given to the Guild of British Newspaper Editors at Coventry by the Director-General of the British Broadcasting Corporation, Saturday 22 October 1977.

44   'BBC Charter renewal: Key issues for the 2015 Parliament', Parliament.uk.

45   Stuart Hood, 'News from Nowhere?', *International Socialism* 68, 1995, Marxists.org.

46   Interview with Michael Bett, 23 June 2011.

47   'BBC to fund provision of free television licences for over-75s', press release, Department for Culture, Media & Sport and HM Treasury, 6 July 2015.

48   Jane Martinson, 'Former BBC chief attacks secret government licence fee deal', *Guardian*, 23 December 2015.

49   Jon Stone, 'The BBC is worryingly close to becoming an arm of the Government, says its own former chair', *Independent*, 6 July 2015.

50   Jane Martinson and John Plunkett, 'BBC to take on £750m cost of subsidy for over-75s in licence fee deal', *Guardian*, 6 July 2015.

51   Born, *Uncertain Vision*, 33.

52   Reflecting broader patterns in social mobility and equality, the Board of Governors also became somewhat more representative in the decades following the Second World War. But even when Britain was at its most equal, in the '60s and '70s, the number of governors originating from low-income families was

still tiny, while the proportion who had attended one of the top public schools (catering to just 0.2 per cent of the population) still stood at 23 per cent (down significantly from a remarkable 41 per cent in the interwar period). The proportion who were privately educated, meanwhile, still stood at 60 per cent (though again this was a relative improvement on the interwar period, when all but a handful of governors were privately educated). Harold Perkin, 'The recruitment of elites in British society since 1800', *Journal of Social History* 12:2, 1978, 222–34.

53 Social Mobility and Child Poverty Commission, *Elitist Britain?*, London, 2014, 12–15, 40, 71–2.

54 BBC Annual Report and Accounts 2014/15, 110, downloads.bbc. co.uk/annualreport/pdf/2014-15/bbc-annualreport-201415. pdf.

55 Nicholas Hellen and Robin Henry, 'Cash keeps rolling in for BBC's six-figure big shots', *Sunday Times*, 2 March 2014, 8–9.

56 'About the BBC, News Group, Senior Managers' Salary Bands', downloads.bbc.co.uk/aboutthebbc/insidethebbc/management structure/seniormanagement/sm_salaries/sm_salaries_news_ 2015.pdf.

57 The Sutton Trust, *The Educational Backgrounds of Leading Journalists*, London: Sutton Trust, 2006.

58 Schlesinger, *Putting 'Reality' Together*, 162, 180.

59 Stuart Hood, *A Survey of Television*, London: Heinemann, 1967, 50.

60 David Hendy, *Life on Air: A History of Radio Four*, Oxford: Oxford University Press, 2005, 30.

61 Burns, *The BBC*, 195.

62 Cited in Krishan Kumar, 'Holding the Middle Ground: The BBC, the Public and the Professional Broadcaster', *Sociology* 9:1, 1975, 67.

63 Schlesinger, *Putting 'Reality' Together*, 137, 195–6.

64 Burns, *The BBC*, 195.

65 BBC Written Archives Centre, T62/97/1 News and Current Affairs Policy Coverage General 1968–1976, Meeting minutes, 30 January 1970.

66 National Archives, PREM 161516 BBC, 'Financing the BBC – TV licence fee increases', Note of dinner hosted by Lord Aldington attended by Harold Wilson, R. T. Armstrong and Sir Michael Swann. Huw Wheldon, in addition to being one

of the most influential personalities in BBC television, was also the closest friend of the influential American neoconservative Norman Podhoretz. See Norman Podhoretz, 'On the death of a friend', *The Times*, 22 March 1986, 8.

67 BBC Written Archives Centre, R78/1,826/1, 'M. Swann (1973)', Note by the chairman on a lunch with Harold Wilson on March 20, written March 21. Cited in Freedman, *Television Policies of the Labour Party*, London: Frank Cass, 2003, 84–5.

2. The BBC and the Secret Service

1 *Radio Times*, 26 April 1935, 52.

2 National Archives, KV2/1385, Letter from Vernon Kell to Chief Constable Major Stanley Clarke, 27 October 1933.

3 *Radio Times*, 15 March 1935, 58.

4 Peter Stanford, *C Day-Lewis: A Life*, London: Continuum, 2007, 142.

5 National Archives, KV2/1385, MI5's 'Summary of contents' of letter from Cecil Day-Lewis to F. N. Roy, dated 3 May 1935.

6 *The Diaries of Captain Malcolm Duncan Kennedy, 1917–1946* (Thursday 1st November 1934), sheffield.ac.uk/library/libdocs/kennedy_diaries.pdf.

7 National Archives, KV4/121, Note by B. re liaison with Col. Dawnay of the BBC, 20 December 1933.

8 National Archives, KV4/121, Copy of note handed to D.S.S. for D.M.O. & I., 6 July 1934.

9 National Archives, KV4/121, Note by B. re liaison with Col. Dawnay of the BBC, 20 December 1933.

10 Paddy Scannell and David Cardiff, *A Social History of Broadcasting: Volume One, 1922–1939*, Oxford: Basil Blackwell, 1991, 290.

11 Quoted in Richard Overy and Peter Pagnamenta, *All Our Working Lives*, London: British Broadcasting Corporation, 1984, 216.

12 'Undelivered broadcast speech', *The Times*, 6 March 1934, 11.

13 National Archives, KV4/121, note re. interview with Col. Dawnay, 14 March 1934.

14 Ibid.

15 National Archives, KV4/121, note re. further interview, 23 March 1934.

16 National Archives, KV4/121, to Col. Dawnay, forwarding report, 16 October 1934.

17 National Archives, KV4/121, note to D.S.S. re. discussion with Col. Dawnay, 24 October 1934.

18 National Archives, KV4/121, note re. interview with Col. Dawnay, 14 March 1934.

19 National Archives, KV4/121, Extract from Admiralty file GW. 8334/1934, 16 October 1934.

20 'General Post at BBC', *Guardian*, 31 May 1935, 11.

21 Hilda Matheson, 'Changes at the BBC', *Observer*, 14 July 1935, 8.

22 National Archives, Arrangements made by DSS with Admiral Carpendale, 3 April 1935.

23 National Archives, KV4/121, note re. discussion with Col. Dawnay and Capt. Graves, 23 August 1935.

24 'Controller Of BBC Programmes Mr. Cecil Graves's New Post', *The Times*, 31 May 1935, 16.

25 National Archives KV4/121, note re. discussion with Col. Dawnay and Capt. Graves, 23 August 1935.

26 Ibid.

27 MI5 would for a period vet individuals appearing on BBC programmes – 'actors, speakers etc' – for a period during the Second World War. But the practice was soon discontinued and 'special arrangements' were made for the BBC to censor scripts and to supervise contributors. James Smith, *British Writers and MI5 Surveillance, 1930-1960*, Cambridge: Cambridge University Press, 2012, 91–2.

28 'Formalities – The Way Ahead', R.I. Stonham to Director of Personnel, 31 January 1983. Released by the BBC under the Freedom of Information Act.

29 'Vetting of BBC Staff', memo for Director of Personnel, 7 March 1985. Released by the BBC under the Freedom of Information Act. Unlike those holding counter-subversion posts, those holding access posts were subject to criminal records checks as well as political vetting. Up until August 1974, all individuals going through 'formalities' were subject to the same procedure, including a criminal records check. The development of the separate procedures and the 'Access List' itself stemmed from a decision by the Criminal Records Office in 1972 that it would only run criminal records checks for staff with access to

confidential information. Discussion paper for meeting on 18 May 1983 between Box 500/BBC representatives, 18 May 1983. Released by the BBC under the Freedom of Information Act.

30 'Vetting of BBC Staff' memo.

31 Discussion paper for meeting on 18 May 1983 between Box 500/BBC representatives, 18 May 1983. Released by the BBC under the Freedom of Information Act.

32 Report of a meeting held in Broadcasting House between representatives of the BBC and the Security Service on 18 May 1983 on 'Vetting for the British Broadcasting Corporation'. Released by the BBC under the Freedom of Information Act.

33 Christopher Andrew, *The Defence of the Realm: The Authorized History of MI5*, London: Allen Lane, 2009, 591.

34 'Formalities – The Way Ahead', Annex B, R.I. Stonham to Director of Personnel, 31 January 1983. Released by the BBC under the Freedom of Information Act.

35 Discussion paper for meeting on 18 May 1983 between Box 500/BBC representatives.

36 The freelance list was initially vetted every two years, but this was reduced to every four years in June 1980 after a cut in Special Duties staff. 'Formalities – The Way Ahead'.

37 'Counter-subversion post review', 5 January 1984. Released by the BBC under the Freedom of Information Act.

38 'Vetting for the British Broadcasting Corporation'.

39 'Formalities – The Way Ahead'.

40 Ibid.

41 'Vetting of BBC Staff' memo.

42 'Formalities – The Way Ahead'.

43 Quoted in 'History of Vetting', R. I. Stonham to Director of Personnel, 7 February 1984. Released by the BBC under the Freedom of Information Act.

44 Jean Seaton, *Pinkoes and Traitors: The BBC and the nation, 1974–1987*, Kindle edition, London: Profile, 2015.

45 'Formalities – Historical 1950-82', BBC News Formalities, Box 500, 21 March 1979, R154/9/1, quoted in Seaton, *Pinkoes and Traitors*.

46 Discussion paper for meeting on 18 May 1983 between Box 500/BBC representatives.

47 'Formalities – Historical 1950-82', BBC News Formalities, Record of a meeting between J.H. Arkell DSA and Sir Roger

Hollis, Box 500, 30 July 1959, R154/9/1, quoted in Seaton, *Pinkoes and Traitors*.

48 Andrew, *Defence of the Realm*.

49 Ibid., 397.

50 'Formalities – The Way Ahead'.

51 Discussion paper for meeting on 18 May 1983 between Box 500/BBC representatives.

52 'Formalities – The Way Ahead'.

53 Ibid.

54 'Counter-subversion vetting', Notes on Chairman/Vice Chairman Views, 12 April 1985. Released by the BBC under the Freedom of Information Act.

55 Notes of a meeting held in Broadcasting House, London on 18 May 1983 to discuss vetting of BBC staff.

56 Discussion paper for meeting on 18 May 1983 between Box 500/BBC representatives.

57 Notes of a meeting held in Broadcasting House, London on 18 May 1983 to discuss vetting of BBC staff.

58 'Formalities Review', Ronald Stonham to Director of Personnel, 14 October 1983. Released by the BBC under the Freedom of Information Act.

59 'Vetting of BBC Staff', memo.

60 'Counter-subversion post review', 5 January 1984. Released by the BBC under the Freedom of Information Act.

61 'Formalities – Defensive Brief', R. I. Stonham to Director of Personnel, 9 March 1983. Released by the BBC under the Freedom of Information Act.

62 Memo from Director of Administration, John Arkell, to Mr Berry, 1 March 1968, and attached brief on BBC Recruitment. Released by the BBC under the Freedom of Information Act.

63 David Leigh and Paul Lashmar, 'Revealed: How MI5 vets BBC staff', *Observer*, 18 August 1985, 1.

64 David Leigh, 'Secret spookery still under wraps', *British Journalism Review* 2:2, 2010, 39.

65 Leigh and Lashmar, 'Revealed: How MI5 vets BBC staff'.

66 'Newspaper Claims MI5 Security Service Has Veto Power Over BBC Hiring', Associated Press, 18 August 1985.

67 Ronnie Stonham to R. A. Harrington, 21 October 1985. Released by the BBC under the Freedom of Information Act; R. L. Stonham to R. A. Harrington, BBC Security Vetting

(Draft), no date. Released by the BBC under the Freedom of Information Act.

68   Draft letter from Christopher Martin to Judge Mason QC, 17 August 1988, and 'Appointment of Vetting Ombudsman/ Monitor Terms of Reference', 26 May 1988. Released by the BBC under the Freedom of Information Act.

69   'Appointment of Vetting Ombudsman/Monitor Terms of Reference'.

70   Notes of a meeting held in Broadcasting House, London on 18 May 1983 to discuss vetting of BBC staff.

71   Leigh, 'Secret spookery still under wraps'.

72   'Formalities – The Way Ahead'.

73   Chris Hastings, 'Revealed: how the BBC used MI5 to vet thousands of staff', *Daily Telegraph*, 2 July 2006.

74   'Formalities – Defensive Brief'.

75   Andrew, *The Defence of the Realm*, 397.

76   Quoted in 'History of Vetting'.

77   Discussion paper for meeting on 18 May 1983 between Box 500/BBC representatives.

78   Andrew, *Defence of the Realm*, Kindle edition

79   'Vetting: Current Position', A Paper by C. A. to D. Pers, 7 October 1985. Released by the BBC under the Freedom of Information Act.

80   Notes on a meeting on 19 November 1985 with Ronnie Stonham and Joan Reader. Released by the BBC under the Freedom of Information Act.

81   Joan Reader to P.O. Box 500, 29 October 1985. Released by the BBC under the Freedom of Information Act.

82   David Witherow to Ronnie Stonham, Bulgarian Section, 24 October 1985. Released by the BBC under the Freedom of Information Act.

83   Hugh Greene, *The Third Floor Front: A View of Broadcasting in the Sixties*, London: Bodley Head, 1969, 123.

84   Stephen Dorril, *MI6: Inside the Covert World of Her Majesty's Secret Intelligence Service*, New York: Simon & Schuster, 2000, 624.

85   Cited in Scott Lucas, 'COLD WAR: The British Ministry of Propaganda', *Independent*, 26 February 1995.

86   Director of Operations, Secret, Director No.16, 'Propaganda Policy and Organisation', cited in Leon Comber, *Malaya's Secret*

Police 1945-60: The Role of the Special Branch in the Malayan Emergency, Singapore: Institute of Southeast Asian Studies, 2008, 158.

87 Paul Lashmar and James Oliver, *Britain's Secret Propaganda War*, Stroud: Sutton Publishing, 1998, 58.

88 Simon M. W. Collier, 'Countering Communist and Nasserite Propaganda: the Foreign Office Information Research Department in the Middle East and Africa, 1954–1963', PhD thesis, University of Hertfordshire, 2013, 167.

89 Alban Webb, 'Auntie Goes to War Again', *Media History* 12:2, 2006, 127.

90 Lashmar and Oliver, *Britain's Secret Propaganda War*, 62.

91 Ibid., 61.

92 Webb, 'Auntie Goes to War Again', 123.

93 Lashmar and Oliver, *Britain's Secret Propaganda War*, 58–9; John Jenks, *British Propaganda and News Media in the Cold War*, Edinburgh: Edinburgh University Press, 2006, 83.

94 Collier, 'Countering Communist and Nasserite Propaganda', 211.

95 WAC, R34/399, 'News Items from the FO', Memorandum from DES to NENE, 1 April 1947, quoted in Webb, 'Auntie Goes to War Again', 124.

96 Collier, 'Countering Communist and Nasserite Propaganda', 13, 38, 245.

97 Mark Leonard, Catherine Stead and Conrad Smewing, *Public Diplomacy*, The Foreign Policy Centre, 2002, 34.

98 Frank Gardner, *Blood and Sand*, 10th anniversary edition, London: Bantam Press, 2014, 292–3.

99 Alan Travis, 'Revealed: Britain's secret propaganda war against al-Qaida', *Guardian*, 26 August 2008.

100 Oliver Luft, 'Al-Qaida row: BBC admits security correspondent met anti-terror officials', *Guardian*, 28 August 2008.

101 Emma Briant, *Propaganda and Counter-terrorism: Strategies for Global Change*, Manchester: Manchester University Press, 2014, 113.

102 BBC, BBC Monitoring Scheme, March 2013, downloads. bbc.co.uk/bbctrust/assets/files/pdf/regulatory_framework/ protocols/2013/bbc_monitoring_scheme.pdf.

103 House of Commons Foreign Affairs Committee, *The future of*

the BBC World Service. Ninth Report of Session 2013–14, HC 1045, HMSO, para.19.

104 Rajesh Mirchandani and Abdullahi Tasiu Abubakar, Britain's International Broadcasting, Los Angeles: Figueroa Press, 2014, 17.

105 HM Government, National Security Strategy and Strategic Defence and Security Review 2015: A Secure and Prosperous United Kingdom, Cm 9161, November 2015, HMSO, paras. 5.17 and 1.3.

106 BBC press release, 'Statement on newly announced Government funding of the World Service', 23 November 2015, bbc. co.uk.

3. When Auntie Goes to War

1 Kamal Ahmed, 'MI6 chief briefed BBC over Iraq arms fears', Observer, 6 July 2003.

2 Kenneth Bloomfield, The BBC at the Watershed, Liverpool: Liverpool University Press, 2008, 140–1.

3 Greg Dyke, Inside Story, London: HarperCollins, 2004.

4 'BBC statements in full', BBC News Online, 29 January 2004, bbc.co.uk.

5 The Pollard Review, 18 December 2012, para. 65, 60, downloads.bbc.co.uk/bbctrust/assets/files/pdf/our_work/pollard_review/pollard_review.pdf.

6 The Pollard Review Transcripts, Stephen Mitchell (Part 1), 19 November 2012, 26–28, downloads.bbc.co.uk/aboutthebbc/insidethebbc/howwework/reports/pdf/pollard/stephen_mitchell_1.pdf.

7 The Pollard Review, para.57.

8 Ian Burrell, 'Hutton Inquiry: Alistair Campbell, Andrew Gilligan and Greg Dyke look back 10 years on', Independent, 27 April 2013.

9 Steven Barnett, The Rise and Fall of Television Journalism: Just Wires and Lights in a Box?, London and New York: Bloomsbury, 2011, 171, 177, 179–181.

10 Review of Intelligence on Weapons of Mass Destruction, Report of a Committee of Privy Counsellors, HC 898 London: HMSO, 2004, para. 331.

11 Report of the Inquiry into the Circumstances Surrounding the

Death of Dr David Kelly, HC 247, London: HMSO, 2004, para. 177.

12 Richard Norton-Taylor, 'An unguided missile: MI6's view of Alastair Campbell is revealed', *Guardian*, 14 July 2011.

13 Tony Currie, *The Radio Times Story*, Tiverston: Kelly Publications, 2001, 42.

14 James Curran and Jean Seaton, *Power Without Responsibility: Press, Broadcasting and the Internet in Britain*, seventh edition, Abingdon and New York: Routledge, 2010, 118.

15 Paddy Scannell, 'The BBC and foreign affairs: 1935–1939', *Media Culture & Society* 6, 1984, 16.

16 Ibid.

17 Nick Robinson, *Live From Downing Street: The Inside Story of Politics, Power and the Media*, London: Transworld, 2012, 79.

18 Scannell, 'The BBC and foreign affairs', 6, 7.

19 BBC Written Archives Centre, R34/44, 9 March 1937. Quoted in W. J. West, *Truth Betrayed*, London: Duckworth, 1987, 39–40.

20 Philip M. Taylor, *Munitions of the Mind: A History of Propaganda*, Manchester: Manchester University Press, 2003, 199. Seaton concurs that the BBC was 'almost certainly the most important instrument of domestic propaganda'. Curran and Seaton, *Power Without Responsibility*, 120.

21 Taylor, *Munitions of the mind*, 191.

22 Curran and Seaton, *Power Without Responsibility*, 134.

23 Taylor, *Munitions of the mind*, 191.

24 The BBC Archive, Record of Conversation with Sir John Reith, 23 February 1940, bbc.co.uk/archive/hawhaw/8921.shtml?page=txt.

25 National Archives CAB 67/6/38, Memorandum from Duff Cooper, 24 May 1940.

26 Taylor, *Munitions of the mind*, 199.

27 National Archives CAB 67/6/38, Memorandum from Duff Cooper.

28 James Smith, *British Writers and MI5 Surveillance, 1930–1960*, Cambridge: Cambridge University Press, 2013, 92.

29 Record of interview at the Ministry of Information, 12 August 1940, BBC WAC R49/106/2. Quoted in Robert Mackay, '"No place in the Corporation's service": the BBC and conscientious objectors in the Second World War', *Media History* 12:1, 2006, 43.

30 Gerard Mansell, *Let the truth be told: 50 years of the BBC external broadcasting*, London: Weidenfeld and Nicolson, 1982, 69.

31 National Archives CAB 66/14/21, Memorandum from Kingsley Wood.

32 Taylor, *Munitions of the mind*, 201.

33 Curran and Seaton, *Power Without Responsibility*, 140.

34 Siân Nicholas, 'War Report (BBC 1944–5) and the Birth of the BBC War Correspondent', in *War and the Media: Reportage and Propaganda, 1900–2003*, Mark Connelly and David Welch (eds), London: I. B. Tauris, 2005, 139–61, 145.

35 Ibid., 146–7.

36 Curran and Seaton, *Power Without Responsibility*, 123.

37 Siân Nicholas, 'The People's Radio: The BBC and its Audience, 1939–1945', in *Millions Like Us: British Culture in the Second World War*, Jeff Hayes and Nick Hill (eds), Liverpool: Liverpool University Press, 1999, 63.

38 Michael Balfour, *Propaganda in War, 1939–1945*, London: Routledge and Kegan Paul, 1979; Ian McLaine, *Ministry of Morale*, London: Allen and Unwin, 1979; Siân Nicholas, *The Echo of War: Home Front Propaganda and the Wartime BBC*, Manchester: Manchester University Press, 1996.

39 Siân Nicholas, '"Brushing up your empire": Dominion and colonial propaganda on the BBC's home services 1939–45', *The Journal of Imperial and Commonwealth History* 31:2, 2003, 208.

40 James Curran, *Media and Power*, London: Routledge, 2002, 5. The media historian Andrew Crisell, for example, writes that while the BBC's 'political broadcasting grew more incisive' with the arrival of ITV in 1955, it was the 'Suez crisis of 1956 which marked the beginning of the end of the old relationship between politicians and broadcasters'. Andrew Crisell, *An Introductory History of British Broadcasting*, second edition, London: Routledge, 2002, 177.

41 Tory MPs complained of anti-government bias at the BBC and called for a Commons debate, 'BBC Charter – Political Balance', on 14 November 1956. Tony Shaw, *Eden, Suez, and the Mass Media: Propaganda and Persuasion During the Suez Crisis*, London: I. B. Tauris, 1996, 148.

42 Tony Shaw, 'Eden and the BBC During the 1956 Suez Crisis:

A Myth Re-examined', *Twentieth Century British History* 6:3, 1995, 341.

43   Ibid. 325 and Shaw, *Eden, Suez, and the Mass Media*, 118.

44   Shaw, 'Eden and the BBC During the 1956 Suez Crisis', 339, 340.

45   Ibid., 342.

46   Ibid., 324.

47   Ibid., 321, 323.

48   Tony Shaw, 'Cadogan's Last Fling: Sir Alexander Cadogan, Chairman of the Board of Governors of the BBC', in *Whitehall and the Suez Crisis*, Anthony Gorst and Saul Kelly (eds), Abingdon and New York: Frank Cass, 2000, 135.

49   Asa Briggs, *The History of Broadcasting in the United Kingdom: Volume V: Competition*, Oxford: Oxford University Press, 2005, 85–6.

50   Shaw, 'Eden and the BBC During the 1956 Suez Crisis', 327.

51   Ibid., 328.

52   Ibid., 332.

53   Ibid., 328.

54   Shaw, *Eden, Suez, and the Mass Media*, 121.

55   Ibid., 119, 127, 130.

56   Shaw, 'Cadogan's Last Fling', 138.

57   Shaw, 'Eden and the BBC During the 1956 Suez Crisis', 336.

58   Steven Barnett, for example, concludes of the whole episode that 'the ethos of independent journalism [which] had become more internalized amongst the BBC hierarchy' won the day. Barnett, *The Rise and Fall of Television Journalism*, 40.

59   Briggs, *The History of Broadcasting in the United Kingdom: Volume V*, 97.

60   Shaw, 'Cadogan's Last Fling', 139–140.

61   Briggs, *The History of Broadcasting in the United Kingdom: Volume V*, 85.

62   Anthony Adamthwaite, 'Nation shall speak peace unto nation: The BBC's response to peace and defence issues, 1945–58', *Contemporary British History* 7:3, 1993, 557.

63   BBC Written Archives Caversham, R34/997, cited in Peter Goodwin, 'Low Conspiracy? – Government interference in the BBC', *Westminster Papers in Communication and Culture* 2:1, 2005, 101.

64   Ibid., 104.

65   Ibid., 105.

66 National Archives DEFE 13/71, cited in Goodwin, 'Low Conspiracy?', 105.

67 BBC Written Archives Caversham, R34/997 Jacob, 28/2/55, cited in Goodwin, 'Low Conspiracy?', 106.

68 National Archives, PREM 11/1089A, cited in Goodwin, 'Low Conspiracy?', 112.

69 BBC Written Archives Caversham, T16/679/1 Normanbrook, 27/9/65, cited in Goodwin, 'Low Conspiracy?', 115.

70 BBC Written Archives Caversham, T16/679/1, cited in Goodwin, 'Low Conspiracy?', 115.

71 John Cook, 'The War Game: how I showed that BBC bowed to government over nuclear attack film', 2 June 2015, theconversation.com.

72 Quoted in Mike Wayne, 'Failing the Public: The BBC, The War Game and Revisionist History: A Reply to James Chapman', *Journal of Contemporary History* 42:4, 2007, 627.

73 Gordon Corera, 'Secret service pressed BBC to censor Panorama-papers', BBC News, 30 December 2011, bbc.co.uk; National Archives, PREM/19/587.

74 News and Current Affairs meeting, 11 May 1982, quoted in Glasgow University Media Group, *War and Peace News*, Milton Keynes: Open University Press, 1985, 14.

75 Ibid., 16. For other analyses of television reporting of armed conflict, see Greg Philo and Greg McLaughlin, *The British Media and the Gulf War*, Glasgow: Glasgow University Media Group, 1993; Greg Philo and Mike Berry, *Bad News from Israel*, London: Pluto Press, 2004; and Greg Philo and Mike Berry, *More Bad News from Israel*, London: Pluto Press, 2011.

76 Ibid., 200, 202–5, 211–12, 270, 274.

77 Email from Kevin Marsh to Stephen Mitchell, 27 June 2003, news.bbc.co.uk/1/hi/uk_politics/3147091.stm

78 Barnett, *The Rise and Fall of Television Journalism*, 174.

79 Richard Sambrook, evidence to the Hutton Inquiry, 13 August 2003, hutton.softblade.com/transcripts.php?action=transcript &session=7&witness=9.

80 BBC News, Letter from Mark Laity to Richard Sambrook, Director of BBC News, 21 August 2003, bbc.co.uk/pressoffice/ pressreleases/stories/2003/08_august/21/laity_correspondence. shtml.

81 Daniel C. Hallin, *The Uncensored War: The Media and Vietnam*, Oxford: Oxford University Press, 1986; Lance Bennett, 'Toward a Theory of Press–State Relations in the United States,' *Journal of Communication* 40:2, 1990, 103–25; Jonathan Mermin, 'Television news and American intervention in Somalia: The myth of a media-driven foreign policy', *Political Science Quarterly* 112:3, 1997, 385–403; John Zaller and Dennis Chiu, 'Government's Little Helper: US Press Coverage of Foreign Policy Crises, 1945–1991', *Political Communication* 13:4, 1996, 385–405.

82 David McQueen, 'BBC's Panorama, war coverage and the "Westminster consensus"', *Westminster Papers in Culture and Communication* 5:3, 2008, 47–68. See also David McQueen, 'BBC TV's Panorama, conflict coverage and the "Westminster consensus"', PhD dissertation, Bournemouth University, 2010.

83 Cited in Justin Lewis, 'Television, Public Opinion and the War in Iraq: The Case of Britain', *International Journal of Public Opinion Research* 16:3, 2004, 295–310.

84 Justin Lewis et al, *Shoot First and Ask Questions Later: Media Coverage of the 2003 Iraq War*, New York: Peter Lang, 2006, 125–6.

85 Justin Lewis, 'Biased Broadcasting Corporation', *Guardian*, 4 July 2003, 27.

86 Quoted in Bloomfield, *The BBC at the Watershed*, 144.

87 Ibid., 134

88 Quoted in Ian Sinclair, *The March that Shook Blair: An Oral History of 15 February 2003*, London: Peace News, 2013, 156.

89 Ibid., 155–64.

90 Ibid., 160–1.

91 Ibid., 157–8.

92 Letter from Tony Blair to Greg Dyke, 19 March 2003. Quoted in Dyke, *Inside Story*, 253.

93 Gavyn Davies, 'These threats to the BBC are serious and sinister', *Daily Telegraph*, 23 July 2003.

94 Letter from Richard Sambrook to Alastair Campbell, 28 June 2003, telegraph.co.uk.

95 Dyke, *Inside Story*, 256.

96 Greg Dyke, letter to Tony Blair, 21 March 2003, news.bbc.co.uk.

97 Email from Richard Sambrook to News Editorial-Board-Editors Cc: Stephen Whittle-and-Chris; Mark Damazer; Mark Byford & PA, 6 February 2003, spinwatch.org/index.php/issues/more/item/16-dissent-under-pressure-on-the-bbc.
98 Dyke, letter to Tony Blair, 21 March 2003.
99 Letter from Sambrook to Campbell, 28 June 2003.
100 Kamal Ahmed, 'Dyke: Blair's world of "lies and bullying"', *Observer*, 29 August 2004.
101 Email from Kevin Marsh to Stephen Mitchell, 27 June 2003, news.bbc.co.uk.
102 Curran and Seaton, *Power Without Responsibility*, 383.
103 Tony Blair, *A Journey*, London: Arrow Books, 2011, 461.
104 Bloomfield, *The BBC at the Watershed*, 156.
105 Quoted in ibid., 145–6.
106 Gavyn Davies, 'These threats to the BBC are serious and sinister', *Daily Telegraph*, 23 July 2003.

4. Politics, Power and Political Bias

1 Jack Seale, 'Robert Peston: there's no left-wing bias at the BBC', *Radio Times*, 24 June 2014, radiotimes.com.
2 Peter Ayton and Howard Tumber, 'The rise and fall of perceived bias at the BBC', *Intermedia* 29:4, 2001.
3 Ibid.
4 'Broadcasting and Politics: Sir J. Right on BBC Policy', *The Times*, 2 March 1933, 9.
5 Ibid.
6 'Impartiality Of The B.B.C.', *The Times*, 16 March 1937, 16.
7 Quoted in Ayton and Tumber, 'The rise and fall of perceived bias at the BBC'.
8 Ibid.
9 Michael Cockerell, *Live from Number 10: The Inside Story of Prime Ministers and Television*, London: Faber and Faber, 1988, 7.
10 Martin Durham, *Sex and Politics: The Family and Morality in the Thatcher Years*, Macmillan, 1991, 9.
11 Stuart Hall, Chas Critcher, Tony Jefferson, John Clarke and Brian Roberts, *Policing the Crisis: Mugging, the State and Law and Order*, London: Palgrave Macmillan, 1978, 247.
12 Amy C. Whipple, 'Speaking for Whom? The 1971 Festival of

Light and the Search for the "Silent Majority"', *Contemporary British History* 24:3, 2010, 327.

13   Durham, *Sex and Politics*, 94–5.

14   Ibid., 95–6.

15   Mary Whitehouse, *Whatever Happened to Sex?*, Hove: Wayland, 1977, 17.

16   Keith Joseph, 'Our human stock is threatened', speech at Edgbaston, 19 October 1974, margaretthatcher.org.

17   Douglas Hurd, *Memoirs*, London: Little, Brown, 2003, 332.

18   Margaret Thatcher, 'Keith Joseph Memorial Lecture. Liberty and Limited Government', 11 January 1996, margaretthatcher.org.

19   Marmaduke Hussey, *Chance Governs All*, London: Macmillan, 2001, 208.

20   Preface by Norman Tebbit in Sir Alfred Sherman, *Paradoxes of Power – Reflections on the Thatcher Interlude*, Exeter: Imprint Academic, 2005, 8.

21   Margaret Thatcher, *The Downing Street Years*, London: HarperCollins, 1993, 634.

22   John Campbell, *Margaret Thatcher Volume Two: The Iron Lady*, London: Vintage, 2008, 401.

23   Paul Johnson, 'Not Everyone Likes Redheads', *The Spectator*, 3 March 1990, 26.

24   Norman Tebbit, 'The BBC doesn't invent lies against the Government', *Independent*, 30 June 2003.

25   The BBC Story – The Libyan Bombing 1986, bbc.co.uk/history ofthebbc/resources/pressure/libyan.shtml.

26   Cited in Alasdair Milne, *DG: The Memoirs of a British Broadcaster*, London: Hodder and Stoughton, 1989, 253.

27   Cited in ibid., 252. For a critical assessment of Tebbit's dossier see Greg Philo, *Seeing and Believing: The Influence of Television*, London and New York: Routledge, 1990, 205.

28   Norman Tebbit, *Upwardly Mobile*, London: Weidenfeld & Nicolson, 1988, 249.

29   Tebbit, 'The BBC doesn't invent lies against the Government'.

30   Woodrow Wyatt, *The Journals of Woodrow Wyatt, Volume One*, Sarah Curtis (ed.), London: Macmillan, 1998, 79.

31   HC Hansard, Volume No. 478, Part No. 118, 25 June 2008: Column 82WH.

32   Wyatt, Sarah Curtis (ed.), *The Journals of Woodrow Wyatt, Volume Two*, London: Macmillan, 1999, 492.

33 Wyatt, *The Journals of Woodrow Wyatt*, Volume One, 146.
34 'Pedigree of a TV Watchdog', *Daily Telegraph*, 20 November 1986.
35 Quoted in Greg Philo, 'Television, politics and the rise of the New Right', in *The Glasgow Media Group Reader, Vol. II: Industry, Economy, War and Politics*, Oxon, Abingdon: Routledge, 1995, 202.
36 Godfrey Hodgson, 'The BBC and the Politicians', *Observer*, 13 December 1987.
37 Cockerell, *Live from Number 10*.
38 Ian Gilmour, *Dancing with Dogma: Britain Under Thatcherism*, London: Simon & Schuster, 1992, 253.
39 Ibid., 254.
40 Julian Lewis, 'Monitoring Works', *Daily Telegraph*, 3 July 1999.
41 Colin Seymour-Ure, *The British Press and Broadcasting Since 1945*, Oxford: Blackwell, 1991, 196–7.
42 James Curran and Colin Leys, 'Media and the Decline of Liberal Corporatism in Britain', *De-Westernizing Media Studies*, in James Curran and Myung-Jin Park (eds), London: Routledge, 2000, 205.
43 Ayton and Tumber, 'The rise and fall of perceived bias at the BBC'. See also Steven Barnett, 'TV: The political bias?', *British Journalism Review* 1, 1990, 63–7.
44 Quoted in Louise Jury, 'BBC row: Elite's favourite show takes the flak from politicians', *Independent*, 13 December 1997.
45 Gilmour, *Dancing with Dogma*, 252.
46 Kevin Marsh, 'Is the BBC really left wing?', *Independent*, 13 July 2004, 8.
47 Wyatt, *The Journals of Woodrow Wyatt*, Volume Two, 252, 258.
48 Charles Moore, 'Time to watch the BBC bias that costs each of us £116 a year', *Daily Telegraph*, 9 September 2003.
49 Minotaur Media Tracking Ltd, Annual Returns made up to 8 July 2005; 'Former TV-am boss dies', BBC News Online, 8 September, 2000, bbc.co.uk.
50 Kathy Gyngell, 'Mrs Thatcher, the woman I met and got to know and like', Centre for Policy Studies, blogpost, 8 April 2013, cps.org.uk.
51 Campbell, *Margaret Thatcher Volume Two*, 572.
52 Robin Aitken, *Can We Trust the BBC?*, London: Continuum, 2007, 209n.19.

53 Morrison Media Consultants, 'BBC Governors' inquiry into the impartiality and accessibility of BBC coverage of the EU, Content Analysis', January 2005, 21.

54 Ibid., 23, 26.

55 *Independent Panel Report – BBC News coverage of the European Union*, January 2005, 3, downloads.bbc.co.uk./bbc trust/assets/files/pdf/our_work/govs/independentpanelreport. pdf.

56 'The European Union – Perceptions of the BBC's Reporting: Management's Response', March 2005, 5, downloads.bbc. co.uk/bbctrust/assets/files/pdf/our_work/govs/eu_management_response.pdf.

57 Peter Oborne and Frances Weaver, *Guilty Men*, London: Centre for Policy Studies, 2011, 58, 26, fn.58.

58 Ibid., 27.

59 Ibid.

60 Ibid., 28–9, fn.60.

61 Michael Buerk, 'Books: Blowing the BBC's Gaff', *Standpoint*, April 2011.

62 John Bridcut, *From Seesaw to Wagon Wheel: Safeguarding Impartiality in the 21st Century*, BBC Trust, Appendix D 'Impartiality: Fact or Fiction – Friday 22nd September 2006 Seminar Agenda and Transcript', http://downloads. bbc.co.uk/bbctrust/assets/files/pdf/review_report_research/ impartiality_21century/d_seminar_transcript.pdf.

63 Aitken, *Can We Trust the BBC?*, 60–1.

64 David Keighley and Andrew Jubb, *Impartiality at the BBC? An investigation into the background and claims of Stuart Prebble's 'Independent Assessment for the BBC Trust'*, Civitas: Institute for the Study of Civil Society, 2014, 2–3.

65 Bridcut, *From Seesaw to Wagon Wheel*.

66 BBC Freedom of Information Request – RFI20110825, 11 August 2011, downloads.bbc.co.uk/foi/classes/disclosure_logs/ rfi20110825_staff_age_disability_ethnicity_30062011.pdf.

67 BBC, Data Tables for 2014/15 Equality Report, downloads.bbc. co.uk/diversity/pdf/appendix-data-tables.pdf.

68 Ibid.

69 *The Educational Backgrounds of Leading Journalists*, London: Sutton Trust, 2006; *Elitist Britain*, London: Social Mobility and Child Poverty Commission, 2014.

70 Oborne and Weaver, *Guilty Men*, 1.

71 Ibid., 38, 31.

72 Mike Berry et al., 'The controversial business of researching BBC impartiality', theconversation.com, 9 May 2014.

73 Mike Berry, 'How biased is the BBC?', theconversation.com, 23 August 2013.

74 Karin Wahl-Jorgensen et al., *BBC Breadth of Opinion Review: Content Analysis*, Cardiff: University of Cardiff School of Journalism, Media and Cultural Studies, 2013, 5.

75 Berry, 'How biased is the BBC?'

76 Wahl-Jorgensen et al., *BBC Breadth of Opinion Review* 64.

77 Berry et al, 'The controversial business of researching BBC impartiality'.

78 Wahl-Jorgensen et al., 11, 48–9.

79 Ibid., 53, 63, 64.

80 'Can Democracy Work', Episode 1, BBC Radio 4, 13 Jan 2015.

81 Hugh Muir, 'There are people that not even a president should cross. Mel is one of them', *Guardian*, 26 February 2009, 31.

82 Nick Robinson, *Live From Downing Street: The Inside Story of Politics, Power and the Media*, London: Transworld, 2012, 21.

83 Paul Donovan, *All Our Todays: Forty Years of the Today Programme*, London: Jonathan Cape, 1997, 100.

84 Brian Wheeler, 'Dyke in BBC "conspiracy" claim', BBC News Online, 20 September 2009, bbc.co.uk.

85 David McQueen, interview with Greg Dyke, 16 October 2009.

86 Andrew Marr, *My Trade: A Short History of British Journalism*, London: Macmillan, 2004, 184.

87 John Birt, *The Harder Path: The Autobiography*, London: Time Warner, 2002, 303.

88 Georgina Born, *Uncertain Vision: Birt, Dyke and the Reinvention of the BBC*, London: Random House, 2004, 394–396.

89 John Arlidge, 'BBC fears "hacking" by Labour insiders', *Observer*, 4 April 1999, theguardian.com.

5. The Making of a Neoliberal Bureaucracy

1 *The Age of Uncertainty*, Episode 9: 'The Big Corporation', broadcast BBC Two, 7 March 1977.

2 Dick Gilling, 'Adrian Malone obituary', *Guardian*, 8 April 2015.

3 Ibid.
4 Churchill Archive Centre: Thatcher MSS (2/1/1/37), Letter from Keith Joseph to Willie Whitelaw, 17 March 1976.
5 Churchill Archive Centre: Thatcher MSS (2/1/1/37), Letter from Keith Joseph to Willie Whitelaw, 10 September 1976.
6 Churchill Archive Centre: Thatcher MSS (2/1/3/9), Letter from Geoffrey Howe to Keith Joseph, 22 March 1976.
7 Churchill Archive Centre: Thatcher MSS (2/1/1/37), Letter from Geoffrey Howe to Keith Joseph, 10 September 1976.
8 John Kenneth Galbraith, *A Life in Our Times,* Boston: Houghton Mifflin, 1981, 533-4.
9 Friedman gave two lectures in London at the invitation of the Institute of Economic Affairs, on 31 August and 1 September 1976, which were published as an IEA occasional paper, Milton Friedman, *From Galbraith to Economic Freedom*, London: Institute of Economic Affairs, 1977.
10 Letter from Keith Joseph to Willie Whitelaw, 10 September 1976.
11 Charles Lichenstein, 27 July 1976, box 149, folder 5, Friedman Papers. Quoted in Angus Burgin, 'Age of Certainty: Galbraith, Friedman, and the Public Life of Economic Ideas', *History of Political Economy* 45:1, 2013, 208.
12 Burgin, 'Age of Certainty', 208-9.
13 Rose D. Friedman, *Two Lucky People: Memoirs*, Chicago: University of Chicago Press, 1999, 475.
14 Antony Jay, *How to save the BBC*, London: Centre for Policy Studies, 2008, 9.
15 In 1972 Jay wrote a pamphlet called *The Householder's Guide to Community Defence against Bureaucratic Aggression* calling on citizens to protest against government planning decisions. *The Times*, 7 September 1972, 9.
16 Friedman, *Two Lucky People: Memoirs*, 476.
17 Ibid., 475.
18 Burgin, 'Age of Certainty', 209-210; Christ Church College, Oxford: Lawson MSS, Lawson 1 (1980), Lawson minute to Margaret Thatcher, 22 February 1980.
19 The title of each segment and the date of its broadcast were as follows: *Free to Choose:1: Power of the Markets* (16 February 1980); *Free to Choose:2: The Tyranny of Control* (23 February 1980); *Free to Choose:3: Anatomy of Crisis* (1 March

1980); *Free to Choose:4: Created Equal* (8 March 1980); *Free to Choose:5: Who Protects the Consumer?* (15 March 1980); *Free to Choose:6: How to Cure Inflation* (22 March 1980). All but *The Power of the Market* were broadcast with discussions hosted by Jay.

20   Thatcher MSS (Churchill Archive Centre): THCR 3/2/22 (45), Margaret Thatcher letter to Milton Friedman, 17 March 1980.

21   The share of national income taken by the rich in Britain had declined to an historic low. But this trend was about to be dramatically reversed. Anthony B. Atkinson, 'The Distribution of Top Incomes in the United Kingdom 1908–2000', in *Top Incomes over the Twentieth Century. A Contrast Between Continental European and English-Speaking Countries*, Anthony B. Atkinson and Thomas Piketty (eds), Oxford: Oxford University Press, 2007, 82–140. For a discussion, see Danny Dorling, 'Fairness and the Changing Fortunes of People in Britain', *Journal of the Royal Statistical Society: Series A (Statistics in Society)* 176:1, 2013, 97–118.

22   Ian Trethowan, *Split Screen*, London: Hamish Hamilton, 1984, 180–1.

23   BBC Written Archives Centre, R1/46/4 BOARD OF GOVERNORS MINUTES 1979, Minutes of Board Meeting held on 13 September 1979.

24   Michael Leapman, *The Last Days of the Beeb*, London: Coronet, 1987, 230.

25   Tom O'Malley, *Closedown? The BBC and Government Broadcasting Policy 1979–92*, London: Pluto Press, 1994, 80.

26   Margaret Thatcher, *The Downing Street Years*, London: HarperCollins, 1993, 634.

27   William Whitelaw, *The Whitelaw memoirs*, London: Aurum, 1989, 263.

28   Ibid., 264.

29   O'Malley, *Closedown?*, 171.

30   Ilde Rizzo and Ruth Towse, 'In memoriam Alan Peacock: a pioneer in cultural economics', *Journal of Cultural Economics* 39:3, 2015, 225–238.

31   Andy Beckett, *When the Lights Went Out: Britain in the Seventies*, London: Faber and Faber, 2009, 338.

32   Alan Peacock, *Report of the Committee on the Financing of the BBC*, London: HMSO, 1986, Cmnd. 9824, para.592.

33 Lisa O'Carroll, 'The truth behind Real Lives', *Guardian*, 12 December 2005.

34 Minutes of a Special Meeting of the Board of Governors to discuss 'Real Lives: At the Edge of the Union', 30 July 1985. Obtained by the *Guardian* under the Freedom of Information Act and available at image.guardian.co.uk/sys-files/Media/documents/2005/12/12/July30Bog1.pdf.

35 Home Secretary Leon Brittan, letter to BBC Chairman Stuart Young, 29 July 1985. Obtained by the *Guardian* under the Freedom of Information Act and available at image.guardian.co.uk/sys-files/Media/documents/2005/12/12/July29A.pdf.

36 BBC Chairman Stuart Young, letter to Home Secretary Leon Brittan, 30 July 1985. Obtained by the *Guardian* under the Freedom of Information Act and available at image.guardian.co.uk/sys-files/Media/documents/2005/12/12/July30A.pdf.

37 Minutes of a Special Meeting of the Board of Governors, 30 July 1985.

38 BOG minutes (special) August 6 1985. Obtained by the *Guardian* under the Freedom of Information Act and available at image.guardian.co.uk/sys-files/Media/documents/2005/12/12/Aug6BogA.pdf.

39 Steven Barnett, *The Rise and Fall of Television Journalism: Just Wires and Lights in a Box?*, London and New York: Bloomsbury, 2011, 99–100.

40 Jean Seaton, *Pinkoes and Traitors: The BBC and the Nation, 1974–1987*, Kindle edition, London: Profile, 2015. Similarly, Hussey writes that his predecessor Stuart Young 'had decided once or even twice that Alasdair Milne should go'. Marmaduke Hussey, *Chance Governs All: A Memoir*, London: Macmillan, 2001, 213.

41 Norman Tebbit, *Upwardly Mobile*, London: Weidenfeld and Nicolson, 1988, 196.

42 Woodrow Wyatt and Sarah Curtis (ed.), *The Journals of Woodrow Wyatt: Vol 1*, London: Pan Books, 1999, 191–193.

43 Hussey, *Chance Governs All*, 210.

44 Simon Jenkins, 'Bias and The Beeb – Does the charge stick?', *Sunday Times*, 5 October 1986.

45 Hussey, *Chance Governs All*, 208.

46 Kim Sengupta, 'The Hamilton Affair: The cost – Right-wing donors united by their loathing of Fayed', *Independent*, 22

December 1999, independent.co.uk.

47 Hussey, *Chance Governs All*, 214.

48 Alasdair Milne, *DG: The Memoirs of a British Broadcaster*, London: Hodder and Stoughton, 1988, 267.

49 Ken Bloomfield, *The BBC at the Watershed*, Liverpool: Liverpool University Press, 2008, 44.

50 Milne, *DG: The Memoirs of a British Broadcaster*, 268.

51 Seaton, *Pinkoes and Traitors*.

52 At the time of Milne's appointment as director general, Winchester, along with Eton, supplied not only the top leadership of the BBC (BBC Chair George Howard was an Old Etonian), but also the editor of *The Times*, the chairs of all the leading banks and the heads of the Foreign and Home Office; Anthony Sampson, *The Changing Anatomy of Britain*, Hodder and Stoughton, 1981, 127, cited in Patrick Joyce, *The State of Freedom: A Social History of the British State Since 1800*, Cambridge: Cambridge University Press, 2013, 308–9.

53 Milne, *DG: The Memoirs of a British Broadcaster*, 141.

54 David Hendy, *Life on Air: A History of Radio Four*, Oxford: Oxford University Press, 2007, 284.

55 Curran and Seaton, *Power Without Responsibility*, 209, 217.

56 Hussey, *Chance Governs All*, 218.

57 Ibid.

58 Ibid.,149.

59 John Birt, *The Harder Path: The Autobiography*, London: Time Warner, 2002, 149.

60 Ibid., 152.

61 Ibid., 149.

62 Beckett, *When the Lights Went Out*, 275.

63 Birt, *Harder Path*, 155.

64 Ibid., 244.

65 John Birt, 'Broadcasting's journalistic bias is not a matter of politics but of presentation', *The Times*, 28 February 1975, 14.

66 John Birt and Peter Jay, 'Why television news is in danger of becoming an anti-social force', *The Times*, 3 September 1976, 6.

67 Birt, *Harder Path*, 261.

68 Ibid., 281.

69 Interview with James Long, 28 May 2014.

70 Birt, *Harder Path*, 278, 291.

71 Ibid., 263.

72 Ibid., 292–3.
73 Churchill Archives Centre, The Papers of Peter Jay, PJAY 4/6/9. Letter from Liz Horgan to Peter Jay, 29 December 1987.
74 Georgina Born, *Uncertain Vision: Birt, Dyke and the Reinvention of the BBC*, London: Random House, 2004, 387.
75 Birt, *Harder Path*, 264–5.
76 Ibid., 278.
77 Ibid., 303.
78 Interview with former BBC Producer, date withheld.
79 Rachid Errtibi, 'Closure of the White City building', About the BBC Blog, 28 March 2013, bbc.co.uk.
80 Greg Dyke, *Greg Dyke: Inside Story*, London: HarperCollins, 2004, 211.
81 Curran and Seaton, *Power Without Responsibility*, 215.
82 Ibid., 310.
83 Ibid., 312–3.
84 Ibid., 215.
85 BBC Written Archives Centre, R162/45/1. Implementation of Producer Choice.
86 Birt, *Harder Path*, 320.
87 BBC Written Archives Centre, T62-358-1, Producer Choice – Cliff Taylor Papers, Michael Starks, Financial Management under Producer Choice, 4 September 1992. Emphasis in original.
88 Michael Starks, 'Producer Choice in the BBC', in *From Hierarchy to Contract*, Anthony Harrison (ed.), Hermitage, Berkshire: Policy Journals, 1993, 170.
89 Ibid.
90 BBC Written Archives Centre, T62-357-1, Producer Choice – Cliff Taylor Papers, Michael Starks/Alan Hammill Double-Spend: Risk Management, ND.
91 Starks, 'Producer Choice in the BBC', 171.
92 BBC Written Archives Centre, T62-358-1, Producer Choice – Cliff Taylor Papers. Property Reduction Strategy.
93 Ibid.
94 Birt, *Harder Path*, 324.
95 Starks, 'Producer Choice in the BBC', 175.
96 BBC Written Archives Centre, T62-355-1, Producer Choice: Project masterplan, nd.
97 BBC Written Archives Centre, T62-358-1, Producer Choice –

Cliff Taylor Papers, The Shape and Size of the Training Need, 8 November 1991.

98 Peter Cloot, 'BBC Producer Choice: A Case Study', Major Projects Association Briefing Paper Number 16, 1994, 27; BBC Written Archives Centre, R162/45/1. Producer Choice Regional Directorate Training Needs Analysis, Update Paper, 8 January 1992.

99 BBC Written Archives Centre, T62-355-1, Producer Choice: Project masterplan, nd.

100 Ibid.

101 BBC Written Archives Centre, R162-45-1, Producer Choice – Rewards and Incentives.

102 BBC Written Archives Centre, R162-46-1 Michael Starks, 'Incentives: A Discussion Paper, 16 July 1993. BBC staff objected to the introduction of financial incentives, which they felt called into question their loyalty and professional commitment. The Producer Choice Evaluation Study noted: 'It was implicitly clear that most discussants were uncomfortable with the thought they should be offered incentives to make Producer Choice a success. They already had a high degree of commitment to the organisation, and were committed in principle to the thinking behind Producer Choice and its aims.' R87-197-1, Producer Choice: Evaluation. Key Messages from the listening exercise. Office for Public Management, 16 July 1993.

103 Birt, *Harder Path*, 328–9. Emphasis added.

104 For staff perceptions of Producer Choice, see BBC Written Archives Centre, T62-358-1, Producer Choice – Cliff Taylor Papers, Chris Trynka, The BBC's Equal Opportunities Policy and Changes in the Organisation of Resources to Make Programmes, 19 March 1992, and R87-197-1, Office for Public Management, Producer Choice Evaluation, the Key Questions, nd.

105 Ibid.

106 Michael Grade, 'The Future of the BBC', in *Television Policy: The MacTaggart Lectures*, Bob Franklin (ed.), Edinburgh: Edinburgh University Press, 2005, 163; interview with former BBC producer, date withheld.

107 BBC Written Archives Centre, R87-197-1, Producer Choice: Evaluation, 16 July 1993.

108 Birt, *Harder Path*, 326.

109 Laurence Marks and Maurice Gran, 'Rewarding Creative Talent: The Struggle of the Independents', in *Television policy: the MacTaggart Lectures*, 208.

110 BBC Written Archives Centre, R162-46-1 Rodney Baker-Bates, Producer Choice Simplification, 12 July 1993.

111 BBC Written Archives Centre, R87-197-1, Office for Public Management, Producer Choice Evaluation, The Key Questions, nd.

112 BBC Written Archives Centre, R87-197-1, Producer Choice: Evaluation, 16 July 1993.

113 Quentin Letts, *50 people who buggered up Britain*, London: Constable, 2009, 33.

114 Ibid., 35.

115 David Graeber goes as far as to argue that the tendency of reforms 'intended to reduce red tape and promote market forces' to 'have the ultimate effect of increasing the total number of regulations, the total amount of paperwork, and the total number of bureaucrats … 'can be observed so regularly that I think we are justified in treating it as a general sociological law'. David Graeber, *The Utopia of Rules: On Technology, Stupidity and the Secret Joys of Bureaucracy*, New York: Melville House, 2015, 9. For other critiques of neoliberal bureaucracy, see Mark Fisher, *Capitalist Realism: Is There no Alternative?*, London: John Hunt Publishing, 2009; and Ronald Amann, 'A Sovietological view of modern Britain', *The Political Quarterly* 74:4, 2003, 468–480.

116 Starks, 'Producer Choice in the BBC', 166.

117 Ibid., 168.

118 Born, *Uncertain Vision*, 128, 178.

119 Brian McNair, *News and Journalism in the UK*, fifth edition, Abingdon and New York: Routledge, 2009, 118.

120 Birt, *Harder Path*, 330.

6. Public Service Broadcasting and Private Power

1 BBC Written Archives Centre, News and Current Affairs Minutes, 27 February 1979.

2 BBC Written Archives Centre, Board of Governors Minutes, 28 June 1979.

3 Michael David Kandiah (ed.), 'Witness Seminar I "Big bang":

The October 1986 stock market deregulation', *Contemporary British History* 13:1, 1999, 104.

4   Leila Simona Talani, *Globalization, Hegemony and the Future of the City of London*, Basingstoke: Palgrave Macmillan, 2011, 62.

5   Interview with Mark Damazer, 20 August 2013.

6   Interview with John Fryer, 10 June 2013.

7   *Report of the Committee on the Future of Broadcasting*, HM Stationery Office, 1977, 272–3.

8   Ibid., 273.

9   Interview with Peter Day, 26 July 2013.

10   Interview with Tom Maddocks, 2 August 2013.

11   Peter Day, 'Peter Day's week', BBC Blog, 30 July 2009, bbc.co.uk.

12   Interview with Tom Maddocks, 2 August 2013.

13   Interview with Peter Day, 26 July 2013.

14   Ed Mitchell, *From Headlines to Hard Times*, London: John Blake Publishing, 2013, 66–67.

15   Interview with James Long, 28 May 2014. Long worked on these *City Press* reports before joining the Financial Unit when it was formed in 1974.

16   Mitchell, *From Headlines to Hard Times*, 67.

17   Ibid.

18   *BBC Staff List*, October 1984.

19   Martin Adeney, '…But will business ever love the BBC?', *British Journalism Review* 12:1, 2001, 51–56.

20   Peter Day, 'Peter Day's week'.

21   Interview with Will Hutton, 3 December 2013.

22   Interview with Richard Tait, 17 May 2013.

23   Tony Harcup, 'Reporting the Next Battle: Lessons from Orgreave', in *Settling Scores: The Media, The Police & The Miners' Strike*, Granville Williams (ed.), London: Campaign for Press and Broadcasting Freedom, 2014, 100.

24   Ibid., 96–7.

25   Ibid., 98, 101.

26   Geoffrey Goodman, 'War without end', *British Journalism Review* 20, 2009, 79.

27   Ibid.

28   Harcup, 'Reporting the Next Battle', 102.

29   Interview with former senior editor, 12 April 2013.

30 Nick Jones, 2009. 'The soul searching of a former BBC correspondent', in *Shafted: The Media, the Miners' Strike and the Aftermath*, Granville Williams (ed.), London: Campaign for Press and Broadcasting Freedom, 2009, 81–2.

31 Ibid., 82–3.

32 For an account of the Wapping dispute, see John Lang and Graham Dodkins, *Bad News: The Wapping Dispute*, Nottingham: Spokesman Books, 2011.

33 Interview with John Fryer, 10 June 2013.

34 In an influential work, the sociologist Geoffrey Ingham described the City of London, the Bank of England and Treasury as the 'core institutional nexus' of British society (Geoffrey Ingham, *Capitalism Divided? The City and Industry in British Social Development*. Basingstoke, Palgrave Macmillan: 1984, 9). The concept was adopted by Peter Cain and Anthony Hopkins in their work on imperialism (*British Imperialism: Crisis and Deconstruction, 1914–1990*, London: Longman, 1993) and by Inderjeet Parmar (*Special Interests, the State and the Anglo-American Alliance, 1939–1945*, London: Routledge, 2013, 52) as well as by Michael Mann in *States, War and Capitalism* (Oxford: Blackwell, 1988, 218). Adopting a more instrumentalist perspective, Frank Longstreth argued that the Bank of England and the Treasury represent the institutionalisation of the power of finance capital within the state (Frank Longstreth, 'The City, industry and the state', in *State and economy in contemporary capitalism*, Colin Crouch (ed.), London: Croom Helm, 1979, 157–90).

35 Mitchell, *From Headlines to Hard Times*, 79.

36 Ibid., 81–2.

37 Interview with Nicholas Jones, 25 February 2013.

38 Interview with Peter Day, 26 July 2013.

39 Interview with BBC business journalist, 17 July 2013.

40 Mitchell, *From Headlines to Hard Times*, 80.

41 Interview with Richard Quest, 28 February 2013.

42 Interview with former BBC business journalist, 29 July 2013.

43 John Birt, *The Harder Path: The Autobiography*, London: Time Warner, 2002, 264.

44 Churchill Archives Centre, The Papers of Peter Jay, PJAY 3/14/3. Letter from Ian Hargreaves to Peter Jay.

45 Interview with John Fryer, 10 June 2013.

46 Adeney, '…But will business ever love the BBC?', 51–56.
47 Interview with Richard Quest, 2 April 2013.
48 LinkedIn, Daniel Jeffreys, uk.linkedin.com/in/danieljeffreys.
49 Interview with Will Hutton, 3 December 2013. Hutton's successor at *Newsnight* was Graham Ingham, a former Treasury official recruited from the World Service who would later became an advisor at the International Monetary Fund and the Federal Reserve Bank of New York. LinkedIn, Graham Ingham, uk.linkedin.com/pub/graham-ingham/a/36/4b8.
50 Ibid.
51 Andy Beckett, *When the Lights Went Out: Britain in the Seventies*, London: Faber & Faber, 2009, 339.
52 Churchill Archives Centre, The Papers of Peter Jay, PJAY 3/14/3. Letter from Vin Harrop to Peter Jay, 5 April 1990; Churchill Archives Centre, The Papers of Peter Jay, PJAY 3/14/4. Fax from Peter Jay to Chris Cramer, 23 January 1996.
53 Churchill Archives Centre, The Papers of Peter Jay, PJAY 3/14/3. Letter from Ian Anne Strickland, Group Hospitality Co-ordinator, Barclays, to Peter Jay, 27 January 1992. Churchill Archives Centre, The Papers of Peter Jay, PJAY 4/8/23. Letter from Ellen Miller to Peter Jay, 4 March 1999. Jay's 'outside interests' led to an ill-tempered exchange with the BBC management when he was offered a column at the *Sunday Business* at the rate of £1,000 per article. Jay claimed that he 'pressingly need[ed] the money' explaining that it 'could educate my children!', but the management did not grant permission because of the concern to maintain impartiality in the run-up to the 1997 general election. See Letter from Vin Harop to Peter Jay and Fax from Peter Jay to Chris Cramer.
54 Interview with Peter Jay, 26 April 2013.
55 Churchill College Cambridge, British Diplomatic Oral History Programme (BDOHP), Peter Jay interviewed on 24 February 2006 by Malcolm McBain.
56 Interview with former BBC economics and business journalist, 12 August 2013.
57 Ibid.
58 Interview with Rory Cellan-Jones, 18 July 2013.
59 Interview with Evan Davis, 7 May 2013.
60 Quoted in James Collard, 'Fiscal attraction', *The Times*, 8 September 2001, 37.

61 Interview with Evan Davis, 7 May 2013.
62 Aeron Davis, *Mediation of Power*, London and New York: Routledge, 2007, 23.
63 Gorkana, 'Gorkana meets the BBC's Business Unit', Gorkana. com.
64 Interview with Rory Cellan-Jones, 18 July 2013.
65 Interview with Peter Jay, 26 April 2013.
66 Interview with Paul Gibbs, 7 May 2013.
67 BBC, *The BBC Trust, Impartiality Review Business Coverage: The BBC Journalism Group Submission to the Panel*, 23 January 2007, 15, downloads.bbc.co.uk/bbctrust/assets/files/pdf/review_report_research/impartiality_business/f1_journalism_submission.pdf.
68 Interview with Paul Gibbs, 7 May 2013.
69 Interview with former senior editor, 12 April 2013.
70 Interview with Pauline McCole, 6 September 2013.
71 Nicholas Jones, 'TUC Congress Guide 1990', quoted in *The Lost Tribe of Fleet Street: Whatever happened to the labour and industrial correspondents?*, Nicholas Jones (ed.), London: Nicholas Jones, 2011, 23–4.
72 Interview with Richard Quest, 2 April 2013.
73 Interview with former BBC business journalist, 29 July 2013.
74 Interview with Richard Tait, 17 May 2013.
75 Interview with former BBC business journalist, 29 July 2013.
76 Birt, *Harder Path*, 303.
77 LinkedIn, Daniel Dodd, uk.linkedin.com/pub/daniel-dodd/3/b01/a5.
78 Interview with former senior editor, 2 August 2013.
79 Interview with Stephen Coulter, 9 January 2014.
80 Interview with Martin Greig, 27 March 2014.
81 'DYKE, Gregory', *Who's Who 2014*, London: A & C Black, 2014.
82 Interview with Mark Damazer, 20 August 2013.
83 Birt, *Harder Path*, 265.
84 Interview with Mark Damazer, 20 August 2013.
85 Interview with Evan Davis, 7 May 2013.
86 Jon Rees, 'Dyke orders BBC to tune into business', *Sunday Business*, 16 July 2000, 14.
87 Interview with Greg Dyke, 28 May 2014.
88 Interview with former senior editor, 2 August 2013.

89 Interview with Evan Davis, 7 May 2013.

90 'Randall becomes first BBC business editor', *Broadcast*, 6 November 2000.

91 'BBC promises more business news', BBC News Online, 6 November 2000, bbc.co.uk.

92 'The Beeb tunes in to business', *Daily Mail*, 7 November 2000.

93 Quoted in Michael Harrison, 'Dyke appoints "£250,000-a-year" editor to re-vamp business news', *Independent*, 7 November 2000, 5.

94 Ibid.

95 'BBC promises more business news', BBC News Online.

96 'RANDALL, Jeff William', *Who's Who 2014*, London: A & C Black, 2014. 'Up close with the Barclays' "consigliere"', *Observer*, 15 January 2006.

97 Jeff Randall, 'A liberal agenda set by patronising do-gooders', *Sunday Business*, 21 May 2000. Reprinted in the *Independent*, 7 November 2000, 5.

98 Vincent Graff, 'You want me to slag Murdoch off', *Guardian*, 17 September 2007.

99 Julie Tomlin, 'BBC creates 20 new posts as Jay heads for retirement', *Press Gazette*, 1 August 2001, pressgazette.co.uk; Leigh Holmwood, '£2m boost for BBC news', *Broadcast*, 3 August 2001, broadcastnow.co.uk.

100 Churchill Archives Centre, The Papers of Peter Jay, PJAY 3/14/6. Letter from Richard Sambrook to Peter Jay, 27 January 2000.

101 Churchill Archives Centre, The Papers of Peter Jay, PJAY 4/8/32. Letter from Richard Sambrook to Peter Jay, 4 December 2001.

102 Churchill Archives Centre, The Papers of Peter Jay, PJAY 4/8/34. Email from Evan Davis to Peter Jay, 16 September 2002.

103 Harrison, 'Dyke appoints "£250,000-a-year" editor to re-vamp business news', 5; Raymond Boyle, 'From Troubleshooter to The Apprentice: the changing face of business on British television', *Media, Culture and Society* 30:3, 2008, 415–42.

104 'Up close with the Barclays' "consigliere"', *Observer*, 15 January 2006.

105 Interview with Greg Dyke, 28 May 2014.

106 Interview with BBC business journalist, 14 June 2013.

107 Interview with former BBC economics and business journalist, 12 August 2013.
108 Interview with former senior editor, 2 August 2013.
109 Interview with Richard Griffiths, 27 February 2013.
110 Ibid.
111 Interview with Rory Cellan-Jones, 18 July 2013.
112 Interview with John Fryer, 10 June 2013.
113 Interview with Greg Dyke, 28 May 2014.
114 Interview with former senior editor, 2 August 2013.
115 Ben Dowell, 'Media: Show me the money', *Guardian*, 8 September 2008, 'Media' section, 7.
116 Independent Panel, *Report of the independent panel for the BBC Trust on impartiality of BBC business coverage*, downloads.bbc.co.uk/bbctrust/assets/files/pdf/review_report_research/impartiality_business/business_impartiality_report.pdf.
117 Interview with Richard Tait, 17 May 2013.
118 *Report of the independent panel for the BBC Trust on impartiality of BBC business coverage*, 3.
119 Michael Svennevig, *BBC Coverage of Business in the UK: A Content Analysis of Business News Coverage*, Leeds: Institute of Communications Studies University of Leeds, 2007, 7.
120 Ibid., 29.
121 BBC, *BBC Trust Impartiality Review Business Coverage*, 16.
122 *Report of the independent panel for the BBC Trust on impartiality of BBC business coverage*, 3, 16.
123 Ibid.
124 Blinc Partnership, *BBC Governors' Review of Impartiality in Business News: Integrated Qualitative and Quantitative Research Report*, 2007, 7–8, downloads.bbc.co.uk/bbctrust/assets/files/pdf/review_report_research/impartiality_business/a_blinc_partnership.pdf.
125 Ofcom, 'New News, Future News: The challenges for television news after Digital switch-over', discussion document, Ofcom, 2007, 25, stakeholders.ofcom.org.uk.
126 Gorkana, 'Gorkana meets the BBC's Business Unit', Gorkana.com.
127 Karin Wahl-Jorgensen et al, *BBC Breadth of Opinion Review: Content Analysis*, Cardiff: University of Cardiff School of Journalism, Media and Cultural Studies, 2013, 80.

128 Mike Berry, 'The Today Programme and the Banking Crisis', *Journalism* 14:2, 2013, 253–270.

130 Mike Berry, 'No Alternative to Austerity: How BBC Broadcast News Reported the Deficit Debate', *Media Culture & Society*, forthcoming.

131 Interview with Will Hutton, 3 December 2013.

Conclusion

1 Nick Robinson, 'Nick Robinson: My beef with Russell Brand', *Radio Times*, 12 January 2015, radiotimes.com.

2 Nick Robinson, 'Marital problems', Nick Robinson's News Log, 30 January 2006, bbc.co.uk.

3 Robinson, 'Nick Robinson: My beef with Russell Brand'.

4 Asa Briggs, *The BBC: The First Fifty Years*, Oxford: Oxford University Press, 1985, 54.

5 Paddy Scannell and David Cardiff, *A Social History of Broadcasting: Volume One 1922–1939, Serving the Nation*, Oxford: Basil Blackwell, 1991, 8.

6 Quoted in W. J. West, *Truth Betrayed*, London: Duckworth, 1987, 116, footnote 24.

7 Scannell and Cardiff, *A Social History of Broadcasting*, 13, 14. Scannell subsequently extends this argument to television also, echoing these very same claims in Paddy Scannell, 'Public Service Broadcasting and Modern Public Life,' *Culture and Power: A Media, Culture and Society Reader*, Paddy Scannell, Philip Schlesinger, and Colin Sparks (eds), London: Sage, 1992.

8 Scannell, 'Public Service Broadcasting and Modern Public Life,' 335, 344.

9 Quoted in D. L. LeMahieu, *A Culture for Democracy: Mass Communication and the Cultivated Mind in Britain between the Wars*, Oxford: Oxford University Press, 1993, 147.

10 Ian McIntyre, *The Expense of Glory: Life of John Reith*, London: HarperCollins 1995, 218.

11 Marista Leishman, *My Faher. Reith of the BBC*, Edinburgh: Saint Andrew Press, 2006, 150, 2.

12 Andrew Boyle, *Only the Wind Will Listen: Reith of the BBC*, London: Hutchinson, 1972, 251.

13 John Reith, *Broadcast over Britain*, London: Hodder and Stoughton, 1924, 220.

14 Scannell and Cardiff, *A Social History of Broadcasting*, 9.

15 Paddy Scannell, 'Public Service Broadcasting: The History of a Concept', in *Understanding Television*, Andrew Goodwin and Garry Whannel (eds), London and New York: Routledge, 2005, 14.

16 *Report of the Committee on the Future of Broadcasting*, HM Stationery Office, 1977, 79, 429.

17 BBC Written Archives Centre, R78/1,204/1 NEWS POLICY, Extract from the Verbatim Report of the Proceedings of the General Advisory Council on 6 February.

18 BBC Written Archives Centre, T62/97/1 News and Current Affairs Policy Coverage General 1968–1976. 'How Should We Broadcast News and Current Affairs?', Discussion Paper by Chief Assistant to the Director-General, 8 July 1975.

19 BBC Written Archives Centre, R78/1,204/1 NEWS POLICY, *The Task of Broadcasting News*, revised draft paper for the General Advisory Council, 11 December 1975.

20 Ibid.

21 Colin Crouch, *Post-democracy*, Cambridge: Polity, 2004; Colin Crouch, *The Strange Non-Death of Neo-Liberalism*, Cambridge: Polity, 2011; Colin Leys, *Market-Driven Politics: Neoliberal Democracy and the Public Interest*, London and New York: Verso, 2003.

22 Scannell and Cardiff, *A Social History of Broadcasting*, 17.

23 Dan Hind, *The Return of the Public: Democracy, Power and the Case for Media Reform*, London: Verso, 2012.

Acknowledgments

The long process that eventually led to this book began eight years ago when I started researching for a PhD in sociology. Since it draws on my thesis, the debts I have already acknowledged there bear repeating here. The first note of thanks then must go to my friend and colleague David Miller, who as my PhD supervisor provided invaluable support and encouragement, and who has contributed inestimably to the development of my sociological imagination over the years. Trish Hayes at the BBC Written Archives in Caversham was extremely helpful, and I would also like to thank all those who agreed to be interviewed over the course of my research. They not only provided some of the raw material for this book, but also offered thoughtful reflections and analysis that helped me develop my own thinking.

Mark Hollingsworth provided me with interesting and flexible work during the first few years of my PhD research, without which I do not think I could have completed this study, and later provided some useful material on political vetting. Others who have helped with this book by providing material or giving context include John Cook, Stephen Dorril, Tony Harcup, David Malone, David McQueen, Seumas Milne and Ian Sinclair. Thanks are also due to my friend Jamie Stern Weiner, and to Leo Hollis, my editor at Verso, for giving this book focus and clarity.

Acknowledgments

Special thanks must go to my parents Andrew and Becky for their love and support over the years. They would never expect me to repay the huge debt of gratitude I owe them, which is just as well because I could never hope to. The final word of thanks goes to my wife, Carrie. She suffered more rants and monologues about the BBC and neoliberalism than anyone should have to endure and put up with me working on my thesis and then on this book when I should have been spending time with her. Her love and support has been invaluable, and it is to her, and to Toby, that I dedicate this book, if they want it.

Index

Index

259

Index

Index

Index